# Secret Beaches
## of Greater Victoria

VIEW ROYAL TO SIDNEY

THEO DOMBROWSKI

VANCOUVER · VICTORIA · CALGARY

Heritage House Publishing Company Ltd.
www.heritagehouse.ca

LIBRARY AND ARCHIVES CANADA CATALOGUING IN PUBLICATION

Dombrowski, Theo, 1947–
Secret beaches of Greater Victoria: View Royal to Sidney / Theo Dombrowski.

Includes index.
ISBN 978-1-894974-98-1

1. Beaches—British Columbia—Victoria Region—Guidebooks. 2. Beaches—British Columbia—Saanich Peninsula—Guidebooks. 3. Recreation areas—British Columbia—Victoria Metropolitan Area—Guidebooks. 4. Recreation areas—British Columbia—Saanich Peninsula—Guidebooks. 5. Victoria Metropolitan Area (B.C.)—Guidebooks. 6. Saanich Peninsula (B.C.)—Guidebooks. I. Title.

FC3845.S22D64 2010 796.5'30971128 C2009-906919-9

*editor*: Lenore Hietkamp
*proofreader*: Lesley Cameron
*designer*: Jacqui Thomas
*maps, artwork and photographs*: Theo Dombrowski

This book was printed on FSC-certified, acid-free paper, processed chlorine free and printed with vegetable-based inks.

Heritage House acknowledges the financial support for its publishing program from the Government of Canada through the Canada Book Fund (CBF), Canada Council for the Arts and the province of British Columbia through the British Columbia Arts Council and the Book Publishing Tax Credit.

Printed in Canada

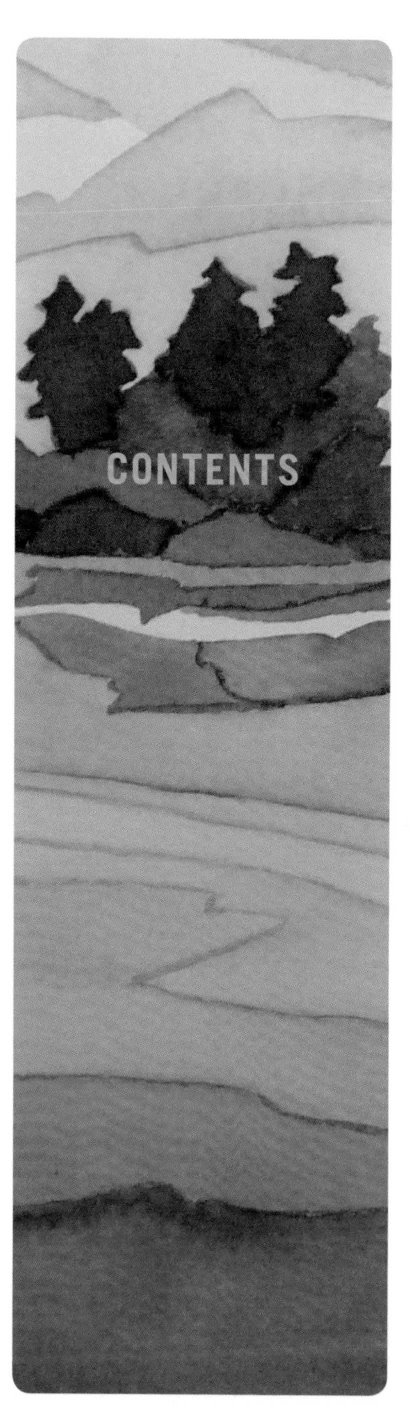

# CONTENTS

# INTRODUCTION

An unusual gift from an unexpected source refreshes our appreciation of life. Such a gift enhances the plot of wonderful stories: when life is at its most depleted, a character receives a small fortune, a magic goblet or a pet with peculiar eating habits via a long-lost and now thoroughly dead great aunt, a crumpled lottery ticket or a neighbour with a suspect sense of humour. The magic happens in real life, too, but sometimes the unusual gift has been there all along, just outside our field of vision—we just need a guide to show us how to find it.

Simply by turning the pages of this book, you can discover wonderful beaches that you never dreamed existed. The shoreline of Saanich Peninsula and Victoria is full of magic doors onto hidden or little-known beaches.

Once you start to explore this area's hidden beaches, you will discover a beach for every occasion. If you're in the mood for an intimate space, try the tiny, rocky cove in Esquimalt, with its fine pebble beach, a curving set of stairs built into the rock and a park bench. If you just want to take in the weather, drive to the spot on Ten Mile Point where, without leaving your car, you can watch the driving rain and the tempestuous hullabaloo in front of you while you sip from your thermos and munch on a blueberry bran muffin. Or, on a blistering hot day, pile the kids, buckets, spades, sunscreen and picnic goodies into the car and head for the wonderful spot north of Sidney for a few hours among magical tidal pools and runways of low-tide sand.

The approaches to these beaches are as diverse as the facilities they offer. Most typically, you will find a wooded strip between shorefront houses, possibly with a directional sign, probably with a flight of stairs made of wood, concrete, stone, aluminum—or even dirt. Although you may find not so much as a park bench at some spots, at others you will find not only picnic tables but also a parking lot and washrooms.

## THE VANCOUVER ISLAND BEACH

As you might have guessed by now, the word "beach" is used loosely, which is the way most people who live on Vancouver Island use the word. For us, a "beach" is simply a shorefront. It can be covered with silvery sand, pebbles, boulders or even solid-rock outcroppings. We have all had visitors who have watched far too many movies about soft-focus encounters on Cape Cod and, as a result, have a sadly restricted notion of a beach. For them a beach is sand. Lots of it. And waves. Lots of them. When you bring such visitors to some of our favourite beaches, they retreat in confusion. They have no idea of the pleasures to be had from nestling among sun-bleached logs in a litter of pebbles with a glossy magazine, a crazy sunhat and a bag of potato chips. They don't know that by peering into rocky tidal pools they can find anemones, ochre stars, hermit crabs, coralline algae, plate limpets, common chitons and all the other familiar creatures of our rocky shores. And they don't know that they actually will encounter acres of sand on our beaches if only they took the time to search or to consult this book.

You could locate these beaches with the aid of land-use or zoning maps obtained from various regional district or municipal offices. Or you could try using a GPS or Google Maps. Any of these guides can be misleading, however, and you can waste considerable hours combing back roads searching for what looks on a map to be a perfectly viable access to the waterfront but turns out to be something altogether different. Sometimes it will be an impassable tangle of blackberry vines blocking a steep descent through heavy brush to a cliff face—not the most enticing approach to waterfront bliss. Sometimes it will look like part of someone's manicured property—leaving you with the distinct impression that you will be trespassing if you take a single step in the direction of the shore. It can also be an enticing, well-beaten path winding through arbutus and oaks to a magnificent view and the perfect picnic spot on a grassy bluff.

## PUBLIC ACCESS

Most of the "public access" routes to the beaches in this book are government-owned land lying between private waterfront lots. These routes lead to shoreline that is free for public use. However, the conscientious beachgoer should know a few further facts. The term "foreshore" is used by the government to describe the beach area between low tide and high tide. Even when the land above the foreshore is private, the public generally has the privilege of using the foreshore and the water beyond it, though not the right to do so. When this area has been granted special status, such as a lease for farming oysters, the public does not have access. Often signs are posted if the public is restricted from using the foreshore.

We have the privilege of enjoying the beaches in this book, a privilege that entails responsibility. This book was written with two key beliefs:

- In keeping with the ideals of the community of which we are all a part, everyone who lives on Vancouver Island (and, indeed, visitors to our paradise) should be able to enjoy waterfront that is, after all, public property.
- The kind of person who will make a point of seeking out a little-known beach will be the kind of person who values quiet beauty and undamaged natural settings.

Those who discover the wealth of waterfront beauty to be had on Vancouver Island will be motivated to help protect it. This introduction explains not only how to use this book to discover the many wonders of southern Vancouver Island's secret beaches, but also how to behave as a conscientious beachgoer.

## BEACH ACCESS WARNING

Quite understandably, many waterfront property owners and other locals want to keep their secret beaches *secret*. Who, after all, doesn't enjoy seclusion by the waterfront, other than, perhaps, those who have been working hard at the gym to build the perfect Beach Body? More important, what property owners welcome cars blocking driveways and high-decibel midnight parties, not to mention rotting litter, aromatic dog excrement, gutted berry patches, depleted clam and oyster beds or ugly firepits? No one finds such abuse acceptable, neither waterfront owner nor visitor. However, the more people who visit the shorefront, the more beachgoers there will be to encourage its preservation. Everyone who loves our shores will doubtless find in the pleasures and peace of the "secret beach" the inspiration to act on behalf of these and all other areas of natural beauty.

## BEACHES IN THIS BOOK

Only about two-thirds of the public access spots in the Greater Victoria area are fully described in this book, and there is little point in writing about the others. Those who are determined to get to *all* access spots possible can obtain an appropriate map from a regional district or municipal office and follow it to their heart's content. They will find that nearly all of the spots excluded from this book exist only in terms of legal status.

Some access points are included that might seem hardly "secret." Three large parks, and a few small ones, are presented in detail because they are so quiet that they could continue to go unnoticed. For example, Macaulay Point Park in Esquimalt, Patricia Bay Park in North Saanich and Island View Beach Regional Park in Central Saanich are significant in size but little known. Also presented in detail are a few pocket beaches immediately off well-known routes, but easy to miss. One such example is the shore with the launching ramp, good for kayaks and tucked into the Victoria Harbour waterfront walk below Russell Street.

Other spots are mentioned only briefly and are introduced by an asterisk. These include those large, well-known beaches that are virtually impossible to miss. No Victorian or visitor to Victoria can miss the scenic drive winding along almost the entire coast from Cadboro Bay to Ogden Point. Nearly as well known is the shorefront walkway that starts near the Johnson Street Bridge and ends in West Bay. Another scenic route, Lochside Road south of Sidney, with its walkway, might be a little off the beaten track, but it is well used. Then there are the big parks—Mount Douglas, Cadboro Bay, Willows Beach and the nearby

Hollydene Park

Esplanade, Gonzales Bay, Cattle Point, even Saxe Point. Each of these is mentioned in just a note.

Some accesses to beaches receive only brief mention because they are near access spots that are more appealing. Although one such shore may be as attractive as another that is fully described, the parking may be difficult or the path steep. Other spots may not be attractive by most people's standards, but are well developed in a particular way. A muddy estuary, for example, rich in bird life but little else, might be serviced by a well-maintained trail. Or the spot might be simply a convenient place to launch a kayak. Others have an idiosyncratic character—the kind of place you might like to visit once every few years, more out of interest than anything else. Some public wharfs are in this group. Still, there is no reason you should trust the value judgements that lard this book: they arise from irrepressible enthusiasm or from mild reservations, not—significantly—from a desire to warp visitors' reactions to their beach experience!

## THE GREAT BEACH EXPERIENCE

Armed with this book, then, and sensitive to the possible impact of beach-going on local residents and the beaches themselves, the adventurous can head out with camera, sunscreen and picnic basket. To be sure that you have a wonderful beach experience, however, consider the following.

**Weather** The first question that anyone with an iota of West Coast experience will ask before going to the beach is, "What will the weather be like?" Even a sunny day does not guarantee a pleasant experience. As any *real* West Coaster will tell you, your beach experience is affected by not just the cloud cover and precipitation, which you can find out from basic weather forecasts, but also the *wind*. Use this book to identify which beaches are partially or fully exposed to which winds. Unfortunately, most radio or newspaper weather forecasters will tell you little or nothing about the wind, except for tossing in the occasional phrase "windy near the water."

Enter the *marine forecast*. This kind of forecast is readily available by telephone as a recording (250-245-8899) or on the Web as printed script at http://www.weatheroffice.gc.ca/. Simply type "marine forecast Victoria," for example, in your browser's search window. Be warned, though—winds around the south of Vancouver Island are sometimes fluky. If a west wind is forecast for the Strait of Juan de Fuca, the most common wind in summer, expect it to be deflected as it passes up Haro

Robert Street—Rainbow Park

Strait into a southwest blow. In fact, some westerlies make for some pretty chilly sunbathing or sandcastle building.

This is where your handy book is so important. Except on the warmest days, and unless you enjoy the exhilaration of beachcombing with wind in your hair, you will have to make some decisions: wait until late morning, when westerly winds may have subsided; bring a sweater; or *look for beaches that are not exposed to west winds* (if they are in the forecast). In general, beaches in Saanich Inlet are least likely to be windy.

But don't avoid all blustery days. You might, in fact, enjoy a strong wind. In a winter storm, for example, when the wind is howling from the southeast, it can be a thrill to drive to some of the spots between Clover Point and the Victoria Golf Course. On a windy day, even in good weather, kite flying can be a great diversion—if you choose your beach carefully. Then, too, there are those (few) stiflingly hot days we have each summer when a windy section of shore feels delightful while everywhere inland feels the opposite.

And don't avoid foul, rainy weather. In even the worst weather, you can, by consulting this book, find some great spots to drive your car in full view of the shore and enjoy a cozy car picnic while simultaneously feeding your soul on the splendours of the wind, waves and gulls. In fact, winter, when we are treated to most of the foul weather, is also the best time for spotting sea lions and many species of waterfowl that spend their summers in the far north. Be careful, though, if you venture onto the shore, since rocks are often more slippery in winter than in summer.

**Sun direction** Do you want to sunbathe on a baking bit of shore or picnic in a patch of cool shade? Use this book to select just the right beach. We tend to think of beaches as being permanently in sun on a sunny day. Because the coast of Vancouver Island has many large trees and many steep shores, however, a particular piece of shore can be deeply in shadow for part of the day. Use this book to consider the right time of day for finding sun or shade on your beach. Most of the beaches on the west coast of the Saanich Peninsula are in shadow until around noon, whereas those on its east coast bask in the morning sun. The south coast of Ten Mile Point and a few spots around Esquimalt can be baking hot and shadeless on a windless afternoon. There are many exceptions to this pattern, though.

And don't forget the seasons. Both the length of shadows and the time of day at which they appear on a beach or disappear from it will vary significantly, even between June and September, let alone December.

**Tides** Beaches can change character completely between high and low tide. This is particularly the case where tides go out a long way. The same beach that is a tempting swimming spot with turquoise waters over sun-dappled pebbles can, at low tide, be a broad swath of oysters, barnacle-covered boulders and tidal pools—or muddy flats. Panting for a swim, you might arrive at a beach to find a nice sandy shore, yes—but also *more than a hundred metres* of this nice sandy shore between you and the water. Conversely, and especially in winter, you might arrive shod and snack-laden for a favourite shore tromp—only to find that the shore is under water. You cannot use this book to predict tides, except in a very general way. You can, however, use it in combination with your tide tables to decide the best time of day or best day of the week to visit your chosen spot.

Learn about tidal patterns. As all Islanders know, we have two high tides each day and, it follows, two low tides. All Islanders also know that the sequence moves forward about an hour each day, so that if, for example, the tide is high at 4:30 p.m. on Tuesday, it will be high at approximately 5:30 p.m. on Wednesday. Not all Islanders, however, are familiar with other patterns. In the summer they tend to follow one pattern, in the winter the reverse.

This seasonal shift should help you in your planning, once you realize that tides are generally *in* during the day in winter and generally *out* during the day in summer. In mid summer, any high tide during the middle of the day will not be very high and will often seem like a half tide. Similarly, any low tide in late afternoon or evening will not be very low; it, too, will seem like a half tide. These are "neap tides." In contrast, if the low tide occurs during the late morning in mid summer, it is likely to be very low, while high tide in mid to late afternoon is likely to be very high. With these tides, called "spring tides," you can launch your kayak easily late morning and come back to the shore a few hours later only to discover that you now have to carry it over a hundred metres of rocks. On the positive side, these tides cause the water to rush in over wide expanses of warmed pebbles or sand and produce the warmest swimming. Locals know, however, that the newly warmed surface water is still "floating" over the comparatively colder water and can be patchy as a result.

This, then, is the pattern of mid summer. In early and late summer, the pattern is a little different. If you're looking for days with extreme tides, in early summer expect an afternoon low tide to be extremely low; in late summer expect a morning low tide to be equally low. Confused? Simply search out one of the dozens of websites that provide tide tables. The most official one is through Fisheries and Oceans Canada (http://www.waterlevels.gc.ca/).

Swimmers are not, alas, the beachgoers who will be happiest in the Saanich Peninsula and Victoria area. Because strong currents sweep past Victoria on their way into and out of Georgia Basin, icy water from the depths is constantly being brought to the surface. Thus some of the most gorgeous beaches you will ever see will not provide the most gorgeous swims you will ever have—unless you are truly Nordic in temperament. The water is at its most bracing around Victoria itself, including the stunning Willows Beach. The water around Cordova Bay is a little better, but not exactly balmy. In general, Saanich Inlet provides the warmest swimming water in this area: an afternoon high-tide swim in Patricia Bay can be very pleasant. For the warmest swimming water, though, you will have to head north to beaches between Qualicum and Mill Bay (see *Secret Beaches of Southern Vancouver Island*).

**Children** We all associate the seaside with children and sandcastles. Public access routes can certainly lead you to many wonderful spots with sand and warm tidal pools. The few large expanses of sand have, thankfully, been snapped up for the big public parks—Cadboro Bay and Oak Bay in particular. If, however, you are using this book primarily as a way of finding places for your children to build sandcastles, you will be restricted.

Nevertheless, one strategy for finding beaches for children away from the big parks is to recognize that even a small area of sand can afford lots of entertainment. Almost half of the spots in this book offer this kind of beach-going experience. Another strategy is to break the stereotypes. Children can play for hours in rocky tidal pools attempting—fruitlessly—to catch "bullheads" (actually sculpins), or building magical little kingdoms of seaweed, rocks and seashells for their shore crab citizens. Likewise, and particularly with adults leading the way, children can, at low tide, discover wonderful creatures under boulders that most beachgoers don't even know exist—the frantically wiggling eel-like blennies, for example, or the porcelain crab with the single giant claw, or the deliciously gooey California sea cucumber. Or the leather star. Or the cling fish. Or...

Some beaches, too, are magical with polished pebbles. Even adults can spend hours sifting through the multicoloured little gems looking for favourites. Other beaches have great skipping stones, or perfect stones for making not sandcastles but rock castles. And don't forget the hours of play that can be had on those shores with fantastic rock formations just begging to be climbed over, conquered or converted into fantasylands.

Because there is nothing much on our beaches that will hurt children, life is made comparatively easy for protective parents. Perhaps the greatest threat is the oyster or barnacle, whose wounds constitute the right-of-passage for all Vancouver Island children. Despite the relative safety of our beaches, remember that antibiotic cream and a colourful Band-Aid, along with the sunscreen, can be useful items in the beach bag.

Not all of the beaches in this book are suitable for children, though. Adults will enjoy a steep path through broken rocks and arbutus to a bluff with a magnificent view of the Gulf Islands and Mount Baker. They will enjoy sipping their favourite drink, pulling out their watercolour set or juicy novel and finding a nest amidst amazing rock formations. They will not, however, enjoy watching a toddler teeter toward the edge of a cliff or wail as he attempts to struggle through a maze of weed-covered giant boulders, crashing and slithering to a bloody-handed halt.

So read the descriptions and advice in this book carefully before you take your children to some of these beaches. If you have a high panic threshold and nimble, adventurous children, you can have a wonderful time at some of the lumpier beaches. Do, however, consider what you will be facing and what decisions you will have to make once you get there. And, of course, be prepared to move on if a beach isn't suitable for your children. One of the delights of this area is that beaches even a hundred metres apart can be wildly different in character.

**Signs** Glorious confusion and amazing inconsistency reign in the world of beach signs. Some beach access spots are heavily burdened with signs. Many have none. Some have one kind, some another. In some places you will find two access spots 100 metres apart, one of them carefully signposted, the other with only a half-hidden path to guide your way.

As you hunt down a remote beach, you will want to know what signs to expect. Signs will help you realize you're not lost. At several locations, in fact, the only indication that you have come to a public access trail is a single sign warning against fires, collecting shellfish, littering or overnight parking.

Signs will also help you plan. If you know that you must leave a shore at 9 p.m., as at most beaches in North Saanich, there's no point selecting the spot for stargazing in the summer. You could take your business elsewhere, to Oak Bay, for example, where you can stay till midnight at most spots. Likewise, if you're planning a wiener roast, you will want to know where fires are not allowed, or where, as at several beaches in Central Saanich, you need a fire permit. Fire restrictions increase in the summer, but in some places fires are not allowed any time of year.

If you're hunting for ingredients for your paella, there's no point coming to a beach with a shellfish warning sign. And dog walkers will want to know where Cuddles must stay on a leash or is not allowed at all. They will want to know where Cuddles may not bring you for a walk from May to September. If the very same Cuddles wants to run wild and free among the exasperated gulls, dog walkers may also want to hunt down places with an off-leash area.

Signs can change quickly, though, so don't treat everything you read in this book as gospel. Below are the signs you are most likely to encounter.

**Public access (or beach access or public beach access)** These vary enormously, mostly between administrative districts, but sometimes within them. Prizes go to North Saanich for the most rustic, artistic and hard to spot, and to Saanich and View Royal for the most decorative. Brentwood Bay tends to go for matter-of-fact displays, if it goes for anything at all, though it has one very pretty sign. Sidney and Victoria also opt for lean and clean functionality. And there are many, many public access routes with nary a sign to indicate that you have found your way to an afternoon's bliss.

**Park** Some parks are merely designated areas, completely undeveloped; others are beautifully managed parks with benches, picnic tables and washrooms. The largest and, generally, most beautiful parts of shorefront you will find in this book are community parks, nature parks, regional parks, municipal parks or even provincial parks. Don't limit yourself to parks, though, or you will miss some real gems.

**Danger/Shellfish area closed** Some of these signs have been in place for decades and are so faded that one wonders about them. Some recent versions of these signs display the skull and crossbones, thereby giving a ghoulish panache to the message. Unless you make some rigorous enquiries, it is clearly best to heed the warning of these signs, even the old, nearly illegible ones.

**Do not dump refuse** Ironically, at some access spots this is the clearest—and only—indication that you have found the right location. In fact, at a few of these spots locals have evidently decided to ignore the sign and gleefully used the area to dump their grass clippings or other garden waste.

**Dead-end road/No turnaround** These are the yellow and black road signs at the beginning of a cul-de-sac that make you feel really, really unwelcome. It is tempting to speculate how these signs found their way to the beginning of some dead-end roads and not others. Occasionally, just occasionally, one wonders about the enthusiasm locals feel for having *outsiders* in their neighbourhood. The alternative NO THRU ROAD, after all, conveys the same information, less threateningly. Not surprisingly, the NO TURNAROUND signs are often misleading. In fact, unless you are driving a semi-trailer or some large Winnebago-beast, you will find yourself perfectly capable of turning around at the end of these roads—you are not condemned to remain, as they suggest, forever jammed at the end of the road in question. In one particularly striking case, a sign declares very vehemently that there is no turnaround, while in fact there is a very *large* turnaround, with a garden in the centre.

**No overnight parking** Again, this is sometimes the only indication that you have found a public access spot. Presumably there have been bad experiences with Winnebago juggernauts blocking such spots or using the landscape as toilets. Otherwise, one wonders what is the harm in a camper van dozing away a few hours on a secluded spot on a secluded road. Still, the sign should be heeded, even if you are hoping to use this

book as a source of get-away-overnight information. Often the hours are posted, again with intriguing diversity. Head to Oak Bay if you want to cuddle, caper or contemplate; in many places there you don't have to leave until midnight. Straitlaced North Saanich, in contrast, requests that you be on your way by 9 p.m. Ironically, many of its access spots facing Saanich Inlet are perfect for viewing late summer evening sunsets.

**Tsunami warning** A few beaches are posted with signs that show a dramatic wave washing ashore. These signs warn beachgoers to move to higher ground in case of earthquake. This is a good warning, but one wonders why this sign appears at one beach and not at a beach 100 metres away with an equally exposed and low foreshore. One may wonder, too, why the signs are mostly confined to View Royal—and at the tops of high banks. Maybe they know something in View Royal.

**No fires (or fire ban or no open fires)** You cannot plan a wiener roast at the vast majority of local beaches. The NO FIRE warnings—sometimes conveyed through words, sometimes through symbols—are, perhaps of all the signs, the most important to heed. Such a sign can appear during a hot summer where you hadn't seen one before. In some spots in Central Saanich you can actually have a beach fire—but you need a "legal permit."

**Dog or pet signs** One assumes the pets in question are dogs. It is hard to imagine what else these might mean. Sometimes the signs tell you to keep your pet on a leash, but more often they are concerned with your pet's excrement. Particularly charming are the signs with the diagram of a squatting dog slashed through with a red line—though, presumably, such a sign is to be interpreted to mean that you should clean up after your dog, not that your dog needs to be warned not to defecate.

Psychologists would have a field day in gauging what lies behind the various levels of genteel circumlocution affected by most sign makers. "Droppings" vies with "excrement" and "defecate," though fortunately never with either "feces" or even the British version, "faeces." Those who hit on the simplest solution, "Clean up after your pet," deserve kudos! At some access points plastic bags are provided. In fact, the creativity and flamboyance of locals in crafting signs for dog owners could make a special study. Waggish exclamations about "pooper scoopers" and invitations to "Paws here, Rover" are rife. Probably most charming of all is the sign in Gonzales Bay, headed PAWS IN PARKS, which employs a nearly life-sized painting of a mournful basset to draw attention to the detailed rules.

**Parking** Whether your access spot is along a through road or at the end of a cul-de-sac, you might find parking is not great. Almost invariably, parking on the shoulder of the road is an option, but rarely can more than two or three cars park there. While the smaller public access spots in this book are not suitable for groups—avoid taking your 64-member family reunion to anywhere other than a public beach—there are some spots where half a dozen cars can park comfortably. You should, of course, be sensitive about blocking driveways and service roads. After all, the reason some spots exist at all as public access routes is that they double as service routes to shorefront utilities such as drainage controls. These spots are occasionally accompanied by warnings that your car will be towed away.

**Facilities** Few of these spots have public toilets. Keep that fact in mind when you plan your outing. The last thing locals or other beachgoers want to face is the unpleasant sight of wild rose bushes festooned with toilet paper.

Remember that the same applies to your toy poodle or your Irish wolfhound—even if there is no "pet" sign. Even worse than festoons of toilet paper is a mound of dog excrement. If you are going to take Fang or Fifi for a little salt air, bring a pooper scooper.

**Boat launching** Use this book to find suitable canoe and kayak launching spots. Only a couple are suitable for launching boats of any weight—say a dinghy with a small outboard—and even in these cases, launching is only easily done at high tide. Many more spots are suitable for launching kayaks and canoes, though you will want to check the information about the length of the trail and the trail's steepness, width and roughness, as well as the extent to which the tide goes out. The best spots for launching kayaks are listed in the final chapter, but other spots can be used, depending on your tides and your determination.

**Cyclists** Some of the most nature-loving, free spirits are those cyclists who use this book to find charming, hidden spots. Any truly motivated cyclist will have no difficulty gaining access to any of these spots, but will probably want to bring a lock in order to leave a bicycle on the road, especially where the path to the beach is steep and difficult. Some of the routes that are particularly well suited to combining cycling touring with beach hunting include the obvious marine drive in Victoria, from Ogden Point to the Victoria Golf Club, the Lochside cycling path in Saanich and, more obscurely, the quiet roads in North Saanich starting at Coles Bay Park and ending in Swartz Bay. If you are intending a circular trip with part of the route away from the coast, plan so you will be cycling on the sea side of the road. For the Lochside path, that means cycling from south to north, and for a North Saanich route, from north to south.

**Flora and fauna** One of the considerable pleasures of many of these spots is not just what is to be found on the shore, but what is to be seen on the way to the shore. This book includes descriptions of distinctive features such as giant old-growth cedars, stands of contorted arbutus, grassy bluffs or splashing streams. At some access points, in fact, you can combine your beach experience with a walk through some wonderful natural woodlands. In North Saanich and Gordon Head carefully signposted walking trails connect shoreside walking with other walking. For the former, read the Parks Guide at www.northsaanich.ca/Welcome_to_North_Saanichton.htm. For the latter, locate the maps at www.gov.saanich.bc.ca/resident/parks/TrailMaps.html.

If you keep in mind the following tips, you may encounter wildlife. Look for sea lions in local waters between October and May and flocks of brant geese in spring. Since many shorebirds spend their summers in the far north and their winters here, consider the pleasures of shorebird identification when the season makes it too cold to picnic or sunbathe. In choppy weather these birds gather in sheltered bays; Roberts Bay Bird Sanctuary north of Sidney is an excellent spot to track them down.

**Beach fires** Don't even think about having a beach fire during fire season, even when you crave s'mores. Enjoy the tranquility and freedom from lungfuls of smoke. Even when beach fires are permitted, be considerate to others and build your fire well below the high tide line. Nothing ruins the pristine pleasures of a shiny pebble beach more than an ugly firepit with ashes smeared into the stones or adjoining logs scarred with burnt areas. In addition, rocks that have been overheated turn an ugly orange-brown, permanently blemishing the beach.

**Beachcombing** Do you most like to use a public access spot as the beginning of an exploration of a piece of shoreline? Whether you enjoy poking through tidal pools or striding along with the wind in your hair, many of these access points will allow you considerable opportunity for uplifting waterfront walks. There are a few things to remember, though, before you set off along the beach. First, technically all land below the high-water mark cannot be privately owned. Don't, therefore, be intimidated if your walk takes you embarrassingly close to someone's front yard. Do, however, respect private property and, as much as possible, keep your distance. Also, be prepared for the heavy development that affects much of the coast around Victoria and Saanich Peninsula.

And don't forget to consider tides. Some carefree rambles can turn into awkward scrambles over bluffs or steep rocks at high tide. At the same time, you needn't worry overly much about tides. It is true that at many points on the island's *west* coast, being trapped at high tide can lead you into dangerous situations. In this area, there are no spots where you will be endangered by high tide approaching—though you might be inconvenienced. Finally, consider the season. Many rocky beaches, easy to stroll along in summer, can be dangerously slimy in winter. Tread carefully when you return in winter to a beach you explored in summer without difficulty.

**Seclusion** You may feel motivated to hunt down a small, remote beach to get away from the madding crowds that throng the big public beaches. If so, you might be unhappy that about two-thirds of the beaches in this book lie between private houses. Take heart! At some of these places you can expect to sit for hours at a time contemplating, undisturbed, the play of light on the waves and the cry of the gulls, or how you are going to tell your partner that he snores.

This book will alert you when an area possesses one of the four key factors that provide that sense of seclusion. First, a few spots border on undeveloped or otherwise "wild" land, such as that belonging to a First Nations reserve. Second, some spots are configured in such a way that rock bluffs, cliffs or the like will screen you from the houses along the waterfront. You will learn from this book that neighbouring houses are sometimes built well back from the bank or behind a high hedge or screen of trees. Third, you can sometimes walk more than half a kilometre out to the low-tide line and so be luxuriously alone with your toes in the sand. Last, as you will discover, some access points are rarely used, even by local residents.

**Mountain views** Islanders often take for granted the fact that, on a world scale, the fantastic views from the coasts of Saanich Peninsula and the Victoria area are actually extremely uncommon. For most places on planet Earth, a "sea view" means perhaps an odd promontory or two, maybe some islands, but beyond that, blank, unadorned horizon. The eye loves the ocean view that involves both movement as well as stillness. The picture-perfect, rare view, with foreground, middle ground and distance—promontories, water, islands, mountains—is typical of the Island's east coast from the northern tip to the south.

The treed bluffs rising above the west shore of Saanich Inlet fill the view from the west coast of North Saanich. These high bluffs can't quite be said to form a mountain, but together are referred to as the Malahat. Their wooded face is interrupted only by a large cleared area at their base; this is Bamberton, formerly a cement works and, if plans go ahead, soon to be a major housing development. Much farther to the east, the heavily developed patch of houses on a low bluff west of the Cherry Point area is Arbutus Ridge, a retirement community.

The rounded crests of Salt Spring Island—especially Mount Tuam—

Saanichton Bay Park

dominate the view from the north coast of Saanich Peninsula. From the east coast of the peninsula, the undulating shapes of the other Gulf Islands form most of the wealth of land contours. North of Sidney, the welter of overlapping reefs, islets and islands large and small is truly astounding. As you move down the east coast of the peninsula, be aware that those islands that appear to be just a short paddle away are actually on the other side of an international border. These islands may, by treaty, belong to the United States, but depending on whose history you read (including that of the oddest war in the history of international border conflict, the Pig War), either those islands rightfully belong to Canada or else the southern part of Vancouver Island—from the forty-ninth parallel in Ladysmith down to Victoria—rightfully belongs to the United States. As it is, we have a whole horizon-full of pretty American islands—just a paddle away.

Those for whom no view is complete without mountains will be heartened to know that from certain perspectives the mainland mountain ranges provide an intriguingly jagged skyline. From the east side of Saanich Peninsula, most spectacular is Mount Baker, well south of the US border. Perpetually white, perpetually awe-inspiring, Mount Baker towers above the surrounding peaks of the

North Cascades and, below, the headlands, islets and reefs of the coast. Captain George Vancouver named the mountain, not very creatively, after his third lieutenant, Joseph Baker. That the mountain is so white, even in the hottest summers, is in part due to the glaciers formed by centuries of enormous snowfalls that never entirely melt—though these glaciers, like others in the world, are gradually shrinking. The bright white is also annually enhanced by snow: in 1998–99 the mountaintop was buried under a record-breaking fall of more than 29 metres. This (not quite extinct) volcano is the northernmost of a sequence of similar volcanoes dotting a geographically unstable region all the way to northern California.

South of the sightline to Mount Baker, and in full view from the coast between Ten Mile Point and southern Oak Bay, stretches what appears to be open horizon. Tucked just out of sight below the horizon is the series of islands and inlets that lead into Puget Sound toward Seattle. To the south of this gap arises as if from nowhere the northern fringe of the Olympic Mountains. These mountains, Victoria's trademark backdrop, reach their maximum height, at 2,427 metres, among the glaciers of Mount Olympus. We expect to see large glaciers on mountains that are either higher or farther from the equator, but the same snowstorms that cover nearby Mount Baker also create huge accumulations of snow, and therefore glaciers, here. In 1774, the Spanish explorer Juan José Pérez Hernandez named the mountain Santa Rosalia. Fourteen years later, British explorer John Meares gave it its current name.

Appearing against the skyline as less a peak than a jagged line, Mount Olympus is flanked by many other, less snowy peaks, among them Mount Angeles and, to its left, Hurricane Ridge. Those who have not taken the ferry to Port Angeles and made their way up Olympic National Park should put the trip on their to-do list. Amazingly, you can drive right to the top of Hurricane Ridge—and then follow the ridge by walking the skyline trail. A better view of the Victoria shoreline is hard to imagine!

**Maps** The numbered beaches start at Gowlland Tod Provincial Park and move clockwise, north up the west coast of Saanich Peninsula and south down the east coast to Victoria, and terminating in View Royal. Unnumbered beaches are described only briefly, in "Also nearby" sections at the end of entries, and shown on the sketch map with an asterisk (*).

When there is more than one beach in an "Also nearby" section, each spot is also given a capital letter to distinguish it (*A, *B and so on). In almost all cases, you'll find these places on the sketch maps between one numbered access point and the next higher one, though occasionally an asterisked spot will appear on the next map.

Unless you know all the significant roads around the Victoria area, you should use the simplified sketch maps in this book in conjunction with a street map. As much as possible, the small maps include major arterial roads or connections to these major arterial roads; for example, West Saanich Road, Cordova Bay Road and Beach Drive. Commercial street maps alone are not very useful for finding your way to some of the more out-of-the-way spots in this book: they either include roads that simply don't exist, except in some planner's head, or they don't indicate roads that do exist, and they can vary from one to another. Online map sites are also not always accurate, and if you are using a GPS, be careful. Often a road exists in several discontinuous sections. Lochside Drive can be particularly confusing, but there are many, many other examples, mentioned here when necessary.

Saanichton Bay Park

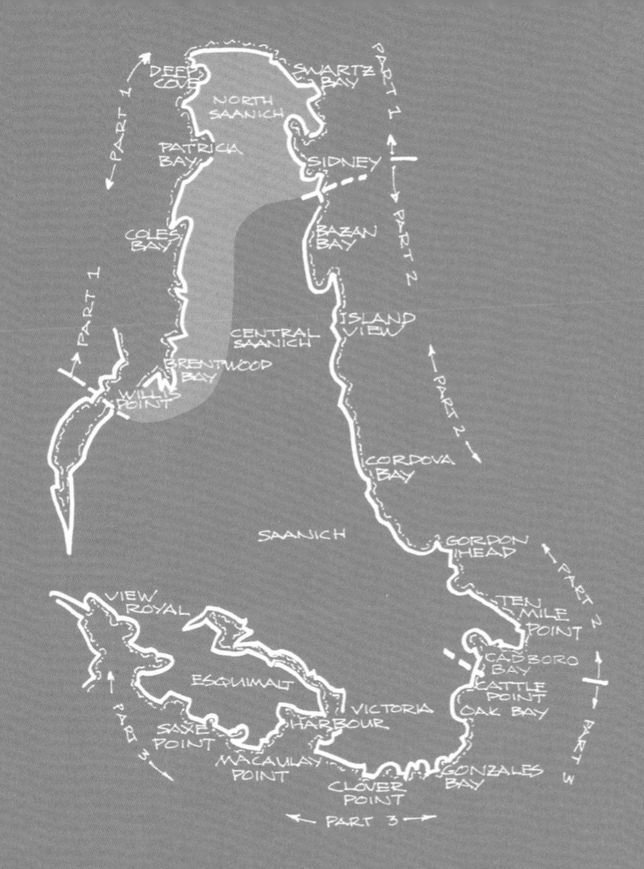


# PART 1 Saanich Inlet to North Sidney

THE HUGE CHUNK OF LAND COMPRISING the lower west side of Saanich Peninsula is still virtual wilderness—and for a very good reason. While the rest of Saanich Peninsula is a largely hospitable area of wooded hills and valleys hosting farms and residential developments, this corner is a high range of rocky, wooded bluffs dropping steeply toward Saanich Inlet. The wonderful walking trails in this rugged corner await lovers of natural scenery, from Goldstream Provincial Park northward into Gowlland Tod Provincial Park.

Access to the shore along the west side of Saanich Peninsula begins with the northernmost of the many trails in Gowlland Tod Park. The beach explorer who starts here and moves north toward the tip of the peninsula will discover that although there are dozens of opportunities to get to the shore, the access routes come in distinct clumps. The tangled byways around Brentwood Bay provide one set of access points. After that, there are few opportunities to gain access to the shoreline until you approach the housing developments toward the tip of the peninsula and along its northern shore.

Fortunately, the shorefront access routes both in North Saanich and north of Sidney are generally well developed, well signposted—and well worth visiting. Those on the west coast of the peninsula provide the warmest swimming water, pretty pebbly coves of light-catching granite rock, lots of afternoon sunshine and great sunsets. The dozen or so access points north of Sidney provide wonderful island views, deep bays with marinas and bird sanctuaries and stretches of low-tide sand.

Throughout the whole area, the character of the beaches varies enormously with the level of the tide. Check the descriptions of individual beaches and consult your tide tables if you want to find just the beach to launch a kayak, take a warm and pleasant swim, explore tidal pools or run with your children barefooted over sand.

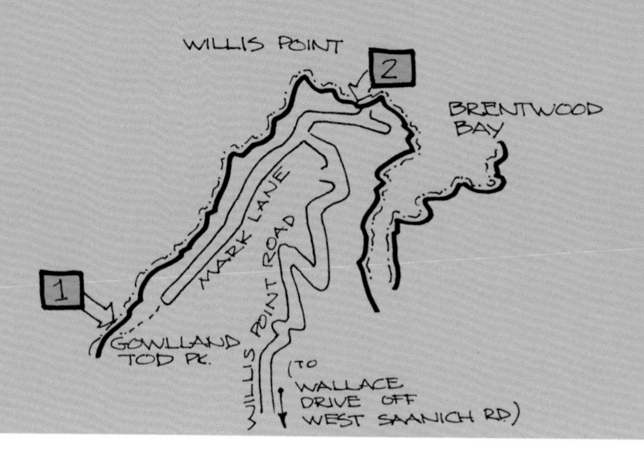

## 1

### GOWLLAND TOD —MARK LANE

**A long, forested walk to an isolated bluff and a tiny pebble beach**

**Location, signs and parking** The access point at the end of Mark Lane within Gowlland Tod Provincial Park may win the prize for the most isolated spot in this book, particularly since the next entry describes the only other shore access for several kilometres. From West Saanich Road, turn off onto Wallace Drive and then follow Willis Point Road as it winds and weaves through many forested kilometres to the steep shores of Saanich Inlet. At the T-junction, turn left onto Mark Lane and follow the signs for GOWLLAND TOD PROVINCIAL PARK to the very end of the road. Be warned, though: there are several other access routes to different parts of this huge park and several enticing signs leading you to these different approaches. This is the only one that goes to the water's edge. You will have no problem parking in the large turnaround area without blocking anyone's drive.

**Path** The path follows the route of a rough track once used by scuba divers and others. It is now used primarily by intrepid trekkers. To find the water's edge, walk 150 m down the wide track as it descends gradually toward the shore running parallel and visible through the trees. Once you are close to the water you will see a narrow path leading to a small, wooded knoll.

**Beach** If you really want a beachy bit of shore on which to flop languidly, try the tiny pebbly cove immediately to the left of the knoll. Since it is set well back into the trees, however, you may prefer to spend your time on the low, rounded rocky area under the arbutus and small firs. The shore drops off quickly here into the depths of the Squally Reach–Saanich Inlet waters, so snorkellers will find it an intriguing spot to make a watery visit.

**Suitability for children** This is not the best spot for wobbly little creatures, but older children who are used to trekking with outdoorsy parents will enjoy this appealing beach. Low tide is most interesting for those who like bothering shore life; high tide is best for those who want to splash and be splashed.

**Suitability for groups** A wedding party or family reunion will not be thrilled by the long drive, the long walk and the limited shore area. Other, smaller groups who know what they're facing will find that the easy parking, beautiful treed views and pleasant shore area are great for picnics and photos. Since the end of the road marks the beginning of the Mackenzie Bight Trail, some will use this approach to start a long walk. From here, trails lead along the shore of the inlet deep into the steep hills of the rest of the park.

**View** This is the deepest into Saanich Inlet you can easily get from this east side of the inlet. Those who have driven up and down Malahat Drive for years will be intrigued by the views of the high, wooded hills of the Malahat not very far away across the inlet. The industrial scar of the former Bamberton cement works, now morphing into a residential area, will be a little less intriguing.

**Winds, sun and shade** The first half of the day is the shadiest, so choose afternoon if you wish to catch some rays to warm up after a dip or to sit in dappled shade under the trees on the promontory. The spot is fairly protected from most winds; when a strong westerly is kicking up a foamy fuss on the east side of Saanich Peninsula, you will be quite sheltered here, though some strong breezes occasionally funnel up and down the inlet.

**Beachcombing** You are on the edge here of a classic fjord sculpted by an ancient glacier. The more you go south, the more you experience the steep, rocky shore. It is possible to pick your way along this shore, especially at low tide—watching out for slippery rocks—but if you want to step out energetically, choose the park trails rather than the shoreline.

**Seclusion** Even on a warm summer's day you can come to this spot expecting to see few people and be seen by few. The long drive is well worth the glorious seclusion you can usually find here.

## 2

### MARK LANE

A broad path to a tiny rocky cove, sometimes used by scuba divers, probably of most interest to kayakers

**Location, signs and parking** Willis Point, on which Mark Lane terminates, extends north into Saanich Inlet. After winding many kilometres along Willis Point Road from Wallace Road off West Saanich Road, you will reach a T-junction with Mark Lane. Turn right and follow Mark Lane almost to the end. No sign or house number exists to help you here, so simply look for a weedy, car-width track leading straight toward the water. There is lots of parking near the beginning of this track, unless you happen to arrive when divers are staggering to or from the shore.

**Path** One of the features that makes this spot usable for kayakers—and divers—is the easy path, gently sloping about 40 m to the shore. At the end of this path, a slight but awkward drop down to the confined space on the rocky shore makes access easier for divers than kayakers.

**Beach** You will find yourself on a rough bit of solid-rock shore with barely enough space to get one kayak at a time into the water. Few enticements beckon the beachgoer to this dark and enclosed bit of shore, other than its usefulness as access to the inlet. Since there is no other nearby launching spot for kayaks or canoes, those who would like to paddle into Saanich Inlet toward Goldstream might be happy to cope with the slight struggle of getting their craft into the water here.

**Suitability for children** Children will find little of interest here, other than the water molecule, of course. They may enjoy the feeling of having discovered an isolated spot, though.

**Suitability for groups** Mostly kayaking or scuba groups will want to stay here for long, though those scouting out views or unusual bird specimens might want to stop by as a slight detour after having been to Gowlland Tod Park (see previous access point).

**View** The view is very pretty, looking as it does up Saanich Inlet and back across the top of Tod Inlet to Brentwood Bay, where the little ferry plies its Mill Bay route.

**Winds, sun and shade** A north or west wind will blow directly onto this shore. If you are a kayaker, keep this in mind when the wind is strong, which is rare, as you will be faced with the prospect of launching a kayak into onshore chop.

**Beachcombing** While you could clamber over the rocks to the right of the access, you will feel little incentive to do so, not least of all because a private jetty largely blocks the shore a short distance away.

**Seclusion** Only a few houses are in this area, generally set well back into the large lots. You will not feel nearly as much in the thick of a suburb as you would at the other similar launching spot to the north off Senanus (see Brentwood Drive access, number 4).

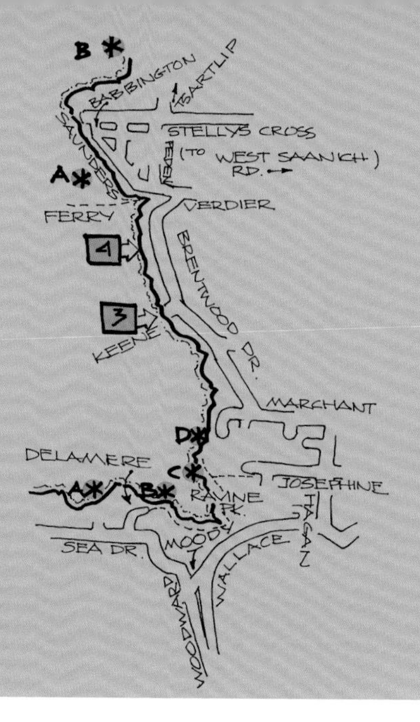

## 3

## KEENE WAY

**A well-maintained approach to a pretty gravel shore in the middle of Brentwood Bay**

**Location, signs and parking** You will see a sign for the very short Keene Way (formerly **Devonshire Road,** the sign informs you) along Brentwood Drive a short distance south of the Brentwood Bay town centre and the ferry landing (easiest found by driving from West Saanich Road to Verdier Avenue, and then left onto Brentwood Drive). Permit yourself to feel a little under siege as you notice that NO PARKING signs line the sides of Brentwood Drive for a considerable distance in either direction. In fact, the gravel shoulders are wide—and dotted with parked cars. If you make the assumption that there is safety in numbers, you will find yourself doing what others do and join them on the roadside. Otherwise, a little more sensibly, you could use the large parking lot near the shore between Josephine and Marchant, a block south of Keene.

**Path** Once you have walked the few metres to the end of Keene Way, you will see a small, business-like rectangular BEACH ACCESS sign atop a pole and a broad gravel path curving, a little oddly, in front of a neighbouring house. Within a few metres, a wooden railing leads to a hilltop park bench and the beginnings of a wooden staircase. Fifteen or so steps take you down these very solid stairs onto a gravel area beside a less-than-pleasant concrete structure.

**Beach** Although many will find that the Brentwood Drive access immediately north of this one is generally more attractive, this beach has some real advantages. Fine gravel extends almost to the low-tide level without a barricade of boulders. In addition, you can find shade from an overhanging oak even late into a blisteringly hot, sunny afternoon. The concrete structure with firmly locked door and warning sign is not one of the advantages, however. Nor is the huge retaining wall backing the beach, though if there has to be a retaining wall it would be difficult to find a more attractive one than this stone and mortar masterwork.

**Suitability for children** Children—and adults, too—will need sturdy water shoes if they are going to enjoy this beach. On a day with cool breezes elsewhere you can bring your little one here for lots of watery fun. Because the shore slopes only gradually, about 15 m or so is exposed at most low tides, so if your child plays with water wings at a mid or high tide you don't have to worry about her suddenly finding herself out of her depth.

**Suitability for groups** A clutch of friends or a hungry family or two could be happily accommodated here. Parking is an obvious issue, however, and the beach area between jetties is not vast.

**View** If you enjoy clusters of jetties and wharfs against a backdrop of wooded hills across the water, you will enjoy the view here—but don't come to this spot expecting to find a lot of natural scenery.

**Winds, sun and shade** Morning time is shade time. Afternoon is generally sunny, but with a little shade. No time is a windy time unless a strong northerly springs up.

**Beachcombing** See the next entry about Brentwood Drive.

**Seclusion** You can't expect much privacy or much sense of isolated wilderness in the middle of a village. You can, however, expect to find few people, if any, on this little bit of shore.

### * Also nearby

**A.** From West Saanich Road, take Wallace Drive west until you reach Moody Street, where you make a sharp turn right and then a sharp turn left where the road leads into **Sea Drive**. Immediate west of the church atop the hill and near the driveway numbered 770, you will see a BEACH ACCESS sign. A dirt track leads down a wooded bank and a flight of almost 30 wooden stairs to a cove and a pretty view of the tiny island in front and northward up Saanich Inlet. The cove has a small beach of pebbles and gravel, but is in shade for most of the day. Local residents use this spot mostly for tying up dinghies and kayaks. On both sides of the cove, jetties project into the bay.

**B.** To reach the end of **Delamere Road**, off Woodward Drive, follow the PUBLIC BEACH ACCESS signs. At the end of the road, walk toward the shore and the beginning of a raised seafront esplanade that passes in front of hillside condominiums and deep into the forested ravine at the

Marchant Road

most recessed part of Brentwood Bay. You are welcome to bring your four-legged friend here, but are requested to clean up "droppings" with the plastic bags provided.

**C.** From near the end of Josephine Road, which runs off Hagan Road via Wallace Drive, a well-signposted network of trails leads into **Ravine Park**, the same forested ravine and shorefront esplanade accessible from Delamere Road. This is the place to come if your primary interest is in the park of large cedars, firs and sword ferns rather than the shorefront walk in front of the condominiums. On the other hand, when you reach the esplanade from here you can start the walk along Brentwood Harbour to your right, ending near Blue's Bayou Cafe.

**D.** A clear route from the end of **Marchant Road**, two blocks north of Josephine, takes you to a public wharf extending out over the water and leading down to a small floating dock. Both diving and swimming from the wharf are forbidden. A sign directed toward dog owners is charmingly illustrated with the smiling face of an animal that can only be a bear. The intriguing waterfront café called Blue's Bayou stands on stilts over the water immediately next door.

## 4

## BRENTWOOD DRIVE

**Probably the best beach in the middle of Brentwood Bay**

**Location, signs and parking** On Brentwood Drive, near the top of the hill immediately south of Verdier Avenue and central Brentwood Bay, and about two blocks north of Marchant Road, is a significant bend in the road. Look for an olive-green wooden pillar on the sea-side bend of the road. A blue and white vertical strip bears the words BEACH ACCESS and points you toward the paved access strip. It is easy to miss the post, so look out for the house numbered 7130 as a further clue. Like almost everywhere else in Brentwood Bay, this spot makes life difficult for those in vehicles. You will have to park on the unpaved shoulder of Brentwood Drive and walk to the brick and asphalt strip leading toward the water.

**Path** From the road, a red brick path soon turns into a smooth dirt and gravel strip between hedges and, after about 30 m, emerges onto an unusual feature for a public access route—a kind of rock and mortar patio jutting out over a rocky bluff. The two picnic benches here invite you to stop and drink in the view. They also contribute to the suitability of this destination as a place for those with difficulty walking to picnic or snack. From this spot about 30 solid wooden steps, complete with handrails, take you under a large fir and onto a gravelly bit of shore.

**Beach** The beach is probably most pleasant at mid to high tide, when the jagged barnacle-encrusted boulders around the low-tide mark are well covered. The gradually sloping mid- to upper beach is made up of rough gravel, though the rock bluff on which the viewing patio is constructed juts forward partway down the beach on the left. The lower slopes of this bluff seem to be a favourite perching spot for local swimmers and sunbathers, but the gravel shore can make for pleasant lounging as well, if you have a beach towel for padding.

**Suitability for children** The protected waters of Brentwood Bay can get more than decently warm, though swimming is clearly best at mid to high tide. At low tide, children will find interesting specimens of shore life under the boulders, and, properly protected with water shoes, can enjoy splashing around—though the water becomes deep quite quickly at the lower end of the beach.

**Suitability for groups** Parking can be something of a problem but otherwise this can be a good spot to bring a family or a small group of friends looking for an unusual picnicking or socializing spot for a few hours. One strategy is to combine a visit to one of the local cafés for lunch with a walk to this beach for a swim or a bit of languid, lazy time.

**View** Because you find yourself in the middle of a busy little series of bays, most of whose shore dwellers love boats and boating, you will see all manner of wharfs and jetties in the immediate foreground of your view—including the dock for the little ferry that plies the water between Brentwood Bay and Mill Bay. You might want to build ferry travel into your plans for exploring this charming and infrequently visited bit of coast. Beyond the man-made structures, the view is surprisingly varied for this side of the Saanich Inlet, since you can see not only Salt Spring Island to the north but also the foreground shores of the opposite side of Tod Inlet, with Butchart Gardens tucked out of sight, and Willis Point beyond.

**Winds, sun and shade** The firs and high bank can cast plenty of morning shadow on the beach. By mid afternoon on a hot day, it can be scorching hot, and all the more because winds are generally light at this sheltered part of the inlet.

**Beachcombing** While it is physically possible to pick your way along the shore for some distance, you will soon run into jetties projecting into the water. Walkers might consider making a tour of the roadways in the whole Brentwood Bay area, including the area of tiny lanes at the north end of the village and shorefront promenades to the south.

**Seclusion** On a warm afternoon, you can't expect to be alone on this pretty little beach, since locals are well aware of its charms. Don't be surprised, however, if you do have it all to yourself.

*** Also nearby**

**A.** From Tsartlip Drive in South Saanich Indian Reserve 1, **Boat Ramp Road** leads to an open shore past the Tsartlip First Nation headquarters. Only some special circumstance would take you there, however, and only after the proper channels had been used to gain permission from the Tsartlip First Nation.

**B.** Although parking is difficult in the incredibly narrow lanes at the northernmost part of shorefront Brentwood Bay, you can walk along the shore for several blocks. Park, for example, near the marina and ferry dock close to the junction of Peden Lane and Verdier Avenue, then find the path, which is apparently **Saunders Lane** on maps, heading northwest past the parking. Then turn up Babbington Lane, the last possible street heading north, and continue your shorefront exploration one block up, down Stelly's Cross Road toward the shore.

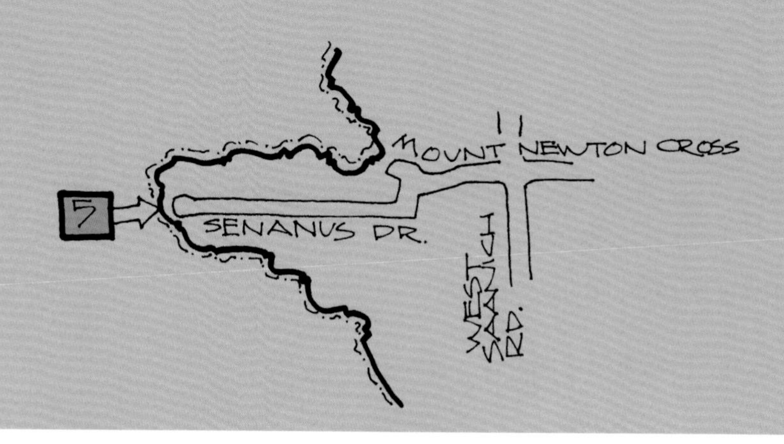

5

**SENANUS DRIVE**

**A short path to a tiny out-of-the-way cove in Saanich Inlet, popular with scuba divers**

**Location, signs and parking** Senanus Drive leads to the tip of a peninsula off Mount Newton Cross Road, which crosses West Saanich Road. Follow Senanus Drive to its end and park in the fairly large turnaround area. While this area is usually empty, it can be packed to the gills with scuba divers' vehicles and shoals of divers climbing in and out of equipment. You are not welcome here overnight, of course, and, as with most other spots in this area, night begins at 9 p.m. and doesn't end until 7 a.m.—so forget those mid summer sunset viewings since, as another sign warns, your car will be towed. Away.

**Path** Part of the reason scuba divers come here is that they don't have to tote their heavy gear long distances or down cliffs. A level gravel path takes you a few dozen metres down a small, fairly steep bit of rock, with a few concrete block steps helping you and, more important, the divers over the last bit.

**Beach** This is a tiny cove wedged in between neighbouring houses, one with a high wooden fence built as far forward as it can possibly go, even over the trunk of a decoratively drooping oak. The uppermost part of the shore is rather wet and set back into the vegetation, so most beachgoers will prefer to move closer to the water and the solid lumps of rock interspersed with patches of pebbles. The tide does not go out far here and the shore drops off fairly quickly, both traits of a typical dive site.

**Suitability for children** This is the kind of mini-beach to visit for a short period. It is not the kind of place where a child will want to stay long, though an older child equipped with mask and snorkel would enjoy a splash and swim.

**Suitability for groups** Since more than a dozen divers can converge here at a time, you may feel that more than a dozen birders can do likewise. While, strictly speaking, this is true, don't forget that divers can spread out into the depths in a way that most birders cannot. Find another spot.

**View** This is about the midpoint of the Saanich Inlet, where the hills of the Malahat are low on the horizon, so the view is still fairly open. From the lower part of the shore you will be able to see some distance south into Saanich Inlet and, in the other direction, out to Salt Spring Island.

**Winds, sun and shade** It can get baking hot here by mid afternoon, especially since shade is scant and few breezes lift the hair or cool the skin.

**Beachcombing** The shore is steep and weed-covered at the low-tide line, and the residents on the right have built a jutting stone arrangement that would make going to the right difficult. Find a different spot on which to walk.

**Seclusion** If you come here when the divers are busy with their bubbles elsewhere, you can expect to be the only one here. The neighbours' houses are sufficiently screened that you can be happily ensconced with your secondhand copy of *War and Peace* on a quiet bit of shore with a pretty view and lots of afternoon warmth.

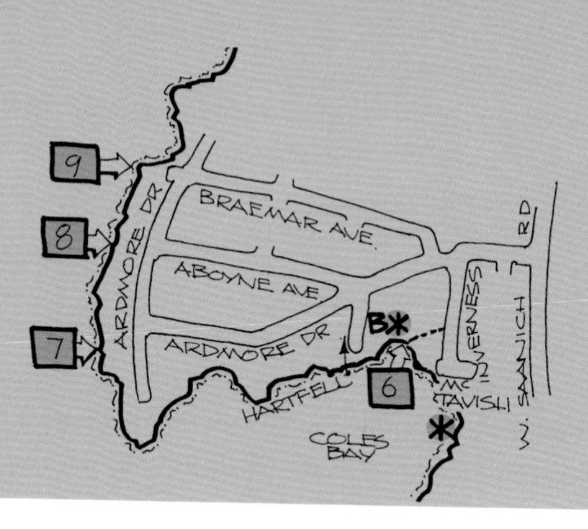

## 6

## COLES BAY REGIONAL PARK

Woodland trails leading to a protected gravel cove with lots of afternoon sun

**Location, signs and parking** From West Saanich Road, turn west onto Ardmore Drive. Take Inverness Road, the second on your left. Partway down, a large sign on your right carved in a rustic manner will tell you that you have, indeed, reached Coles Bay Regional Park. Another prettily painted sign provides a map of the trails in the park and more general information. Other more functional signs tell you not to collect shellfish and not to let your dog or its leavings be unmanaged. Cyclists will appreciate the bicycle rack. Car owners will soberly note the signs about thieves and towing regulations. A large gravel parking area can easily accommodate far more cars than are likely ever to converge on this park.

**Path** For many, it is not the shore itself but the paths to the shore that constitute the most attractive feature of this park. The main path, of well-maintained crushed gravel, meanders with little change in elevation. A side path takes you across a small gorge and then turns onto a parallel route toward the shore. The large firs and maples along the paths are particularly appealing on a sunny day. Less natural features will also be of interest, especially to families—toilet facilities and, closer to the water, picnic tables in an open grassy area.

**Beach** Ironically, the beach in this park is much less attractive than beaches elsewhere along Saanich Inlet whose access and parking are much more limited. As you approach the beach, you will quickly realize why picnic facilities have been provided at the grassy spot before reaching the shore. You'll have trouble finding anywhere, except for a few logs, to perch and eat, let alone contemplate. Most of the small narrow bay is covered with gravel and rocks, though they are surprisingly unsquelchy, given the recessed nature of the shore here. The tide goes out a long way, and so the water can be warm for swimming at high tide. In fact, swimmers may well find that this is the warmest swimming beach in the whole area.

**Suitability for children** Most children would probably be happiest here at mid to high tide, when they can splash and wade in safety. The comparative lack of barnacles, the gradual slope of the beach and the warm water make this a child-friendly beach. The protection from winds and the lack of shade on the shore also help. The major limitation is the lack of anywhere appealing to sit between splashy episodes.

**Suitability for groups** The large parking area and facilities would seem to make this a suitable spot for lots of people to convene. There are only three picnic tables, however, and the shore area is limited. It is unlikely that a large group would want to linger here after walking the pretty trails and admiring the view.

**View** Were it not that the shore is so obviously a tidal one, many visitors might think they were at the side of a lake rather than at the ocean. Although the view is more enclosed that at any other section of this shore, it is attractive. The varied contours of the hills and headlands and the expanses of forest are broken only by Bamberton across Saanich Inlet and a few houses to the right. The Malahat directly in front and the high wooded shores of Saanich Inlet extending down Squally Reach almost as far as Mount Finlayson together make for a prettily framed picture.

**Winds, sun and shade** Even when winds are frisky elsewhere in the area, they are largely absent here. While lots of shade lurks in the forest behind the beach, on the shore itself there is little shade to be found after mid morning.

**Beachcombing** Strollers and explorers can make their way a considerable distance along the gravelly shore to the left, particularly at low tide. To the right, however, the shore narrows to a strip of rock after some distance.

**Seclusion** This is one of the most secluded bits of shore on the Saanich Peninsula, even though there are a few houses on the wooded banks to the north. For most of the peninsula, public access routes are amply provided wherever there are housing developments. Here, access to the shore is provided for the opposite reason—it's in a Capital Regional Park.

### * Also nearby

**A.** Carry on past Coles Bay Park on Inverness Road to the end of the road, then turn right onto the very short **McTavish Road** (not to be confused with the discontinuous McTavish Road cutting across the Saanich Peninsula). From the end of McTavish a public access path leads a short distance down to a gravelly shore. It is possible to launch a kayak from here, though best at high tide.

**B. Hartfell** leads off the section of Ardmore Drive that runs along the north shore of Coles Bay. Parking is difficult on Hartfell, so walk down to the end. From the top of the impressive flight of stone stairs, enjoy the view of Coles Bay and the narrow, wooded and rocky shore. If you decide to go down to the shore, be careful because even in summer groundwater can trickle over the steps and create a slimy patch.

## 7

### ARDMORE DRIVE—SOUTH

**A level, wooded path to an east-facing beach of mixed granite gravel-and-rock outcroppings**

**Location, signs and parking** This little gem is one of the more difficult beach access spots to find. The initial difficulty is sorting out the roads, since Ardmore Drive (currently misnamed on Google Maps) runs west off West Saanich Road, until it comes to an end at a T-junction with—wait for it—Ardmore Drive! The spot you want is on the short spur to the south of this T-junction. Keep your eyes peeled for a small gravel pull-off area, a sign saying NO FIRES PERMITTED and a fire hydrant. Oddly, at the time of writing, no indicator marks the spot, though indicator posts are otherwise scrupulously employed in North Saanich. The road is fairly narrow with little shoulder, so if you are lucky—and you are likely to be—you can park on the small gravel patch near the fire hydrant.

**Path** The path has clearly been maintained. Fresh crushed gravel covers its nearly level surface as it gently meanders some 70 or 80 m through small second-growth woods. A fence on one side will remind you that you are on a wooded strip between private residences. The path ends with a large juniper and Garry oaks, most commonly found on the sun-baked southern shores of Vancouver Island, the west shore of the peninsula and the Gulf Islands. This is one of the only paths on the whole peninsula running virtually at beach level, a fact of potential interest to kayakers.

**Beach** It is hard to account for the particularly appealing nature of the shore here, since the same elements you find here you will find at many other spots on the peninsula: patches of barnacly, broken rock interspersed with bumps and ridges of solid rock dotted with tidal pools at low tide. Because the rock is granite, the underwater patches of gravelly rock appear attractively turquoise—and appealing to snorkellers. Apparently seals are unusually common along this stretch of coast.

**Suitability for children** Properly shod and properly protected from the sun, all but the most sand-minded children should find much to amuse them here. They will, admittedly, have to be sure-footed as they clamber and bounce over some of the irregular features of the beach, but when they make their inevitable, gradual descent into the water, they should find it warmer here than at many other spots on the north and east shores of the peninsula. Be prepared for the lack of toilet facilities and the distance separating your child parked on the beach from your car parked on the road.

**Suitability for groups** Parking is the big issue here. Possibly two families could come here, but much more than that would have a hard time being accommodated.

**View** Though the view is not quite as extensive as at some other points on the peninsula, it is beautifully varied. To the south, the heavily wooded west shore of Saanich Inlet stretches to Mount Finlayson in the distance. The Malahat, complete with the scar of Bamberton, leads to Mill Bay, tucked largely out of sight. The trained eye can pick out Arbutus Ridge (another scar), Manley Creek Park, Cherry Point, Mount Tzouhalem and, to the far right, Salt Spring Island. Most visitors, though, will be happy just to enjoy the intersecting contours—including the tiny rock islets to the south.

**Winds, sun and shade** Largely protected from easterly winds, the shore is somewhat exposed to the northwesterlies that are rarely strong here. Morning shade dapples the upper beach, and the trees hang close to the ground, providing some shelter even in the afternoon. Because the land is low, however, you will never experience the dank and dark upper shore that the highest shorelines create.

**Beachcombing** You won't be hampered by cliffs or squelchy mud flats if you decide to make your way south to Yarrow Point—but even at mid tide, you will find you need to have a bit of an adventurous spirit and sturdy shoes to go the distance.

**Seclusion** Houses dot this section of coast. In the immediate vicinity of the access, however, they are set well back amidst leafy green. As a result, you can enjoy the pleasures of the spot without feeling either intrusive or intruded upon.

## 8

## ABOYNE AVENUE

**A flight of stairs to a shore of mixed rock, gravel, and sand, good for viewing sunsets**

**Location, signs and parking** Aboyne Avenue, like Ardmore Drive, is best described as peculiar. You will have to keep the faith, or pay close attention to a map. Drive from West Saanich Road along the southern branch of Ardmore Drive, looking for Aboyne Avenue. First you will pass Aboyne Avenue to your right shortly after passing Inverness Road. This is *not* the version of Aboyne Avenue that is your beach landmark—this Aboyne doesn't connect to the part you want except by footpath (it connects on some commercial and online maps). Instead follow Ardmore Drive until what appears to be a T-junction, and then turn right…onto Ardmore Drive. Proceed to the first road that joins Ardmore: lo and behold, it is none other than Aboyne…again! Be reassured that you have found the right place when you spot one of the marker posts with the little icon of a white walking figure on a blue square on the sea side of Ardmore directly opposite Aboyne. Ardmore Drive here is fairly narrow, without much shoulder, but it is quiet, treed and rural in feeling. You should have little difficulty finding a spot on the shoulder unless a posse of many other cars accompanies you.

**Path** The well-maintained, open path leads down a gradual but significant slope through light, airy woods. After 70 or 80 m you will come to an enticing spot under some large arbutus leaning over a steep bank—and a flight of 33 wooden steps in two stages.

**Beach** Like two or three other beaches close by, this one is wonderfully bright with light-reflecting granite. Even though a small cliff backs the shore, at places solid, at others formed of large boulders, the general effect is of light, especially where the water shines turquoise over the granite. To one side of the access is a small, sandy beach, but directly in front of the access, slabs of rock underfoot mingle with patches of loose granite boulders. Snorkelling and swimming would be rewarding here. Comfortable picnicking, though possible, is a little less easy to arrange. A charming little mink lives in the area and may provide you with a few photographs and a few smiles.

**Suitability for children** Like so many of the beaches in the area, this one is good for a child who is well shod, does not have sandcastles on the brain and is happy to clamber and splash. If your child is not sure of foot or doesn't like stairs, you would be better off choosing one of the many spots available with a smoother surface underfoot.

**Suitability for groups** Only a two-car-sized group would be easily accommodated here. A picnicking, wandering or birding group is less likely to find this the spot of their dreams than a sketching or photographing group—there are some truly lovely compositions of gnarled arbutus, cliffy rock and turquoise waters.

**View** Because the shore surrounds a small bay, the view is both enhanced and limited by the wooded, rocky land on either side. You will see lovely contours and stretches of wooded shore, both in the foreground and across the inlet, but if you want a panoramic view stretching from the end of Saanich Inlet to Salt Spring, you won't find it here. A single piling gives a little picturesque assertion to the rocky shore to the south. Like other spots on this part of the peninsula, this one is good for sunset collectors.

**Winds, sun and shade** When southeast winds are fuming and fussing away elsewhere, they are largely non-events here. When northwest winds are blowing, though, you will have a much better idea what they are up to. Sun lovers will be happiest coming here in the afternoon—the shore is well submerged in shadow until early afternoon, and then it receives the full brunt of the sun.

**Beachcombing** This is not the place to choose if you want to accumulate kilometres under your walking shoes. If, however, you are interested in exploring tidal pools and picking your way over interesting knobbles and bumps, you will be happy making your way in either direction.

**Seclusion** While you are close to residences on either side, you won't be much aware of them—or they of you. The steep shore and overhanging trees ensure some sense of seclusion.

## 9

### BRAEMAR AVENUE

A few steps to a bank-top view and a park bench before a considerable flight of stone stairs to a mixed shore

**Location, signs and parking** Slightly north along Ardmore from the previous access spot, turn west onto Braemar Avenue. The road ends shortly, in a turnaround area. You will see a NO PARKING sign, but, on closer inspection, will discover that only between 9 p.m. and 6 a.m. are you not allowed to park there—so give up on any ideas of midnight beach parties or Winnebago sleep-fests. If you want to watch a summer sunset—and this is a perfect spot from which to do so—you will have to park along the road. Except for the time restriction, you should have no difficulty parking in the turnaround area, where there is room for several cars. One of the marker posts with the blue and white access icons marks the beginning of the steps to the beach, but is hardly necessary since you can see the shore from the end of the road.

**Path** The road ends at the top of a steep bank in sight of the water, but one of the chief reasons for coming to this spot is the nature of the path. This is a good spot to bring someone who has walking difficulties, because the path goes but a few steps past the parking area to a bench overlooking the shore through an attractive cluster of trees. The stairs to the beach, with a handrail on one side, are a grand stone and concrete affair. After some 18 steps the approach takes an equally grand turn to run parallel to the shore. Kayakers could do worse than make use of this spot, but, of course, will have to be prepared for a little hefting up and down the stairs. A shellfish warning sign is posted on one of the trees above the shore, so you won't be able to get your paella ingredients here.

**Beach** The stairs bring you to the centre of a small gravelly bay with occasional low ridges of rock and rockweed. The shore shelves gradually and over a considerable expanse at low tide. A small rock and concrete retaining wall backs the beach on either side of the access steps, but an area of fine gravel above most high tides is pleasant for spreading out a picnic or settling with a book or easel.

**Suitability for children** The proximity to the car, the safe and solid stairs and the ease with which even unsteady little creatures can negotiate the nearly level shore all make this a reasonable spot to bring little ones. While the range of activities is limited, as long as your child enjoys paddling and picnicking, he or she will be well entertained. There are no toilets, so plan accordingly.

**Suitability for groups** Bring a small group here for a picnic and paddle, by all means, though the area is too limited to bring more than a small group.

**View** Because this access spot is at the head of a small but significantly indented bay, the view is much more limited than that from many other spots along this part of the peninsula. However, the curve of the shore is such that the view toward Mill Bay and extending to Cherry Point is framed by the low, wooded shorefront on either side.

**Winds, sun and shade** Protected from the south and east, the shore is fully exposed to the usually light summer winds from the northwest. Anyone who wants to be warmed by the sun will have to come in the afternoon; anyone who wants to picnic or perch in the shade should come fairly early in the day.

**Beachcombing** Since the beach changes from gravel to solid rock once you leave the end of the bay, beachcombing will be enjoyed most by those who arrive at low tide to explore the crevices and pools of the rock shelf.

**Seclusion** Houses are generally set well back, spaced reasonably apart and sheltered with foliage, to the extent that if you picnic on the upper shore you will neither see nor be seen by the local residents.

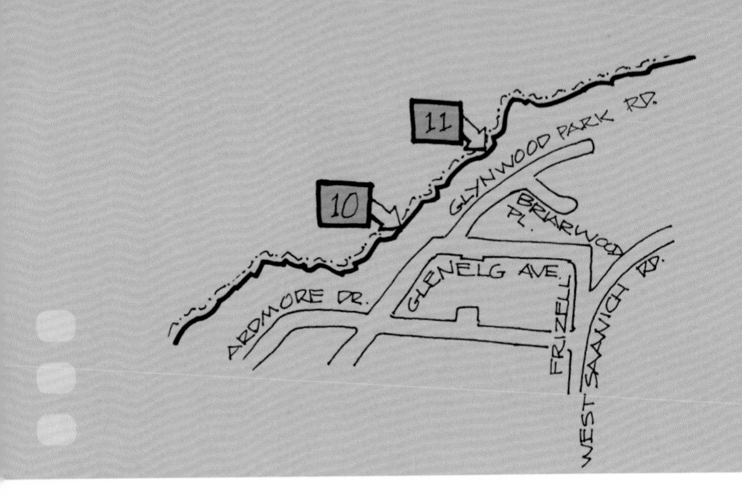

## 10 ARDMORE DRIVE–GLENELG AVENUE

A grassy path between houses and down a set of wooden stairs to a gently sloping beach of granite gravel, boulders, sand and flat rock

**Location, signs and parking** The access path is a little difficult to identify, but look for the T-junction of Ardmore Drive and Glenelg Avenue. Find a parking spot on the shoulder. Beside the STOP sign on Glenelg, you should be able to see one of the beach access posts set well back from the road, adorned with one of the signs prohibiting the collection of shellfish, though you might have to beat your way through some tall grass to get to the path.

**Path** The path goes horizontally nearly 100 m through a narrow strip between houses, partially screened by hawthorns and other small trees. After passing a concrete drainage structure inset in the ground, you will come to a set of 16 wooden stairs taking you to the shore.

**Beach** You will find yourself on a beach with a tangle of logs and mostly fine gravel interspersed with a few angular boulders. To your left is an odd-looking assortment of concrete structures, apparently the sad remains of someone's attempt to build a wharf. To your right you will find a small area of low-tide sand on the gradually sloping beach. It is possible, even pleasant, to relax and sprawl on the upper beach.

**Suitability for children** The appeal of this beach is similar to that of most other beaches in this area. You will want to bring shoes to protect little feet, but otherwise can happily sit back and watch a little one pry under rocks for creatures, throw rocks and splash with always increasing vigour. Most children will probably want to make a beeline for the low-tide sand down the beach to the right, so choose low tide for the most diverse child play.

**Suitability for groups** A group that is interested less in a picnicking beach than a wandering beach will find this one attractive and pleasant. Parking is a little tricky, though, and the shore area isn't huge, but it is isolated and easy enough to explore.

**View** Your view is bounded to the left by a point with some arbutus and shorefront bushes. To the right you can see an extensive sweep of low, treed shore and all the islands beyond the northern end of Saanich Inlet.

**Winds, sun and shade** Like the rest of the beaches in this area, this one is well protected from a southeast wind, but a northwest blow will reach it. Depending on the time of year, the bushes can cast fairly deep shadows well into the afternoon.

**Beachcombing** This is an inviting shore to explore, especially if you bring appropriate footgear and like encountering a mixture of shore types. Alternating areas of low, shelving rocks line the shore in both directions, but particularly to the north. You may be especially interested in heading north in any case, because the housing development ends within a few hundred metres to your right.

**Seclusion** Like most other spots here, this one is in the middle of a housing development. However, the houses are set well enough back and above you on the treed bank that you can come here expecting a quiet time with yourself or someone equally compatible.

# 11

## BRIARWOOD PLACE

A broad gravel slope with a concrete launching pad and some low-tide areas of sand

**Location, signs and parking** Where West Saanich Road curves to follow the shore of Patricia Bay, Frizell Road seems almost like a northern extension of it. If you are approaching from the south, therefore, you will drive straight ahead onto Frizell. If you are approaching from the north you will have to take a sharp turn back onto Frizell. In either case, turn immediately left onto Glenelg Avenue. The first and only right turn will take you onto Glynwood Park Road, and, a very short distance ahead, the intersection with Briarwood Place. Three discouraging signs on the corner declare that not only is there no parking and no harvesting of shellfish, but also that this is a tow-away zone for those who would block driveways. On the other corner, however, is an equally bold but more encouraging BEACH ACCESS sign. Parking is extremely awkward. You are not allowed to park anywhere, anytime, in the short extension of Briarwood that leads directly toward the water—and what appears to be a launching ramp. Your only option is to pull off onto the narrow grassy shoulder on Glynwood Park Road or Glenelg Avenue, being careful not to find yourself in the grass-covered ditch.

**Path** The "path" is really a small stretch of gravel road sloping a few metres toward a concrete ramp and handrail. At this point, those looking for a launching spot for their kayaks will reflect upon the fact that the NO PARKING signs do not say "no stopping," and may want to take advantage of the difference. If you are quick about getting your kayaks off the roof of your car and onto the slope, you couldn't find a much better put-in spot in this area. Those visitors with complicated picnics and cumbersome easels and the like will also note the ease of getting objects onto the shore.

**Beach** Probably more than any other beach on the west or north part of the Saanich Peninsula, this spot comes close to conforming to what most people think of when they hear the word "beach." At low tide the pebbles that make up most of the small bay actually blend into sand. The light colour of the pebbles and smooth, gradual slope of the shore make it particularly beachy in character. Those west coast picnickers who don't feel life is right unless they have a log to lean against will find a few on the upper shore. Retaining walls back the beach on both sides, one of loose granite boulders, the other of concrete.

**Suitability for children** The very qualities that make this a traditional beach also make it a great place to bring children. The lack of toilet facilities should be introduced into the equation, of course, but otherwise you could hardly do better than to bring children here, particularly if their chief mission in life is to splash and make watery mayhem. Do be aware, however, that the farther you head south into Saanich Inlet, the warmer the water is likely to be on any given day.

**Suitability for groups** Parking, the lack of facilities and the proximity of residents limit a group invasion of this spot. Two or possibly three vehicles' worth of picnickers is probably the most that would be comfortable here.

**View** Because this access brings you to the centre of a small bay, it doesn't provide as much scope as some other spots. Two treed points of land in one direction and one in the other, however, frame a pretty view of the north end of Saanich Inlet and part of Salt Spring Island.

**Winds, sun and shade** Well protected from the south and east, the beach is largely exposed to winds blowing from the north down Sansum Narrows. A few large and quite beautiful firs overhang this north-facing shore, so shade covers large patches of the beach well into the afternoon.

**Beachcombing** Most people who come to this spot will probably want to do their wandering along the pebbly or sandy water's edge in the small bay. It is possible, though, to extend your wandering some distance onto the solid-rock shelves beyond the edges of the bay.

**Seclusion** At this point you are close enough to the airport to be disturbed by the sound of airplanes. Also, the approach to the beach looks much more suburban than most on the peninsula; trimmed lawns and immaculate gardens abound. Once on the beach, however, and particularly if you are picnicking on the upper shore, you will not feel you are in someone's front garden, but, rather, on a lovely bit of beach.

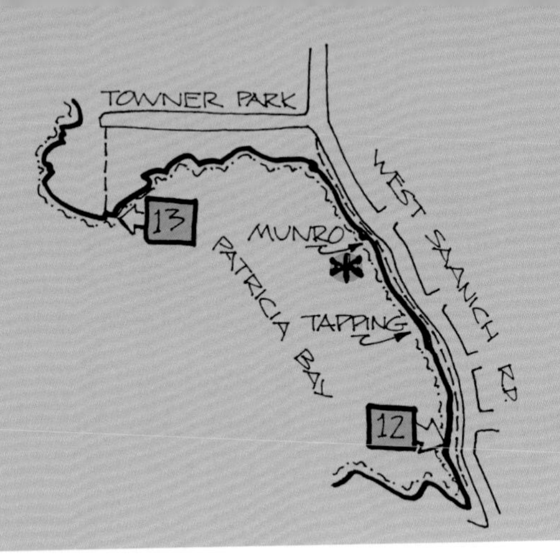

## 12

### PATRICIA BAY PARK

**A long strip of parkland between the road and the shore, with a lawn area, shade trees and picnic tables**

**Location, signs and parking** "You can't miss it," enthusiastic locals often tell us when we ask for directions to a new destination. Often they are wrong. In the case of Patricia Bay Park, though, it would take enormous skill or determination to "miss it." If you can find West Saanich Road, one of the main roads running north–south through Saanich Peninsula, then you will find Patricia Bay Park. At the south end of that section of West Saanich Road where it runs immediately above the shore, a large log with bold, yellow letters emblazoned on it announces that this is, indeed, Patricia Bay Park. A paved parking lot provides ample space for many cars. Immediately adjoining the parking lot is a grassy area with toilets, rubbish bins and a few picnic tables.

**Path** Several paths lead into the park. Some visitors will be primarily interested in the wheelchair accessible one that runs in a roughly circular route starting and ending in the parking lot. Some will be interested in the flight of 15 broad stone and concrete steps leading from the north end of the wheelchair trail down to the beach. Yet others—joggers evidently prominent among them—will seek out Scoter Trail, a gravel track that runs below the road and parallel to the beach the entire length of Patricia Bay. Be warned, however, that the trail is subject to erosion and, therefore, to being closed. In case you're wondering, a scoter is an interesting black seabird that is sometimes mistaken for a puffin because of its thick, colourful bill.

**Beach** Despite the easy access and the various facilities, the beach will not be to many people's tastes, unfortunately. Close to the Institute of Ocean Studies immediately to the south, the beach at low tide stretches a considerable distance over mud flats. The upper shore isn't much more enticing, unless you are attracted to barnacle-encrusted, jagged rocks and gravel. Still, the beach is a long one and changes character along its considerable length.

**Suitability for children** According to one publication from the district, "Children will love exploring the tidal flats at low tide." Since these tidal flats are so squelchy, it is hard to see how this claim will be true of many children. In any case, if you are planning to spend much time here with children, come prepared with sturdy water shoes for the barnacly sections, as well as plenty of sun protection. The grassy area near the picnic tables and, of course, toilets, if not the beach itself, are child friendly.

**Suitability for groups** Some groups will come here if they want to interact with the water in a splashy way. Those who are interested in other qualities of this particular spot—picnickers, joggers and, possibly, sunbathers among them—will find the ample parking, toilet facilities and tables to be significant assets.

**View** Patricia Bay forms a considerable scoop into the west-facing coast of Saanich Peninsula. As a result, the sweep of the shoreline dominates the view. The Institute of Ocean Studies is the prominent feature of the headland to the south, but the general impression elsewhere is of low, wooded undulations dotted with residences. Inland, the airport is clearly visible—and, sad to say, audible.

**Winds, sun and shade** Because the whole of Saanich Peninsula is so low and flat at this point, winds from the southeast can blow directly over the airport and kick up quite an offshore blow. Westerly winds, generally light in summer, blow directly onshore. Sunbathers wanting as many hours as possible of seaside exposure, however, will find exactly that here: the only shade available is under a few small trees in the grassy picnic area.

**Beachcombing** Of all public areas on the west or north coast of the peninsula, this one offers the most to anyone wanting to stride out for several kilometres. Such walkers will find themselves close to the shorefront part of West Saanich Road. They will also find that at many points they will prefer to walk on the shore-hugging Scoter Trail rather than the beach itself. Those who do want to walk near the water's edge should come with sturdy shoes that can get wet and sandy.

**Seclusion** The beach is about as public and exposed as you can imagine, though it usually attracts few people.

* **Also nearby** It is possible to get onto the shore directly from West Saanich Road at several points north of here, such as those opposite junctions with Tapping Street and **Munro Street**. Most sunbathers who want to catch their rays on the beach rather than the grass will find the beach most to their liking directly below a grassy promontory about 100 m north of Munro.

## 13

### TOWNER PARK ROAD

**A long, level walk through mixed woods to the remarkably exposed rocky outcroppings of Warrior Point**

**Location, signs and parking** The directions could hardly be simpler, as long as you don't confuse Towner Park Road with Towner Road. Towner Park Road leads directly off West Saanich Road and needs only to be followed to its end to offer up its beach access path to Warrior Point. The end of the road may be a little ambiguous at first, since a private drive seems at a glance to be an extension of the road. The unpaved shoulder will have to be your parking lot, but the road is quiet and there are few driveways to avoid, so there is plenty of space for a few cars. Instead of the usual blue walking symbol on a post, however, look for a yellow one.

**Path** This is one of the longest approach paths on the peninsula, but a pretty and level one: most won't see it as an obstacle but as an embellishment. In fact, those who like woodland walking may well want to explore the trail in the opposite direction—and, thereby, go all of the way to Towner Road, northwest past Towner Park Road, and the pretty beach access there. Our path to Warrior Point takes you almost half a kilometre through lots of interesting and changing flora, especially pretty in late spring. The tall, almost spindly second-growth firs open out to a bushier mix of hawthorn, oak, wild roses and false lily of the valley. The less charming aspect of our path is that it runs parallel to a private road and, for a while, through a public corridor between two private drives. After remaining level for its entire length, the path opens through a lattice of arbutus and Garry oak onto the top of a flight of 14 wooden stairs.

**Beach** No other bit of publicly accessible shore on the west shore of Saanich Peninsula reveals such a broad swath of low, sun-baked rock shelves and tidal pools. The upper bit of shore has a pebbly section suitable for nestling and picnicking, and batteries of logs for leaning against.

**Suitability for children** This spot will not appeal to all children, of course. For the free-spirited child, sure of foot and entertained by tidal pool life, this bit of shore provides a huge area of safe wandering, prodding and clambering. At low tide, too, this is probably the only spot on the west or north part of the peninsula where kite flying is possible. The cagey parent will want to consider the length of walk to get here, the slightly awkward access to the water at low tide and the lack of protective shade.

**Suitability for groups** Mostly because of the space for moving around on and dispersing along the large shore, this is a good spot for even a fairly large group interested in observing, recording and exploring an unusual and striking piece of shoreline. Mid to low tide is probably most suitable for a larger group.

**View** Like other features of this spot, the view, too, is distinctive. Facing largely south, Warrior Point provides an intriguing perspective on the sweep of Patricia Bay—and the airport behind it. By walking around the point or even toward the low-water line, you will have something like a 270-degree view extending northwest up Saanich Inlet.

**Winds, sun and shade** Just as the spot is wide open to a great sweep of views, so it is exposed to winds from nearly every direction. You might think you are protected from a strong southeast wind because Saanich Inlet lies between you and the wider waters beyond. Alas, you are wrong. In fact, a southeast wind seems almost to be amplified as it blows in over the airport and bay. Batten your hatches!

Except for early morning, you are not going to find much protective shade here at any time of day. Some obliging oaks and arbutus hang low over the bank, though, so you will always be able to find some shade, even if it means retreating to the highest logs.

**Beachcombing** Beachcombing is probably the main reason for coming to this spot. Most will want to wander and explore the extensive rocky shelves and tidal pools of Warrior Point itself, but some will enjoy making their way a considerable distance in either direction, even though the shore narrows considerably away from the point.

**Seclusion** Although the whole area is residential, it is bushy enough, particularly in summer, and the properties are large enough that you will not feel intrusive. Low tide, of course, and the area directly surrounding the beach trailhead provide the greatest opportunities for being on your own.

* **Also nearby** See the next sketch map for these nearby access points.
**A.** From West Saanich Road, take Downey Road or Wain Road to Madrona Drive. At its south end, in the bend where **Towner Road** begins, an access path leads for about 50 m through the slightly wooded shore to a bank and access to a mixed shore of solid and broken rock. With just a little bit of a struggle you can launch a kayak or two here, though parking is a bit of a feat. Towner Road is not to be confused with Towner Park Road, for though they are geographically close they are not easily connected.

**B. Norris Road** is the next street north of Towner Road. It crosses Madrona Drive and takes you nearly to the shore. A flight of steps brings you down to a shore of mixed rock with views southwest and lots of afternoon sun..

**C. Downey Road**, one road up from Norris, ends in an elevated viewpoint through a lattice of trees. Since the view is similar to that at nearby Cromar Road, where you can also easily get to the beach, this viewpoint simply provides another angle from which to see the same coast.

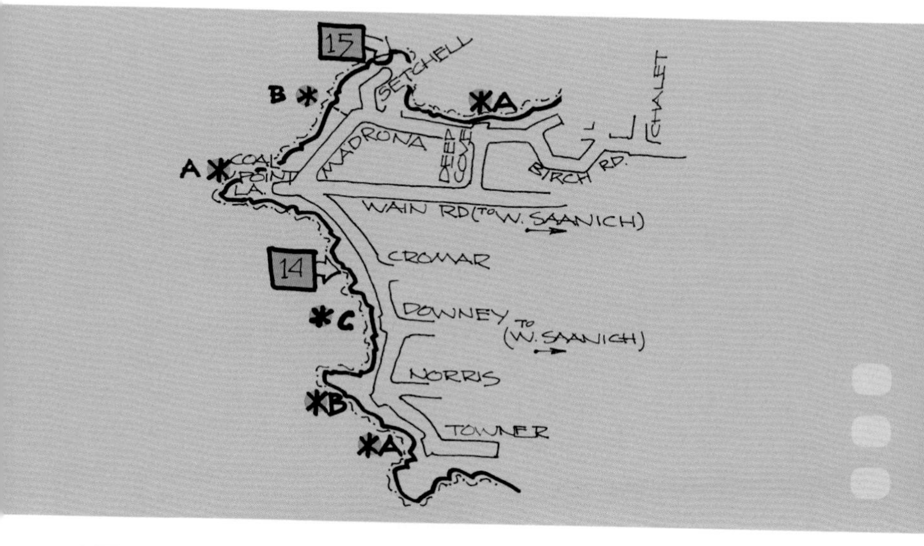

Oct. 3, 2013

## 14

### CROMAR ROAD

A flight of stone steps to a pebbly beach that soaks up afternoon sun

**Location, signs and parking** Take Wain Road or Downey Road west off West Saanich Road just south of Deep Cove, and then Madrona Drive to reach Cromar Road. Parking isn't great, but there are some spots on the shoulder. You should see a simple but assertive BEACH ACCESS sign along with a shellfish warning sign. Your hours of parking (read: beach partying) are restricted, according to the signs. A NO FIRES sign almost covers the other signs.

**Path** A level gravel path about 20 m long runs through a small area of shaggy hedges. From here a flight of very solid staircase leads to the shore at the bottom of the bank.

**Beach** This is a small bay with a rocky, treed headland on either side. A few houses, particularly to the left, are shored up by concrete retaining walls. At low tide, the beach reveals its soft and not so pretty underbelly. The rough pebbly upper beach gives way to an area of slightly larger rocks and gravel and, at very low tide, wet tidal flats of eelgrass, squidgy sand and tidal pools. You can find a place to sit and soak up the blisteringly hot afternoon sun on the pebbly upper beach, but you will probably be most comfortable going a short distance to the right side of the beach where a treed bank, rather than a retaining wall, creates a small level area abutting an area of fairly smooth, solid rock.

**Suitability for children** This beach is too confined and feels too much like a private one for you to be very comfortable with a shouting and jumping battalion of children. Nevertheless, it is a safe place for a child to swim, with its gradually sloping beach and endless hours of warm sun. Compared to the water at the beaches around Victoria, the water here on a sunny day can seem almost balmy. Do, however, make sure you come at a high tide and bring water shoes.

**Suitability for groups** The spot is much too confined and much too overlooked by houses for a group to decide to make its way here.

**View** Framed by the wooded headland on either side, the view is of the forested hills of the Malahat across the widest part of Saanich Inlet.

**Winds, sun and shade** Not only is this a good spot for an afternoon swim because of the hot sun, but also it is protected from most winds.

**Beachcombing** This is not a beach for beachcombing, though it is easy enough to walk back and forth on the 100 m of pebbly beach and, beyond, to the low and undulating sandstone formations. Low tide is a good time to hunt for moon snails, spider crabs, soft-shell macoma clams and like denizens of this kind of ecosystem.

**Seclusion** You could hardly feel less secluded—but you could well be the only ones using the beach.

*** Also nearby**

**A.** Park in a cramped turnaround at the very end of **Coal Point Lane**. Seven wooden steps take you to a grassy glade with a bench and a pretty view through a lattice of willow and firs.

**B.** Just south of the junction of **Setchell Road** and Madrona, a barely visible path is marked by a signpost a few feet away and leads for almost 100 m down a significant descent via a narrow wooded strip between two houses. The beach is a narrow strip of solid rock. A magnificent old juniper tree at the end of the trail is almost enough to make the trek worthwhile.

## 15

## SETCHELL ROAD

**A picturesque access to a viewpoint and steep sandstone shore on a small promontory**

**Location, signs and parking** This point juts out into the southern part of Deep Cove. If you are approaching from West Saanich Road, turn onto Birch Road and follow it past the big bend in the road until it morphs into Madrona Drive. Look for Setchell at the beginning of a significant bend in Madrona. A short drive toward the water brings you to the end of the road and a paved cul-de-sac with parking for a few cars—though not, of course, after 9 p.m. or before 6 a.m. After all, this is North Saanich. From the parking area, the handrail for a set of wooden stairs is clearly visible to the left of a cluster of arbutus and fir.

**Path** The path proceeds in different stages. Fourteen wooden stairs take you to a small and laboriously constructed viewing spot with a rustic but not very comfortable bench cut from logs. At this point you may think that you have come here only to see the view from this bench and not to reach the shore, since immediately below the drop from the viewing spot you will see a wire fence that seems to block further progress. Take heart—after appreciating the view. A small dirt path winds around and proceeds a little steeply but safely enough through rough grass and onto the shore.

**Beach** You will find yourself on a promontory that looks more or less like a large, sandstone serving of mashed potatoes. To your right the shore does a middling imitation of a cliff, but immediately in front you can easily make your way down to the low-tide mark. Be careful; the weeds can make the rocks slippery. While it would be possible to find a perching spot on a dry area of the petrified mashed potatoes, don't expect to find a comfortable area for picnicking or sunbathing. The deep water at the edge of the shore, however, suggests good snorkelling or casting possibilities.

**Suitability for children** Only older children who want a brief clamber and prowl will be happy here. The area is much too confined and rough for most children.

**Suitability for groups** Only a few friends with a specific purpose, such as snorkelling or sketching, would be comfortable here for more than a brief visit.

**View** The view is probably prettiest from the designated viewing spot, but is nevertheless striking from several different angles. The graceful contours of Mount Tuam on Salt Spring Island overlook the high, wooded shores of Deep Cove itself.

**Winds, sun and shade** The promontory is essentially north-facing and scattered with trees, so you will be in shade or patches of shade for most of the day. Occasional northwesterlies cool this spot, but it is protected from most other winds.

**Beachcombing** Few other spots provide as little incentive to wander along the shore, though most explorers will be tempted to prod a little around the low-tide area.

**Seclusion** The spot itself is beautifully secluded, except for a jetty immediately to the left. At the same time, of course, if you find the place occupied by only one other visitor, you could hardly feel less alone!

Setchell Road

## * Also nearby

**A.** Directly opposite the junction of Madrona Drive and Deep Cove Road is a wide gravel parking area and **Deep Cove Road Wharf**, an old, slightly rickety public wharf extending out from the south shore of Deep Cove, propped up high above the water. At present, you can walk partly along the wharf, but the end of the wharf is closed because it is in disrepair.

**B. Tatlow Road** (see next sketch map), partway up Deep Cove and leading off West Saanich Road, crosses Chalet Road and then brings you at its end to a well-developed access path and set of stairs to the middle of a pebbly bay. Surrounded by shorefront houses, the spot is also called Chalet Beach. It is possible to launch a kayak here and to swim at high tide.

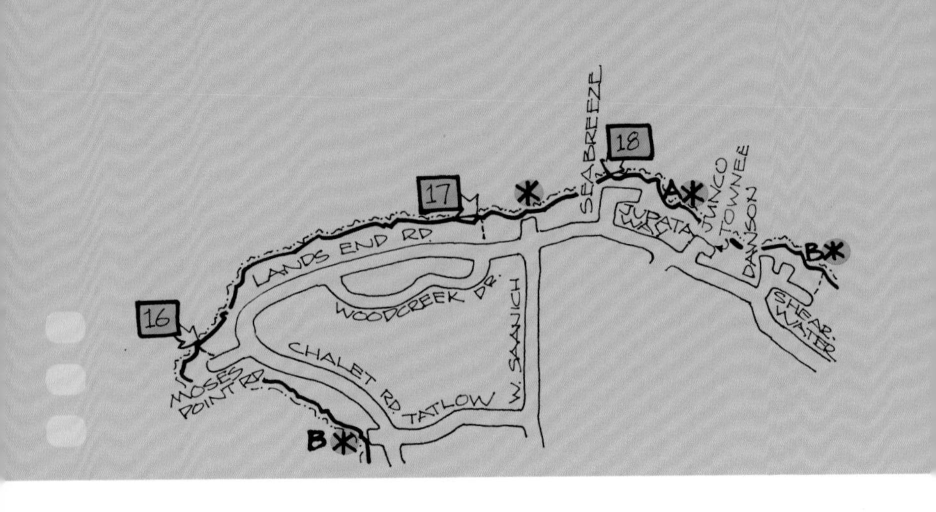

## 16

### MOSES POINT ROAD

**A level, leafy path to a shore with a little bit of everything**

**Location, signs and parking** Moses Point is at the northwest corner of Saanich Peninsula and the northern tip of Deep Cove. Reach Chalet Road from Tatlow, which leads off West Saanich Road. Moses Point Road leaves Chalet Road just before Chalet turns almost 90 degrees east and becomes Lands End Road, the coast-hugging northernmost road. At the end of Moses Point Road, look for a broad, dirt path and three signs. One of them you can expect to see at many public access spots, warning against shellfish gathering. The other two, however, are unusual for Saanich Peninsula: one asserts that you are not to light a fire, the other that though there is a public beach, it is public only below high tide. We can only surmise that local residents have had problems with visitors invading their property—or are worried that they will have such problems. A few cars can tuck in along the side of the road, but only a few.

**Path** The broad dirt path winds almost 100 m more or less horizontally over a few roots and through fairly small firs and maples hedged by a chain-link fence on one side. The chain-link fence extends assertively past the trees and onto the rocks of the upper beach. Point made. Just before the shore is a beautiful arbutus, a bench fashioned from a log and three concrete steps inset into a rounded, sandstone hump. This spot could well be used as a launching spot for kayaks or canoes, especially since it is fairly easy going to the water's edge, even at low tide.

**Beach** The shore is intriguingly diverse, combining areas of fine gravel and pebbles with lumpy ridges of rock covered with rockweed. Two pebble beaches on either side of the access point are very much in the "front yards" of the houses backing them. Moses Point itself, to your left, reveals a broad expanse of sculpted rock and a few tidal pools at low tide. The small curving beach to your right is soft and weedy at low tide, not the kind of place that your children have very firmly in mind as you entice them to the beach.

**Suitability for children** You could do far worse than bring your children to this beach. Older children will like to explore the diverse terrain at low tide, poke in tidal pools, scramble over nobbles of rock and so on. Properly shod and protected from the sun, the right sort of child could be happy here for some time.

**Suitability for groups** A small picnicking group will find a good spot on a small area of pebbles and crushed shells on the upper part of the beach. There is enough space and diversity at low tide—but only at low tide—that a group interested in wandering a little will be able to spread out and explore.

**View** Unfortunately, the spot reached by the path is not actually on the tip of Moses Point, but, rather, in a small bay on the north side of the point. Thus, the view is not quite as expansive as you might anticipate. Still, if you compare the view here with that on other spots around the peninsula, you will appreciate that here you can see both the green contours surrounding Saanich Inlet and the sun-dried slopes of Salt Spring Island to the north.

**Winds, sun and shade** Largely protected from southeasterlies, this spot will be cooled by winds from the northwest. Bring your full arsenal of sun protection if you are planning to stay here for any length of time.

Except for the area around the bench, most of the beach and upper shore are in sun for most of the day.

**Beachcombing** The fact that the tide goes out so far on the solid, ridged rock to your left will mean that—at low tide at least—you will feel most tempted to explore that area. You can extend your wander along the shore to Moses Point proper and thus find your view opening back into Deep Cove and Saanich Inlet.

**Seclusion** It is difficult to feel secluded here. Immediately to your right as you reach the shore you will see a small beach cabin on a concrete base protruding right onto the shore. In the other direction, only by going toward the waterline—at low tide—can you get much distance between yourself and the local residents.

## 17

## WOODCREEK DRIVE

**A long, wooded walk to a north-facing shore of mixed rock**

**Location, signs and parking** The trail to the beach actually leads directly off Lands End Road, but the road sign for Woodcreek Drive more or less opposite the trailhead is a helpful indicator that you're at the right spot. Look for the entrance to Woodcreek Drive closest to West Saanich Road (see map). Once you have a general fix on the location, look on the north side of the road for one of the square posts with the blue walker symbol, and then a small flight of concrete steps complete with handrail. Parking is possible only along the shoulder of Lands End Road. Since there is little traffic and the shoulder is fairly wide, however, you should have no difficulty finding plenty of space, even for several cars.

**Path** The path to the shore is a delight—especially on a sunny summer day. The winding trail through large cedars, with the sun dappling swordferns, is a west coast treasure. Those who don't like to puff, however,

Woodcreek Drive

should note that the path, more than 100 m long, drops considerably as it approaches the water and descends 18 stairs onto the beach. As you walk the path, you will be very aware of the estate-like private houses and gardens on either side of the public strip, but the wooded corridor is ample enough that you shouldn't feel like a peeping Tom.

**Beach** The shore isn't for everyone, but everyone should find it interesting, at the very least—varied surfaces, rocky lumps and bumps, dramatic boulder and patches of barnacled gravel shelving toward the water's edge. At low tide you will have about 20 or 30 m of knobs and gnarls to explore; at high tide, the diverse terrain makes a fascinating snorkelling area, though the water here can be more than a little nippy. It is possible to find a perching spot for a picnic on some of the rock formations, but none encourages a comfortable, restful meal.

**Suitability for children** The longish path might be an issue for some children, especially those who need quick access to the car. Those older children who are just out for a scramble and splash, though, will find considerable diversion along the shore.

**Suitability for groups** The space and variety would make this an attractive spot for a small group whose primary goals include observing, photographing or poking at the natural world. Those who want a picnic would be more comfortable elsewhere.

**View** The immediate view is fairly enclosed, since wooded headlands sprout out of the shore a short distance in either direction. To the west is the Cowichan coast and directly across is Salt Spring Island. Three pilings, the remains of a collapsed or failed construction, punctuate the shore to the north. Some will find these picturesque; others will not.

**Winds, sun and shade** Because of the wooded points of land in either direction, winds are a little reduced here and, in any case, will blow roughly parallel to the shore. Morning is the time to come if you want maximum sun on the upper shore. However, even in the afternoon only the upper part of the shore is shaded.

**Beachcombing** This is the kind of shore where beachcombing is best done at low speed and with much peering and prodding. At the same time, you can make your way for a considerable distance in either direction, particularly if you choose a time with quite low tides.

**Seclusion** Residences on either side are noticeable but, because of the rise of the shore and the enthusiasm of the vegetation, largely unobtrusive. You will mostly be aware of various steps and constructions that allow local residents their private access to the shore.

*** Also nearby** Turn north off Lands End Road onto **West Saanich Road** and drive the few short metres to the very end. It would be difficult to survive a scramble down the steep bank to the shore, but this is a good place to come for a car picnic. From the cozy comfort of your car you can view the rain-lashed waters while enjoying your best-ever tuna sandwiches and tea.

## 18

### SEABREEZE ROAD

**A rough dirt path to concrete steps and a ridged-rock, north-facing shore**

**Location, signs and parking** Turn off Lands End Road onto Seabreeze Road until you come to something akin to a roundabout and take Jupata Way leading off to the right. You will not immediately see the BEACH ACCESS and shellfish warning signs, since some enthusiastic vegetation tends to block both. A quick scan to the left as you face the shore, though, should reveal both the signs and the path.

The roundabout is large enough that you can park along it without much worry of blocking the roadway. Though seeing other people here would be unlikely, several cars could fit into this area. Kayakers, however, and particularly those planning an overnight jaunt, should note that this is one of the few places in the area where you are not forbidden to leave your car overnight.

**Path** This may be a viable spot to launch kayaks, but viable does not mean easy. The undulating dirt path leads through a slightly descending, woodsy strip between houses. After about 40 m you will come to a set of 19 solid but venerable concrete steps that lead you down to the shore. Those who are not sure of foot will find the path easy and will be grateful for the handrail on the steps.

**Beach** Geologists or just plain lovers of rock should be interested in the beach. Essentially flat, the shore is dramatically ridged with eroded layers of sedimentary rock tilting toward the water. Tidal pools, patches of rockweed and barnacle-encrusted gravel are interspersed with the flat areas of ridged rock. Picnickers won't find this a very enticing spot, however, since only a tumble of jagged boulders and a few small patches of fine pebbles comprise the upper beach.

**Suitability for children** The simple path access, the tidal pools and the relatively stumble-proof flat shore will make even small children comfortable. Whether or not their interest will be held by the comparative sameness of the shore, though, will depend on the mood and disposition of the child—as so much in life does!

**Suitability for groups** Only certain—and small—groups would want to choose this spot. Limited parking and lack of inviting picnic spots will discourage many. A few friends wanting to explore and wander along an interesting bit of shoreline, though, would be happy to know about this access.

**View** Keep in mind that Seabreeze Road is a short branch off the aptly named Lands End Road. At the north end of Saanich Peninsula, the shore here looks more or less directly across at Salt Spring Island. At the same time, though, the view opens to the west toward Cowichan and to the east toward Swartz Bay's ferries plying the protected waters. Above the low, rolling profile of Pender Island rise the snowy tops of the mainland mountains not visible from any of the access points to the west and north of Saanich Peninsula.

**Winds, sun and shade** Think about it: Seabreeze Road. While road names in housing developments are often hilariously inappropriate, not so this one. Indeed, sea breezes, no matter what the direction of the wind, waft cheerfully unimpeded onto this shore. Because the lightly wooded bank behind the north-facing shore rises gradually, the shore has little shade, even in the afternoon.

**Beachcombing** Although beach walking is limited in both directions, the relatively flat, ridged rock shelf in combination with the tidal pools make this an appealing place to amble by the water's edge for some distance.

**Seclusion** Houses are close by on either side of the narrow strip of public land leading to the water's edge. However, they are set back enough above and behind leafy screens that you will feel comfortably on your own.

*** Also nearby**

**A.** From **Junco Road**, just off Lands End Road, an intriguing trail and almost 100 steps lead down the high, wooded shore where Junco turns into Townee Road. Although at the time of writing it is closed and posted with a sign to that effect, the height of the road from the shore promises a wind-worn shore below. Check back regularly for the path to re-open.

**B.** Turn down Dawson Way off Lands End Road and right onto **Shearwater Terrace**. On the sea side of the turnaround is an unmarked strip of grass that turns into a wet dirt path and drops onto the shore of a little bay. The beach at high tide has striking views, though underfoot is unattractively squelchy and rocky.

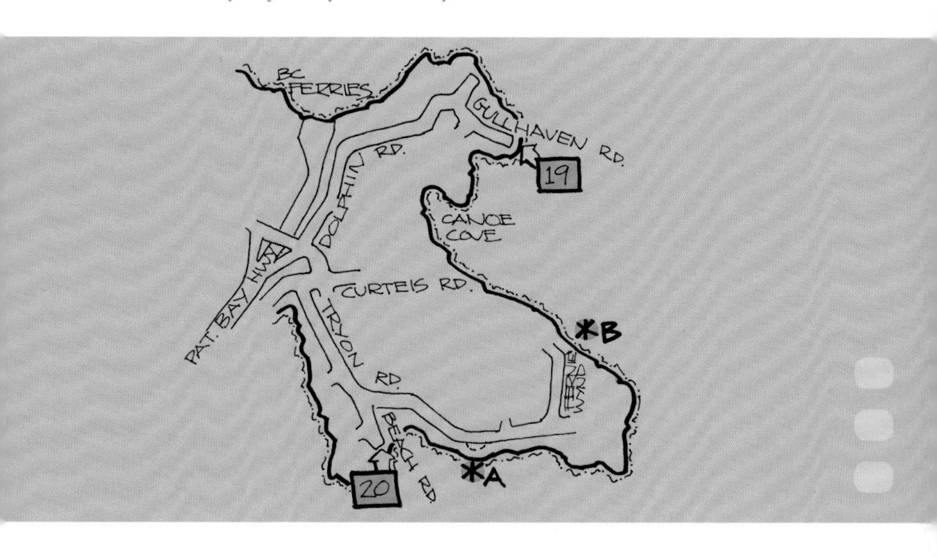

## 19

### GULLHAVEN ROAD

A bluff-top path to a tiny rocky cove with an exceptionally pretty view of reefs, islets and islands

**Location, signs and parking** The route to this tiny but truly worthwhile access spot is convoluted. You will have to thread a maze of disorienting roads over and around the BC Ferries terminal in quest of your goal at the end of Swartz Head. First get onto Dolphin Road by taking the exit ramp from the highway to the terminal just before the overpass or, if you are approaching via Lands End Road, by taking the overpass over the tangle of ferry terminal roads. Even once you are on Dolphin Road, you will feel more than a little odd as you wind behind ferry parking lots.

Persist. As Dolphin Road disappears into a treed residential area, look out for Gullhaven Road and follow it a short distance to its end. There are no signs for the access itself. It seems that while all of the access routes in North Saanich are meticulously maintained on the north and west of the peninsula, those on the east are more randomly handled.

Since there are two private driveways near the end of the small cul-de-sac, you will need to edge your vehicle discreetly onto a grassy shoulder. Very few vehicles can park here, but the likelihood of finding another vehicle is small.

**Path** Look for an opening in the thimbleberry bushes at the end of the cul-de-sac and a dirt path that winds and bumps a short distance over roots and rocks to a rocky promontory a few metres above the shore. It helps to be well shod and sure-footed coming to this spot: forget about bringing a formally clad wedding party for a photo shoot, although you could hardly find a prettier background for any photograph.

**Beach** The beach area, like everything about this spot, is tiny—but, also like everything else here, fascinating and charming. You will need to climb down over sandstone, sometimes blockish and sometimes ridged, to get close to the water or to sit and enjoy the view. A tiny pocket beach immediately to the right of the path's exit is overhung with bushes at high tide and covered with barnacly rocks and pebbles at low tide. Because of the currents sweeping past the shore, the water here is always cold, even in the warmest weather. As the kelp heads bobbing within 1 or 2 m from the shore at low tide suggest, the rocks drop off quickly into deep water.

**Suitability for children** This is not the place to bring children for more than a short visit. Even then, bring them only if they like to clamber, perhaps throw a few rocks, and conclude with eating a peanut butter sandwich.

**Suitability for groups** The spot is suitable only for a very small group in no more than two vehicles and with the express purpose of taking full advantage of the view.

**View** Ah, yes—the view! Probably best in the afternoon or evening when the sun is behind you, the view is nevertheless charming at any time of day. The clusters of islands, islets and reefs, close by and distant, will thrill every photographer and painter. If you like to name what you're looking at, then tick off, from left to right, Knapp, Pym, Goudge and Fernie islands as well as many smaller islets. To your left is Colburne Passage while Iroquois and Page passages lead south to your right. Your view to the south is constrained by a treed bluff—and, a little sadly, a chain-link fence.

**Winds, sun and shade** Completely sheltered from westerly winds, the shore here is somewhat exposed to easterlies, but a little protected by the islands immediately offshore. If you want to picnic or sketch in the sun, you will find some throughout the day down on the rock ridges, but the morning is by far the sunniest part of the day.

**Beachcombing** This is not a spot that invites wandering very far. Restless visitors can explore farther along the coast past the rocky ridges to the left, if they are willing to negotiate a shore of irregular-sized boulders.

**Seclusion** It is, indeed, one of the huge pleasures of this spot that you will feel that you've found a secret portal into a secluded world—so close to the hurly-burly of the ferry terminal. There are, in fact, houses close by but they are nicely buried in thickets of trees.

Gullhaven Road

## 20

### BEACH ROAD

**A well-hidden gravel beach, most attractive at mid to high tide**

**Location, signs and parking** Finding Beach Road, like finding Gullhaven Road, is something of an adventure in navigation. Like Gullhaven Road, it is located on the "island" of residential land surrounded by sea on three sides and, on the fourth, by the tangle of roads and parking lots by the BC Ferries terminal. Don't confuse Beach Road with Beach Drive, the prominent shorefront road connecting Victoria and Oak Bay. If you are approaching on Highway 17, take the last exit before the terminal and the first sharp right onto Land's End Road. Follow this up with another sharp right onto Curteis Road and an even sharper left onto Tryon Road. Continue past the marina on your right until Beach Road angles down a short distance. Very near the end of Beach Road, along with a NO PARKING sign on one side, you will see a somewhat battered PUBLIC ACCESS sign and a shellfish prohibition sign. Parking is difficult—unless yours is the sole car in the little patch of paved shoulder at the trailhead.

**Path** The gravelled smooth path runs beside a wire fence by a large, privately owned field. Although the path drops only slightly, take care, since the gravel can be loose underfoot at one little dip toward the end. The path, some 50 m long, ends with a thoroughly engineered set of 10 concrete steps inset into a solid chunk of retaining wall.

**Beach** You will find yourself more or less in the middle of the shallow scoop of Bryden Bay, a couple of hundred metres wide. As is the case with many beaches on the east side of the Saanich Peninsula, the fine pebbly upper beach is generally the most pleasant, so the beach is most appealing at mid to high tide. Low tide reveals a combination of barnacle-encrusted rock and squelchy, muddy sand. Some rock ridges run toward the water and thus break up the general slope of the gradually shelving beach. Log lovers will be happy that logs line almost the entire length of the uppermost beach.

**Suitability for children** The beach is at its best at mid to high tide for children with water play on their minds. Water shoes are a good idea, along with the usual protection against sun. This is also a perfect beach to play games involving running along logs, searching for multicoloured pebbles and skipping stones.

**Suitability for groups** Parking is the real issue for groups. If spots can be found along the shoulder without blocking the driveways of local residents, then two or three cars' worth of families and picnickers will find the beach itself capacious and secluded enough for a very pleasant, beachy experience.

**View** Like other spots near to and north of Sidney, this one offers a fascinating combination of harbours, marinas and islets, peninsulas and inlets. In this particular case you will be looking primarily across Tsehum Harbour toward Thumb Point, Armstrong Point and the marina near All Bay. Curteis Point and Kingfisher Point are to your left and right respectively; directly in front, an unnamed reef and, beyond, Little Shell and Ker islands provide decorative touches. Photographers and artists of various hues will find plenty of material for interesting compositions: morning will tend to provide silhouettes and backlighting; late afternoon will bring out maximum colour and depth.

**Winds, sun and shade** The beach is fully protected from westerlies, but winds from the south and east that curve around and over the offshore islands can be felt. Because few trees back the beach, except at the north end, there is little shade at any time of day. In the hottest part of the afternoon some shade can be found left of the access point under some arbutus.

**Beachcombing** Most visitors will feel tempted to walk around the pebbly mid-beach along the curve of Bryden Bay, though the chief attraction is the shifting view and easy stroll, rather than interesting sea life or tidal pools.

**Seclusion** Because of the large properties and houses set well back, this beach provides a considerable sense of seclusion from behind. It is the view of busy marinas and houses across the harbour that makes the spot seem less secluded.

**✱ Also nearby**

**A. HMS Plumper Park** is an undeveloped ecological park just east down Tryon Road. A short path circles through the woods to a viewpoint, but not to the shore.

**B. Fernie Wynd Road** leads off Tryon Road near its end. As you approach the end of Fernie Wynd, a viewpoint opens onto a bit of seascape that you can't see from any other publicly accessible spot.

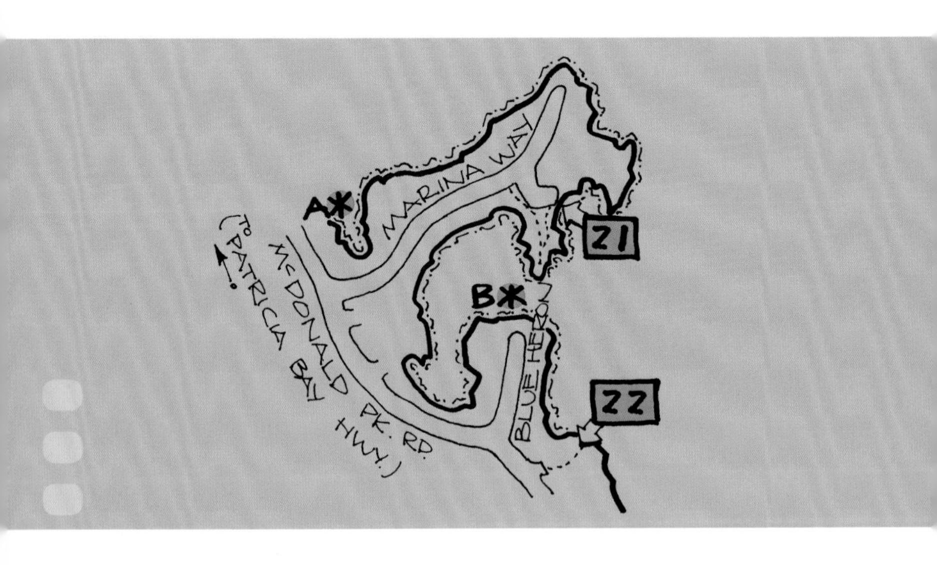

## 21

### NYMPH POINT PARK

A slightly confusing trail to a bluff-top walk with paths to a breakwater and a shore of mixed rock

**Location, signs and parking** Like some other spots near Sidney, this one is a bit tricky to locate—and not least of all because development has encroached on the park. The general approach to Nymph Point Park, from Marina Way, is fairly straightforward once you find your way onto MacDonald Park Road from the highway. It helps that the inland Blue

Heron Park, off MacDonald Park Road, is well signposted from the highway and faces the entrance to Marina Way. Marina Way winds through a residential area toward a yacht club and boat sales near the tip of Wales Point. A few hundred metres past the only side street on this road, Marti Lane, on your left, you will see on your right a large, carved log sign announcing Nymph Point Park (the *Nymphe*, with an *e*, was a nineteenth-century gunboat). Give some thought to parking and you will probably want to ignore this sign. Instead, continue east toward the North Saanich Marina and Yacht Club. It may seem to be possible to park on the edge of the road right beside the log sign for Nymph Point Park, but because there is a paved curb and sidewalk, you cannot pull off onto the shoulder. You are probably better off finding parking in one of the lots immediately off Marina Way up ahead to your right.

**Path** Although the full path leads from Marina Way, it soon emerges from the pleasant woods to exit into a parking lot! Businesslike blue and white signs redirect you to the second section of path leaving the parking lot. Many will prefer, therefore, to park so that they can cross the parking lot and start the walk at this point.

The very pretty trail, with all of its bumps and roots, runs along a neck of land with a busy marina on the right, clearly visible through a screen of arbutus and Garry oaks. On a bluff that looks for all the world like a small segment of a Gulf Island, the path splits as it leads into a system configured roughly as a figure eight. The branch to the right leads down some wooden steps onto a breakwater and an awkward descent onto one recessed bit of rocky shore. The other branch leads to a park bench, and, ultimately, to the more northerly of two bays—the only easy descent to the shore.

**Beach** Like other spots in this section of coast, this one is prettiest at mid to high tide since the lowest part of the shore is somewhat squelchy and slimy. The southern bit of shore, near the breakwater, has lots of sandstone lumps and bumps intersected by pebbly sections. The northerly bay, separated from the other by a small sandstone headland, curves classically along the pebbly upper shore. At low tide, the water retreats a good 50 or 60 m. On the bank behind the beach are piled broken shells, evidence that this was once a First Nations midden—or garbage dump.

**Suitability for children** Smaller children or those who are not sure of foot should be taken only to the northern beach, where access is comparatively easy and where the pebbly shore is easy to walk on. When the water is at least partway in, most children should find themselves comfortably engaged in a world of splashes and pebbles—though the water is warm only at the edge of an incoming tide.

**Suitability for groups** There is enough parking in the adjoining areas and enough paths that a group of considerable size could make this an appropriate spot for an outing and picnic. Opportunities for sketching and photography abound, with the huge diversity of landforms and perspectives on this elaborately indented piece of shoreline. Picnicking is probably best done on the northern beach, though there are no facilities to sustain a long visit.

**View** Because of the system of trails over irregular geography, the views vary enormously depending on where you look. Natural plants and landforms in the park itself contrast greatly with the enthusiastic encroachment of marinas and residences. Blue Heron Basin lies behind the breakwater while Tsehum Harbour opens out toward the open sea. All around are numerous pilings, anchored boats, reefs, islands and peninsulas—all making for a diverse and complex series of perspectives.

**Winds, sun and shade** Largely protected from northwesterlies, this bit of shore is quite exposed to winds from the south and east. On the pebbly beach where any picnicking is likely to be done, shadows—though mostly dappled—move across the shore during the afternoon. Otherwise, the trees are scattered and gnarled enough that they throw no heavy shade at any time of day.

**Beachcombing** This spot is a good one to choose for a half hour or so of walking. If you are to take full advantage of the various paths and the diverse shore, you will be able to combine strolling for some distance with more careful exploration of rocky-shore sea beasts.

**Seclusion** No doubt because of the odd location of this park, it is fairly quiet. You will probably see some other visitors, though, unless you come at an improbable time of day or season. The diversity of the shore means that, even on a hot summer's afternoon, you will have little difficulty finding a nook to feel comfortably away from others.

### * Also nearby

**A.** On some maps, off Marina Way you might see **Tsehum Lagoon Park** marked. It encompasses the land and water of the lagoon tucked in between the north side of Marina Way and the south edge of Patricia Bay Highway. Its overgrown swath of far-too-verdant greenery is enticing, as is its designation as an ecological reserve and bird sanctuary.

**B.** If you are using the North Saanich parks brochure as a guide to finding interesting shorefront trails, note that the access at the end of **Blue Heron Road** is currently overgrown. Since, however, this is the only public access to the south side of Blue Heron basin, and provides a view north to Nymph Point Park, it stands to be of real interest to explorers of this convoluted area of bays and harbours.

## 22

## LILLIAN HOFFAR PARK

**The site of a heritage homestead, now a flat, garden-like promontory with a diverse shoreline**

**Location, signs and parking** If you can find your way onto McDonald Park Road from Highway 17 north of Sidney, you should have little difficulty finding 1.6-hectare Lillian Hoffar Park. More or less directly across McDonald Park Road from Blue Heron Park, it is marked with a large log carved with the name of the park and embellished with slightly odd-looking swans and, possibly, cormorants. In the parking space, another sign will tell you that parking between 9 p.m. and 6 a.m. is forbidden. A beautifully detailed information sign under a roofed shelter provides a wealth of information on, among other things, the Tseycum First Nation and various members of the Hoffar family. The carefully maintained gravel parking rectangle a short distance off the road has room for three or four cars.

**Path** The asphalt path, apparently once the paved driveway to the Hoffar property, leads straight ahead between giant hedges for 70 or 80 m. The path is smooth and level enough that wheelchairs could easily gain access to the park at the end of the strip of asphalt. This drive ends in a loop at the edge of a large, flat, grassy area. A mixture of native and cultivated trees surrounds this area. Seventeen steps, with two strong handrails, lead onto an area of fine shell and pebbles.

**Beach** The park is on something of a promontory surrounded by a highly diversified range of shore features. Most striking, perhaps, is the narrow concrete wall that zigzags out along the solid rock directly in front of you and ultimately acts as a breakwater for the tiny harbour to your left. This harbour gives way to a narrow gravelly bay overhung with various deciduous trees. To the right of the breakwater, the shore is divided into patches of gravel and solid rock with a few tidal pools on the lower part of the beach. One of the most pleasant features is the small area of fine sand and beach grass above the high-water mark and in the shelter of the breakwater. Although there is a picnic table in the grassy area at the top of the stairs, many will understandably prefer to munch on their prosciutto and provolone sandwiches here or on the pebbly upper shore to the right of the stairs.

**Suitability for children** The diversity of terrain is the key to this being a child-friendly destination. Some children will begin with the grassy area, perfect for such serious pursuits as tag and Frisbee throwing, and proceed to the enticingly walk-on-able breakwater. At that point, the child who is in full exploration mode should enjoy the different areas of rock, the tidal pools and the shell and pebble strip leading to the water's edge. In spite of these possibilities, this isn't the most obvious spot to bring a very young child for a simple bit of paddling and splashing.

**Suitability for groups** Groups have used and will no doubt continue to use this welcoming spot for different activities. The small size of the parking lot and the lack of facilities are the major limitations. Otherwise, there is lots of room for a large picnic and a good bit of shorefront exploration.

**View** Like the view from the other spots north of Sidney, this one is really a treat for those who are intrigued by the contrast between wild and rocky bits on the one hand and boats and buildings on the other. Those who enjoy this area will also enjoy seeing the same features from the completely different perspectives of Beach Road and Nymph Point

Park across Tsehum Harbour. At low tide, no fewer than half a dozen rocky reefs embellish the view in the immediate foreground. In the background, Mill Point immediately to the left, Kingfisher Point directly across the harbour and All Bay to the far right are the chief features in the widely varied view.

**Winds, sun and shade** Southeast winds cool virtually the whole shore area. Northwest winds are a little buffered by the land but still curl around and across the harbour. Because of the diversity of lawns, trees and terrain, you can always find patches of both sun and shade. In general, though, the shore faces north and thus does not feel as sun-baked on a hot day as some other spots.

**Beachcombing** Although you can happily explore shoreline for a short distance on either side of the small promontory at the centre of the park, don't plan to make a long walk part of your beach plan. You could, at low tide, go several hundred metres in either direction, but will be walking through dense residential areas if you do so.

**Seclusion** It is unlikely that you will find the park heavily used, so you can always find some spots to perch for a little contemplation or dreaming. At the same time, do not choose this spot if you want your thoughts to be uplifted by the awe of untouched natural vistas.

### * Also nearby

**A. Resthaven Park** is a large playground and grassy romping area, complete with picnic tables and washrooms, alongside Resthaven Road near its junction with Harbour Road. The parking lot is near the adjacent apartment buildings—look for the sign directing you there. Although the park does go down to the water's edge, the shore is largely mud. Few will seek this spot out for the access it gives to the shore. After a game of tennis at the nearby courts, though, you may well enjoy a stroll by the water with its views across a narrow bay and out to clusters of boats tucked into the marina.

**B. Harbour Road** ends in a manicured turnaround by a lodge. Parking is a little tricky since the road is curbed, but from the garden-like grassy area and park bench you can get a bank-top, leafy-framed view of Thumb Point to the right and Curteis Point across Tsehum Harbour.

## 23

### BIGROCK ROAD

A well-marked but slightly awkward approach to a secluded rocky shore on the north side of Roberts Bay

**Location, signs and parking** Four other access points bring you to Roberts Bay, but this one is distinct. Take Resthaven from Sidney and turn right onto Allbay until, on your right, you see a paved area opening onto the water—this is Bigrock Road. You can't park at the end of the extremely short road because of driveways there, but will have no trouble finding a spot on the broad gravel shoulder of the road. Instead of the usual Sidney-area PUBLIC BEACH ACCESS sign, expect a black and white horizontal ACCESS sign attached to the road sign—and no others.

**Path** Although clearly designated, the path can provide a few challenges for those unsteady on their legs or under the burden of paraphernalia. A little rocky track winds through a short section of semi-wild bush before taking you to six weathered wooded steps and a single handrail. Here you will find yourself at a small viewing spot with a park bench—

and an entirely lovely view. It is here that the path becomes interesting. Although perfectly safe, it does require a bit of a steep scramble down solid rock to reach the pebble shore a couple of metres below.

**Beach** If you've just been to any other of the four access points to Roberts Bay to the south, you might find it something of a relief coming to this spot. Here you are well out of the soft tidal flats and onto a rock shelf. Extending several dozen metres to the low-tide line, the rough rock is made of patches of large boulder, tidal pools and rockweed-covered rock. Low tide gives you lots of interesting bits to explore, but high tide makes for a prettier view, especially since there is plenty of space near the access spot to spread out your picnic or suntanning gear among the pebbles. Don't expect much in the way of useful beach logs, though.

**Suitability for children** You will have to be confident and determined to get a small child down the steep bit onto the shore. You will have to be equally confident and determined to cope with the same child's frustrations and falls on the rough shore. Tough little children, however, could have a wonderful time here, especially if prodding at sea stars and rock crabs is among their repertoire of pleasures.

**Suitability for groups** There is room here for two or three cars' worth of visitors, but you will have to make sure that this is the kind of beach your group wants.

**View** The view is one of the prettiest in the area. Overhanging firs of the picturesquely windblown variety, rocky treed promontories and a fine mix of reefs and islands, distant and far, make for some eye-pleasing combinations. If you know what you are looking for, you will be able to pick out not just nearby Braham Rock, but also the various islets of the Little Group, Forrest Island and the tip of Sidney Spit, all framed by Roberts Point across the bay.

**Winds, sun and shade** The shore is fairly exposed to most common winds, but you can find some shelter on the upper shore if the wind is cooler than you like. Toward noon the sun is at its most direct, but you will have to wait until late afternoon to get even a little shade from the few shoreline firs.

**Beachcombing** Some will feel tempted to stumble over the rocky shore toward the much easier walk around the sweep of Roberts Bay Bird

Sanctuary to the south. Others will be happiest poking about on the sometimes slippery but always interesting assortment of rocks and pools in the immediate area.

**Seclusion** The beach is surprisingly secluded. The nearby houses are set back at the top of wooded banks, and the pebbly area is nestled virtually out of sight beneath the little cliff. Enjoy your peace and quiet, confident that any other beachgoer will have to be as intrepid as you!

* **Also nearby** Allbay Road ends at **Armstrong Point** in a small turnaround with a park bench. A dirt path descends a few metres to a tiny pebbly cove, fully in shadow by late morning. The cove is surrounded by a solid-rock shoreline dropping fairly steeply to the water's edge. The view is across Tsehum Harbour to Curteis Point, and to your right, primarily of Coal Island, and partway along its shore, Killer Whale Point.

## 24

### BOWDEN ROAD

**A well-maintained access to the north shore of Roberts Bay with a good view and a long flight of steps to a pebble and gravel beach**

**Location, signs and parking** Resthaven Drive, the main road north from Beacon Avenue in central Sidney, forks off onto Allbay Road at its slightly messy junction with Ardwell. Bowden crosses Allbay and terminates to the north at Harbour Road, and to the south leads a very short distance to a gravelly end. Two or three cars can park at the very end of the road, but parking is restricted to daytime hours, between 6 a.m. and 10 p.m. Another sign tells you to keep your dog well leashed and to "clean up after your pet." The large, decorative ROBERTS BAY BIRD SANCTUARY sign gives particular thrust to the dog-leash warning.

**Path** You can almost use this as a car-picnicking spot, but your view will be narrow and restricted to only a part of Roberts Bay. A few steps take you to a park bench and waste bin and an excellent bank-top view—

for those with difficulty walking and a thermos of coffee, a pleasant destination. Those with a little more energy have 30 solid concrete steps between them and the shore.

**Beach** You will find only a narrow strip of dry, loose pebbles at high tide to sit on and only the odd bit of beach log to lean against. Even so, if you want a pretty place to spend an hour or two, mid to high tide is probably the best time to come. Since it seems the spot receives few visitors, you will have little difficulty finding a pleasant spot to nestle with your blanket and thoughts. At low tide the gradually sloping pebble beach reveals increasingly large rocks covered with weeds and, beyond that, the beginning of tidal flats spreading across the bay to the south.

**Suitability for children** Like other spots on Roberts Bay, this one is a reasonable place to bring a matched set of children at mid to high tide. Properly shod and not too preoccupied with the imperative to build sandcastles, children could well enjoy splashing around in the comparatively warm water near the edge of an incoming tide. In cold weather, a child's options are limited to defying a parent's commands to stay dry and, possibly, hunting for pretty pebbles.

**Suitability for groups** A family or a few friends could be accommodated here, since they are unlikely to be disturbed by other visitors to the spot. This is a prime bird-viewing spot at high tide, and because birds tend not to hold still, bird groups who spot an interesting looking species from the southern part of the sanctuary will doubtless want to come here for a closer … gander.

**View** The view from the top of the bank is worth lingering over. From here your fir-framed view allows you to appreciate the nearly full circle created by the deeply inset Roberts Bay, since you are viewing the bay from near its northern tip. From the shore, because you are behind Armstrong Point, your view is restricted to looking across the bay.

**Winds, sun and shade** A southeast wind can blow freshly onto the shore here, but otherwise expect few winds to flap the pages of your novel. Expect more or less full sun throughout a sunny day.

**Beachcombing** If you keep to the upper shore, you can walk around the entire circuit of Roberts Bay. As you walk you will find that the loose pebbles of the upper shore are interrupted every few metres by a low rocky strip of rock. You will probably want to stay away from the low-tide flats since the shore there is generally very soft.

**Seclusion** You are at the bottom of a bank on this beach, and well hidden from houses above and behind you, particularly on your right. At the same time, though, there is a beachfront summerhouse on your left that extends right over the beach, so don't expect to feel hidden.

* **Also nearby** **Seagrass Road**, one street south down Allbay from Bowden, has a well-developed set of stairs down to the pebbly upper shore of the centre of Roberts Bay. The access is difficult to spot, though there is a PUBLIC BEACH ACCESS sign planted in what looks like an area of private garden just north of the junction of Allbay and Resthaven. You will need to march purposefully across the lawn to find the stairs.

## 25

### ARDWELL AVENUE

**The main access to Roberts Bay Bird Sanctuary, and its most park-like setting**

**Location, signs and parking** Although getting here from downtown Sidney is extremely easy, the road signs can be confusing. Once you have found your way to Resthaven, a major road running north from the core of Sidney, you need only drive until you reach Ardwell Avenue, your destination. The confusion arises only because one sign will point out that this is the "East End of Ardwell"—which is what you want, anyway—and other signs tell you that this same road, Ardwell, is also the location of houses officially on both Resthaven Road and Allbay Road.

Simply drive the very short distance down Ardwell to the end and park in one of the several spots where the pavement abuts a grassy park area. One sign tells you there is no parking at all and immediately below it is one telling you can park for one hour. Permit yourself a smile. As it happens, this is the only beach access on the Saanich

Peninsula with a one-hour parking limit, so make sure you are fairly efficient with scoffing your picnic, watching your ducks or soaking up those sun rays. As befits the location, dogs are to be kept on a leash. You will see one of the small, business-like PUBLIC BEACH ACCESS signs common to Sidney, and, much more interestingly, a large illustrated interpretative guide to 24 different species of shorebird you can look for—in the 60 minutes allowed.

**Path** There is no path to speak of. You can virtually drive onto the beach, and were it not for a log, could physically do so, were you seized with that desire. Keep this fact in mind when looking for a shore access for those in wheelchairs or extreme difficulty walking. Also keep it in mind when the winter storms are howling and you want a restorative spot to gaze out to sea, sip from your thermos and munch your roast duckling sandwiches. In the grassy area beside the parking spots you will see a rubbish bin and a park bench.

**Beach** The low-tide area of the beach is not all that pleasant, though not nearly as muddy as those at the Third or Fifth Street approaches to Roberts Bay. The tide goes out almost 200 m, exposing a large area of small gravel, but also areas of eelgrass and slightly muddy sand. The upper beach, in contrast, backed by a fine stand of seagrass, provides some of the loose pebbles, coarse sand and logs required for a round of sunbathing or picnicking. The largest and most appealing area, though, is immediately to the left of the access, nearly in front of a neighbouring house.

**Suitability for children** The beach is level and easily negotiated with a minimum of peril to unsteady little legs. This, in combination with its proximity to the family-mobile, makes it a comfortable and convenient place for a child. You will probably want to come at high tide, however, when the water is easily accessible—if not exactly warm. The low-tide sandy areas are not appealing for conventional sand play. In any case, in your desire to give sanctuary to the grebes and geese, you will no doubt feel you need to curtail the shrieking and running—without which a visit to the beach can be no fun at all!

**Suitability for groups** There isn't a huge amount of parking, but otherwise the area itself is well suited for a few cars' worth of beach explorers.

**View** Although the house-lined shores of the nearly circular bay enclose the view, the size of the bay and the overlapping sequence of islands directly across from the access spot make for a certain kind of beauty. If your purpose in coming here is to soak up some view before a week in the office, you will find a good deal of therapeutic beauty.

**Winds, sun and shade** One of the attributes of the bay that makes it attractive to the feathered world is its protection from strong wind and waves, though on a windy day even both they and you can be blown about a little.

**Beachcombing** The upper shore of pebbles and small rocks at this end of the bay is long enough to be explored pleasantly for a few hundred metres in either direction. You will probably want to stay near the high-tide line, though, since the lower beach is soft and almost muddy in some areas.

**Seclusion** Houses surround you, and the bank is low. The garden of one adjoining house is virtually contiguous with the public area of grass. The spot is quiet, nevertheless, and off the radar for beach-seekers.

Ardwell Avenue

## 26

### FIFTH STREET

**A low, level access to a little-used shore of beach grass, sand and logs along the south shore of Roberts Bay**

**Location, signs and parking** Fifth Street runs north from Beacon Avenue, the main street of downtown Sidney. Simply follow it to its end and then look for a parking spot along the fairly narrow shoulder on either side, since you are restricted from parking at the very end. You will see two other restrictive signs, one telling you that the area is closed to shellfish harvesting, and the other, bearing a regal silhouette of a fine hound, telling you to keep your dog on a leash and "clean up after your pet." Although you are not told so at this point, the leash makes particular sense given that the whole bay is a bird sanctuary. Think about it...

**Path** There is no path to speak of—for some, one of the chief attractions of this access. You will find a park bench and a waste bin at the edge of a section of enthusiastic beach grass, and you need take only a few steps onto the shore.

**Beach** The shore onto which you step and to your left is probably the most appealing part of the beach for most visitors. Although the section of dry loose sand and pebbles isn't large, it is enough that you can spread out your sunbathing or munching wares, though without the benefit of more than the odd bit of beach log. To your right, most of this dry beach area has patches of vegetation. The upper beach to your left is covered with a dense area of high beach grass and curves toward a low grassy point extending over the tidal flats. Because the tidal flats here, as throughout Roberts Bay, are somewhat muddy, they aren't pretty—or easily traversable. Most visitors will be happiest at mid to high tide.

**Suitability for children** Come at mid to high tide with children. At such tides, even little ones can splash cheerfully around in the comparatively warm shallow water of an incoming tide. Water shoes are a good idea, though not strictly necessary. The area in which children can romp isn't huge, but if they are content with a little water play, they could be happy here.

**Suitability for groups** A family or few friends could find this an unusual and probably private picnic or chatting spot. Birders, of course, will be keen to come at high tide to see whether the long-tailed ducks or mergansers barely visible from the other spots in the sanctuary are closer here.

**View** Most of your view is taken up with the large sweep of the nearly circular bay, lined with houses atop low bushy banks and set among occasional trees. Armstrong Point is on your left, Roberts Point on your right. The view of the islands outside the bay, dominated by Killer Whale Point and Coal Island, is—photographers take note—exquisite.

**Winds, sun and shade** This spot provides no protection from sun throughout the day, though during the afternoon the sun will be largely behind you. Since the shore is protected from all but the strongest winds, a hot day can be very hot here and even a cool day can be warm.

**Beachcombing** It is possible to walk around the edge of Roberts Bay, though the flats themselves don't make for easy walking and the dry upper shore can be a little awkwardly loose underfoot. Appropriate footgear will make a huge difference to your pleasure. At regular intervals you will be crossing low patches of rock extending toward the lower beach. The stream hidden from view a short distance to your left could present a minor obstacle if it happens to be full.

**Seclusion** Given that you are at the edge of a giant fishbowl of house after house looking into the bay, this particular spot is surprisingly secluded. The house to your left is set well back, and that to your right is behind a high hedge. In addition, this access is generally less used than the several other access routes to Roberts Bay.

## 27

### THIRD STREET

Park-like access to the east end of Roberts Bay Bird Sanctuary

**Location, signs and parking** From Sidney's centre, the route could hardly be easier. Simply drive north to the end of Third Street and park in one of several spots that directly abut a sizable chunk of trimmed lawn overhung with a few evergreens. A short distance ahead you will see a large, colourful sign announcing this to be the Roberts Bay Bird Sanctuary. Don't be confused if you see exactly the same sign elsewhere since the sanctuary is a large sandy bay with more than one access route. Two other signs will tell you to keep your dog on a leash, not least of all because birds looking for sanctuary don't expect to be hounded by hounds. Another, smaller sign, perhaps redundantly, declares this to be a PUBLIC BEACH ACCESS. A third sign warning you against collecting shellfish is posted on the piling of a private jetty on the beach itself.

**Path** A level, kempt, gravel path leads straight ahead maybe 30 m through the grassy area to a set of 18 concrete steps. If you are planning to rest or picnic at this spot, you might want to stop at the park bench at the top of the steps before going on to the less comfortable beach.

**Beach** You will find yourself at the east end of a large, flat bay. The very qualities that make this a great place for our ducky friends to shelter and picnic also make this the kind of beach where you cannot engage in typical beachy activities. Because this end of the bay is protected, the several hundred metres of tidal flats are mostly muddy sand, interspersed with the odd barnacle-covered rock. The low-tide edge of the shore is thick with eelgrass, a great source of snacks for the duck world. High tide comes virtually up to the small retaining wall at the access steps, leaving little of the upper beach zone and few logs, so crucial for most good picnics. All of this is to say that you probably want to come here at mid to high tide if you want the most attractive view and the best chance of sighting buffleheads and Pacific loons.

**Suitability for children** Almost all children will be much more approving of their parents if they take them to nearby Beaufort Road or Goddard Road access.

**Suitability for groups** This is a good spot for two or three cars' worth of beach explorers to spread out a picnic on the grass. Most groups, however, will be happiest here if their purpose is linked to the bird sanctuary rather than a public beach in the conventional sense.

**View** From this end of Roberts Bay you will have the visual impression that you are on the edge of what seems to be almost a lagoon. From the point immediately to your right, behind you and most of the way around, you will see a sequence of houses backed by a low, wooded shore. The circle is completed by the string of Fernie, Goudge and Coal islands extending behind Armstrong Point nearly opposite and punctuated by Braham Rock and its signal light.

**Winds, sun and shade** You won't find many places more protected from virtually all winds—or more exposed to all-day sun, except, of course, under the trees in the grassy area.

**Beachcombing** Unusually for this kind of enclosed shore, it is not so overhung with shorefront vegetation as to make walking along the upper shore at high tide difficult. Most will not choose this bay as the site for a long walk; birders are the obvious exception.

**Seclusion** There are not many places where you can see so many shorefront houses at a glance—or be seen by them. Nevertheless, this is a quiet spot, not much visited by those from beyond the immediate area.

## 28

### BEAUFORT ROAD

**An easy approach to an east-facing shore that exposes a large area of sand, tidal pools and reefs**

**Location, signs and parking** From Third Street north of Sidney's town centre, take the last road on your right, Beaufort, and follow it as it swings left, nearly to the road's end. Keep your eyes open for a fire hydrant and a square, white and green PUBLIC BEACH ACCESS sign atop a metal pole to the right of two closely set hedges. Permit yourself a small "Eureka!" You will see no other signs, so simply pull over onto a suitable section of shoulder on this quiet road.

**Path** The level, groomed path leads some 30 m through the narrow-set hedges. The latter part of the trail is concrete. Remarkably, it skirts both sides of a fir growing in exactly the middle of the path. Nine concrete steps and a single metal handrail lead to a small solid-rock shelf. You will have to negotiate your way past a few boulders to reach the pebbles of the upper shore on your right.

**Beach** This beach is prettiest at high tide but reveals its wonderful qualities only at low tide. Decide, therefore, whether you plan to sit and soak up the view or explore the low-tide critters. For the former, you will probably want to take a few steps along the upper zone of solid rock and find a spot in the loose pebbles among the logs. For the latter, if you want to explore the full range of the shore, make sure you are wearing shoes that you don't mind getting a little wet. Because of the diversity of the beach, this is a perfect spot to come armed with a copy of a guide to the intertidal zone so you can identify all the anemones, sea stars, crabs and so on. Areas of boulders merge into sandbars with tidal pools, and weed-covered reefs extend 70 or 80 m into the water.

**Suitability for children** This is a great place to bring your beach-loving children, especially if they are old enough to enjoy rambling and scrambling. The two essential ingredients for a great child's beach, large areas of sand and an easy path to and from the car, make for a good afternoon's play here. Be prepared, though, for the lack of facilities. In addition, be sure you have water shoes of some sort and, even in cold weather, a change of clothes. The chances of a child remaining dry for very long are small.

**Suitability for groups** The beach here is only a narrow access between shorefront houses, not a large public area. If you remain sensitive to that fact, you could bring a couple of cars' worth of friends or family members, especially if you also come at low tide and are interested in spreading out and along the beach.

**View** Since this access spot opens onto the east-facing shore immediately south of Roberts Point, your view spreads along the chains of islands from Coal Island in the north, past the Little Group to the north part of Sidney

Spit in the south. Morning light creates a beautiful pattern of misty blue overlapping contours. Choose early afternoon if you want to see the islands thrown into full relief against the backdrop of distant Mount Baker.

**Winds, sun and shade** Westerly winds can fan the shore lightly, but easterlies hit the shore more or less directly. In either case, though, moving toward the waterline exposes a bare arm to more wind; shifting to the upper shore increases the warmth from the sun, particularly during the first half of the day. Come prepared to protect yourself from UV rays: if there are any to be had, this virtually shadeless shore will have them.

**Beachcombing** You will feel most drawn to walk in the direction of Sidney since the shore curves into a gentle bay and offers a sequence of sandbars and rocky areas. Low to mid tide and appropriate footgear will, of course, give you the most options. Expect to stroll rather than stride, however. The shore requires a little care at some spots.

**Seclusion** The shoreline is low and the houses are everywhere. The comparatively large lots and plentiful shorefront vegetation, however, allow you to feel that you are not an intruder.

* **Also nearby** If you keep driving to the **end of Beaufort Road**, you will encounter a paved turnaround and a slightly cleared area with a park bench. The view looks northeast toward the cluster of islands.

## 29

### GODDARD ROAD

**Easy, level access to a small shallow bay with a smooth rock upper shore and interesting tidal flats and reefs**

**Location, signs and parking** Follow Third Street north from Sidney. Near its end turn right onto Beaufort and, after a short distance, immediately after the road angles to the left, turn right onto Goddard. At the end of the road behind a small grassy area between hedges, a pair of cars can park easily, but only a pair. The usual parking sign will remind you that you are not welcome here between 10 p.m. and 6 a.m. Now that you've found the spot without benefit of a public access sign on the GODDARD signpost, a small rectangular sign will confirm that this, indeed, is PUBLIC BEACH ACCESS. Unusually for this area, there are no signs about bylaws and their rulings on dogs, or their leashes or droppings, so you will be obliged to use plain old consideration for others as your guiding principle.

**Path** A level gravel path leads through a small grassy area past a waste bin to a park bench. A few concrete steps take you onto the more or less smooth rock of the upper shore. The easy access to the upper shore makes launching a kayak possible, but do so at high tide unless you want a squelching trek across low-tide flats. Unwieldy beach bags or family members are easily got onto the shore.

**Beach** The beach has a little of everything. The upper beach of the small, shallow bay is solid rock immediately below the concrete steps but turns to pebbly sand to the right. The mid-beach of boulders and barnacle-covered rocks yields, at low tide, to eelgrass among sand flats and low, rounded reefs, one of them just offshore. Of primary interest to would-be picnickers or loungers is the patch of soft, dry sand intermixed with some beach grass and the occasional all-purpose beach log. Be aware, however, that immediately behind this area is a metre-high retaining wall and, at the back of a large lawn, a private house.

**Suitability for children** Older, curious children will find that the mixture of tidal pools, sand, logs and rocks provides plenty of amusements. Don't forget your Band-Aids and water shoes, however, since the active child could well come a cropper on some of the rocks. The gradual slope of the shore makes for comparatively safe water play, but the water is usually cold for swimming and the shore is rough underfoot at the mid-tide level. There are, of course, no facilities.

**Suitability for groups** The area is too small and the amusements too limited for more than a car or two's worth of family folk or friends.

**View** The view of islands and reefs could hardly be prettier. If you know what you're looking at, you can pick out (from left to right) Coal Island, Forrest Island and Sidney Island.

**Winds, sun and shade** You will be partially sheltered from any strong winds blowing up Haro Strait, but expect other winds to be onshore. There is no shade throughout the day, except the smattering from a shorefront fir to the right of the access in the afternoon.

**Beachcombing** You will enjoy strolling along both the upper and lower beaches at low tide. It is possible to go farther to the south, along the bay that you can also reach from the Amherst Avenue access. The going can be a little awkward over the rougher stretches of shore, however, so come properly shod and expect more of a shore exploration than a beach walk.

**Seclusion** Like all other access routes in this area, this one brings you to a much-appreciated shore lined with houses. The lots are fairly large, however, and the houses are generally set well back. You will encounter few others here, so enjoy the quiet.

* **Also nearby** **Surfside Place** leaves Beaufort Road immediately south of Goddard Road. A PUBLIC BEACH ACCESS sign directs you to a short, level path between hedges and a park bench beside a utility structure. A few concrete steps bring you down on a gravel-and-rock coast facing southeast.

## 30

### AMHERST AVENUE

**Easy parking and access to one of the prettiest mixed beaches immediately north of downtown Sidney**

**Location, signs and parking** Third Street runs roughly parallel to the shore north of Sidney town centre and feeds many different access routes. Amherst Avenue leads directly toward the shore. Look for a black and white PUBLIC BEACH ACCESS sign on the AMHERST AVENUE signpost. At the end of Amherst, one sign indicates where you are not to park at any time. Another, beside a wide gravel area especially designed as a parking space for several cars, will tell you that there is no parking between 10 p.m. and 6 a.m., and, unusually, adds that there is no parking anytime for "vehicles over 6.1 m," presumably the size of larger RVs. Dog owners are not given instructions about the use of leashes, but a green and white sign depicts a dog in telltale defecation position and asks you to "pick up after your pet"—without being ungenteelly specific about what is to be picked up.

**Path** A level, well-maintained gravel path leads through an open grassy area and past no fewer than four park benches. From the end of the grassy area a few concrete steps take you down to the shore.

**Beach** You will find yourself standing on loose, high-tide sand toward the south end of a beautiful little bay. Picnickers and sun worshippers take note: a fine, white, sandy upper shore is backed by a metre-high concrete retaining wall and lined with a few beach logs. The beach ends with a low, picturesque rocky bluff on either end. Low tide reveals less pretty sand and weed punctuated by a few boulders and, to the left, a low-tide reef some 20 or 30 m long and protruding toward the deeper water. There is enough shore at most high tides to allow picnicking or perching, but the beach is at its most photographable or sketchable at mid tide and most interesting—biologically—at low tide. Kayakers could put in their craft at high tide but would not much enjoy slogging over the low-tide flats.

**Suitability for children** Come at mid tide to maximize most children's pleasures. At this point you can stand back and supervise the building of castles, reprimand the throwing of sand and smile at the splashing of water. Since the shore shelves so gradually, you needn't worry overmuch about the next generation disappearing into the abyss. You will, however, be justified in worrying about hypothermia if your child goes very far from the warm edge of the water into the comparatively icy depths.

**Suitability for groups** Because of the relatively easy parking and the general seclusion of the area, a small group could be happy here, especially because there are extremely pretty views to observe or record.

**View** The overlapping profiles of low, wooded islands across the waters are too numerous to list, but among them you might pick out, from left to right, Fernie, Coal, Forrest and Sidney. Lovers of mamma nature will be grateful that a groomed promontory to the south obliterates the view of Sidney itself.

**Winds, sun and shade** The bay is deep enough that you will be largely protected from westerlies, particularly toward the south end of the bay, though some winds do strike the shore directly. There is little protection from sun throughout the day, though the sun in the afternoon is largely from behind so will seem a little less blistering than otherwise.

**Beachcombing** You will find yourself automatically strolling back and forth around the 100 m curve of the bay. You will, however, feel little temptation to go beyond, even though it is possible to make your way over more rugged terrain, particularly to Roberts Point to the north. Low tide is great if you want to search for moon snails, thin-shelled clams and other denizens of eelgrass beds.

**Seclusion** This is the middle of a suburb, so don't expect any real privacy. On the other hand, don't be surprised if, nestled in the soft sand or strolling along the beach, you are alone or nearly alone.

* **Also nearby** Shoreacres Road leaves Third Street and terminates at **Memory Lane** where parking is extremely difficult. A PUBLIC BEACH ACCESS sign indicates a narrow cleared strip between a hedge and a fence, concluding with 12 concrete steps that deposit you on a steep bit of solid rock. A little fancy footwork brings you onto a mixed shore of broken and solid rock with views across to Sidney Island and south toward Sidney Harbour.

## 31

### ROTHESAY ROAD

**A level, paved path to a shore of solid rock and pebble with morning sunshine and views of nearby Sidney Harbour**

**Location, signs and parking** Once you've found your way onto Third Street north of downtown Sidney, turn onto Rothesay Road, the third on the right from Beacon Avenue. Parking is a little tricky because of the various restrictions on how long you can park and where, but the grassy shoulder of this narrow road is wide enough that you can find a spot for a car—or a few. Along the path to the shore are one of the little, square, matter-of-fact PUBLIC BEACH ACCESS signs and a NO PARKING sign, though inconveniently not visible from Third Street.

**Path** The wide, flat paved path is considerably more welcoming than the parking or signs. In fact, those with difficulty walking or even those in a wheelchair will find this a good spot: at the end of the 30 m walkway is a pleasant, low, grassy knoll with a park bench and waste bin. Also, alas, there is a hideously functional metal utility structure, but you can easily ignore it. From here there are but a few steps down a grass slope, usually trimmed, onto the shore itself.

**Beach** You will step down onto the south end of a gently curving little bay, the upper shore of which is a pleasant strip of pebbles and sun-bleached logs. Immediately in front, the shore is entirely different. At low tide this bay virtually empties to reveal patches of broken rock and gravel, and you will see a lot of exposed rock shelf, mostly covered with barnacles and rockweed, interspersed with patches of tidal pool and mixed gravel and boulders. In addition, the mysterious remnants of a low concrete wall extend directly toward the water. Most visitors looking for a spot to soak up some sun or finish off a hair-raising chapter of their overdue library book will head left and find a blissfully comfortable spot among the pebbles and logs. Choose high tide and morning for probably the prettiest visit; choose low tide for the most fun exploring the sea stars, shore crabs, chitons, limpets and other creatures in the pools and under the rocks.

**Suitability for children** Unless toilets and sand are part of your checklist of required elements, you and your children should find this spot good for a pleasant hour or two. Keep in mind that the water is generally cold here, and that the nature of the shore varies considerably with the tides. In any case, though, make water shoes and sun protection part of your beach bag contents.

**Suitability for groups** A family or a few friends could spend a wonderful hour or two, eating, chatting or wandering along the low-tide shoreline. Do not, however, plan for more than that. If parking can be managed, consider this spot for a great family photo or even a wedding photo since the easy walking and grassy patch would smooth the way for the group to say cheese.

**View** The view, like the shore, is enormously varied. Much of it is taken up with the gentler side of civilization. The end of the breakwater for Sidney

Harbour is directly offshore, and the harbour's forest of masts spreads toward the town centre. All around you comparatively unassertive houses nestle back behind the beach grass and low, bushy bank. To your left, though, your view is entirely different. A magical array of overlapping islands line the horizon and leads far into the distance toward the US islands.

**Winds, sun and shade** Although the area is fairly exposed to southeast winds, and less so to northwest ones, the upper shore of the pebbly beach gives considerable protection. No such protection is available from the sun, though during the morning hours the sun shines most directly onto the shore.

**Beachcombing** At low tide you will feel drawn to explore the remarkably indented shoreline of rocks and pools. You can walk for a considerable distance to the north if you are not looking for easy striding. To the south you can gain access to a shorefront promenade that leads to the centre of Sidney, and, if you're feeling self-indulgent, a latte and cinnamon bun.

**Seclusion** You are more or less in full view of a dozen houses here. However, because nearly all are discreetly set back behind lawns and low trees at the edge of a low bank, you won't feel as if you have stumbled into a closed neighbourhood of front gardens, as you do at some similar access spots.

* **Also nearby** Opposite the house numbered 9960 Third Street, a narrow brick walkway between two wooden fences takes you to the end of the concrete esplanade that leads around **Sidney Harbour** to the centre of Sidney—and beyond, all the way down Lochside.

## 32 TULISTA BOAT RAMP AND PARK

**A pretty, citified park immediately south of the town centre, good for beginning a seaside walk or launching a kayak**

**Location, signs and parking** No map accompanies the directions to this park since it is easy to find. Maintained by the Town of Sidney, the Tulista Boat Ramp and Park is located where Lochside Drive turns inland

and morphs into Fifth Street. Signs to the adjacent Anacortes ferry will help you pinpoint the spot. Those wishing to park after using the boat ramp will have to read the detailed sign carefully. The website for the park says that there is free parking here, but that applies to the parking area at the south side of the park, near the washrooms. The information sign by the launching area will tell you about the need to buy a ticket for parking here. In addition, if you are planning an overnight kayaking trip, you will need to park across the road in the gravel Iroquois Park parking lot, and even then, you are allowed a maximum of three days' parking. Dog walkers will likewise want to know that their eager new puppy must be kept on a leash and, of course, must leave no evidence.

**Path** The launching ramp leads directly from the parking lot. Kayakers can choose between the concrete ramp, where they can use the wooden ramp-side floats to get into and out of their kayaks, or the gravel shore beside the ramp, where they can take their time in loading gear into their kayaks. Those who want to get some kilometres under their belts while drinking in sea air will find this a great place to begin a walk south. They can choose between remaining on the paved pathway or, occasionally, descending a few concrete steps onto the gravel-and-log shore.

**Beach** The beach by the parking area is much too jagged, busy with boat launching and encrusted with sea life to be of interest to beachgoers. If you wish to picnic or ponder by the lapping waves rather than in the kempt and flowery park, use the parking area to the south of the park and walk south until you find a patch of gravel beach that suits you.

**Suitability for children** The presence of a playground with lots of colourful swings, slides and the like could be used as an enticement by parents bringing children here for a walk along the esplanade. Washrooms and drinking fountains likewise make for a child-friendly spot. While the shore itself isn't perfect for children, the gently sloping shore to the south of the playground area is well suited to picnicking, throwing rocks and soaking shoes that shouldn't be soaked.

**Suitability for groups** The park is probably more (sub)urban than most groups will want. However, the easy parking by the washrooms, the facilities and the walkway make this a great starting spot for a group stroll.

**View** To the north, the landing for the Anacortes ferry is the most obvious feature, while to the south, your eye will be drawn to the broad sweep of Bazan Bay toward Cordova Spit. The big island directly across is Sidney Island and that immediately south is James Island.

**Winds, sun and shade** The area is fairly exposed to all winds, and those blowing up Haro Strait can be quite strong. If you are seeking shade, you can find a little on the lush lawns under a few trees in the park, but otherwise can expect to be in full sun as long as there is sun in the sky.

**Beachcombing** Most wanting to walk long distances will prefer to stay on the paved esplanade running immediately above the beach and along the side of Lochside Drive. Those who don't mind stumbling and sliding a little while they look for flotsam can walk the same distance along the shore or, if they prefer, onto and away from the shore at several spots provided with steps. It is possible to keep to the shoreside and walk all the way into, and indeed, north of, Sidney itself. Those looking to punctuate or conclude a walk or paddle with a cappuccino might build this into their planning.

**Seclusion** The whole area is surrounded by houses. The walking options are extremely popular with retired strollers, joggers and dogs towing their owners, most of them happy to exchange a cheerful greeting and a few views on the weather.

*** Also nearby** The **shorefront walk** leads north from here past the prettified gardens and benches of Eastview Park, with access from Eastview Drive off Oakville or Bevan. The path heads to Beacon Park right in the centre of the Sidney waterfront. From here you can carry on north around the harbour and past downtown Sidney.

If you want to start at the south end of the walk, it officially begins a short distance south of Captain's Walk along Lochside Drive. A Rotary Club sign promotes this 2.5 km walk as a "Heart Smart" exercise.

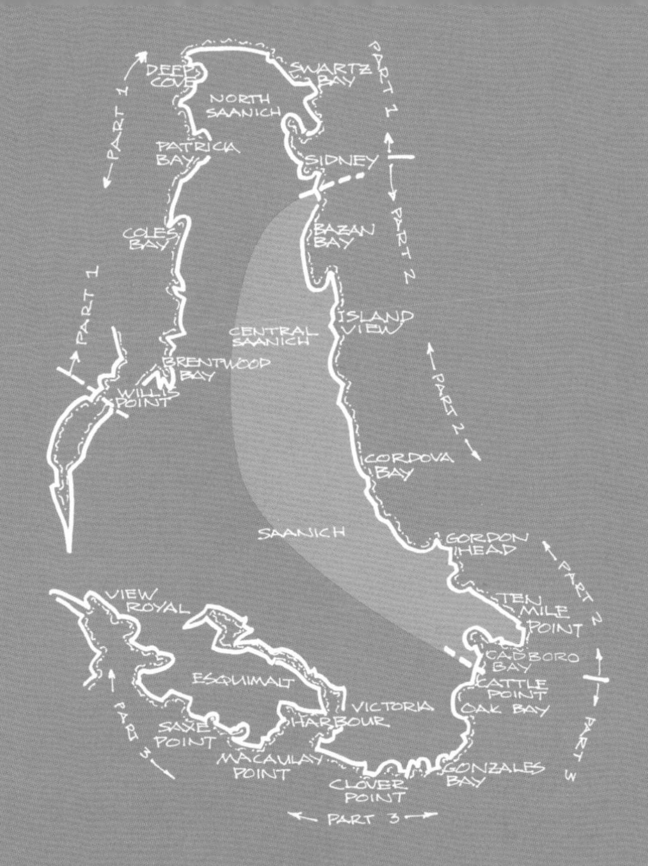


# PART 2 Sidney to Cadboro Bay

THE DIVERSITY OF BEACHES IN THIS SECOND section could hardly be greater. At one extreme you will find long, level beaches that seem to go on for ever; at the other are rugged and weathered headlands with elevated views of distant US islands and shores.

If you start just below Sidney and work your way south along the coast toward Cadboro Bay, you will encounter three main areas. The first of these, the east coast of Saanich Peninsula immediately south of Sidney, including Bazan Bay and Cordova Bay, is generally level and low, offering lots of opportunities for walking along the shorefront. A long stretch of high, sandy cliffs starting south of Island View Beach and continuing to Parker Road makes public access to the shore far below impossible.

The second main area reaches from Mount Douglas Park to the tip of Ten Mile Point, with beaches generally facing north and generally shady. This is an area of gracefully curving bays overhung by wooded banks, tiny shady coves and windswept headlands. Often you will have to be in full navigational mode to wend your way through some of the more complex labyrinths of narrow residential streets. Although a few of the spots in this area are great for children, especially Hollydene Park and Telegraph Bay, most of them will appeal to adults looking for a quiet, hidden beach or a splendid place to photograph.

The last section, from the tip of Ten Mile Point to Cadboro Bay, is a place for lovers of sun-baked, rugged little coves and views of the Olympic Mountains. With lots of options for car picnicking, sunbathing and launching kayaks, the wonderful, child-centred beach at Cadboro Bay and its little-known access routes brings this section to an end with a grand flourish.

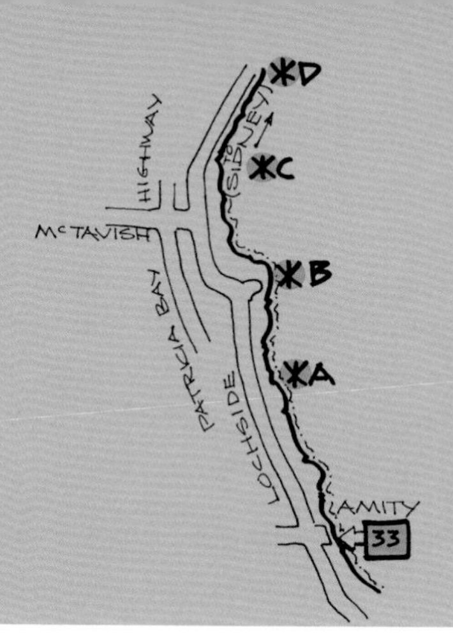

# 33

## AMITY DRIVE

**A solid flight of stone stairs to a mixed shore of solid rock and small loose rocks, with a view of Sidney and James Island**

**Location, signs and parking** Since exits and entrances from nearby Patricia Bay Highway are limited, you should use Lochside Drive for all of your beach explorations of the east coast, as far south as Lochside Drive extends. Near the southern border of North Saanich with Central Saanich, Amity Drive crosses Lochside Drive and from there proceeds but a short distance to the beach. At this point you will be a little put off by the battery of sinister-looking metal constructions and a gate, but you may also be drawn by the clear visual line to the open coast. Parking along the shoulder is easy, though be careful not to block the drives near the end. The NO PARKING sign applies to the area in front of the gate and utility structures. The familiar looking shellfish warning sign is a clear indication—and the only one—that this is a shorefront access spot.

**Path** Past the humming utility structures a magnificent flight of about 25 stone and mortar steps heads down an open grassy bank. At the bottom, a few more steps take you onto a level area of small, loose rock.

**Beach** The beach is composed of a gradually sloping area of rough solid rock, tidal pools and stretches of mostly small, loose boulders covered with rockweed and barnacles at lower tides. The access spot itself is backed by a retaining wall of the same rock and mortar construction as the steps and, farther along, by a tumble of giant shore-stabilizing boulders. Although not hugely inviting, this area is level and dry enough that you could sit here awhile or set up an easel.

**Suitability for children** The tidal pools in the area of rock shelf will amuse most children, particularly if those children enjoy prodding at and exclaiming over tiny sculpins and hermit crabs—and most do. The rocky area is level enough that they can do so without risking life and limb in the process. The shore on either side, though, with its small boulders, will make for a lot of stumbling. It will not rank high on the child-pleasure scale.

**Suitability for groups** While there is room for a group to park and wander, most groups will prefer to go farther north where both are easier.

**View** Because Amity Drive emerges onto the southern curve of Bazan Bay, it provides a pleasant view, to the north, of the town of Sidney. You might puzzle a little about what mountain is looming over Sidney. What you are looking at is actually Mount Tuam on Salt Spring Island. Immediately east, across the water is the low, wooded profile of James Island. To the south, a giant boulder on the shore provides a striking visual element to the otherwise even shoreline.

**Winds, sun and shade** The morning sun shines most directly on the beach, but there is no shade here at any time of day.

**Beachcombing** You could walk from here all the way to Sidney, several kilometres to the north, with the knowledge that the closer you get to Sidney the easier it is to walk. The first kilometre or so of shoreline is rough, though, and you may feel that it's not worth risking a twisted ankle. You'd have to go at low tide, as well, since at high tide the shoreline is generally not wide enough to walk along for any distance.

**Seclusion** Houses line the shore here, but the lots are fairly large and the houses are mostly set back among trees at the top of the bank. In addition, you are likely to see only a few locals bringing their dogs to check out the resident sea star population.

### * Also nearby

**A. Cy Hampson Park** is such a well-signposted and prominent park along this section of Lochside Drive below McTavish Road that it hardly requires a separate description. In case visitors haven't noticed it, however, they may well want to find their way to this beautiful seaside park about 1 km south of the junction of McTavish and Lochside Drive. Dog walkers might be interested in the off-leash area across Lochside from the shore. Note the tap and bucket to quench your dog's thirst.

A solid strip of bush shelters a large area of grass from the shore. Here you will find several picnic tables and a toilet. You might want to postpone your picnic until you get to the shore, where there is one table on a grassy knoll. Those with walking difficulties will be glad to know that the park is wheelchair accessible. A gradual ramp leads down to the shore to the left of the grassy area, while a set of stairs leads down from your right. The shore of Bazan Bay here is mostly rock and rounded boulders at high tide, tricky for strolling along, but at low tide sandbars allow for much more vigorous exercise.

**B.** Just north of Cy Hampson Park and just south of McTavish, where Lochside takes a sudden turn inland, a short, wide **service road** (unnamed, beside a house numbered 8929 Lochside Drive) approaches the shore. A paved path leads from the end of this road toward the shore of Bazan Bay, but is heavily eroded at the lowest part. At the time of writing, the path is closed, a sign says, but perhaps the path will soon be rebuilt.

**C.** A short distance north of the intersection of **McTavish Road** and Lochside, a roadside pull-off area leads through blackberry bushes to a rickety but usable set of seven wooden stairs. This is actually a kind of miniature estuary with interesting gravel bars breaking up the otherwise smooth curve of the beach. The upper beach is backed by seagrass and is thick with bleached logs among the pebbles.

**D.** A **broad, grassy strip**, looking almost like a road, alongside the house numbered 8527 Lochside, leads to an impressive set of stone stairs descending to a shore of broken rock and a fairly enclosed view dominated by James Island.

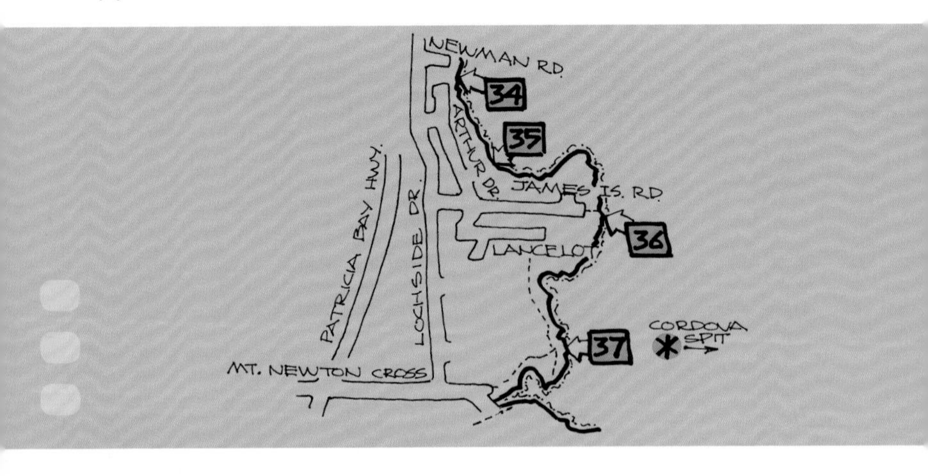

## 34

### NEWMAN FARM PARK

**Historic farm buildings and boathouses on the rocky shore of Ferguson Cove**

**Location, signs and parking** Newman Farm Park, the historic homestead of the Newman family, is easy to spot, signposted from the side of

Lochside Drive less than a kilometre north of the drive's starting point at Mount Newton Cross Road. Parking, however, is a minor nightmare since you are not allowed to stop along Lochside Road and there is no place to pull off near the park. You would do best to turn down Newman Road to the north of the park and stop on the fairly accommodating shoulder of the road. Other than the small sign for Newman Farm Park immediately in front of it, don't expect other information or guidance. If you are interested in the history of this Finnish pioneer family's farm, search the parks and recreation area of the District of Central Saanich website at http://www.centralsaanich.ca/.

**Path** No clear path will lead you through the rough, grassy field, but it is easy enough to walk either along the edge of the field or directly toward the wooded bank and clearly visible stair railings. A new set of 35 very solid wooden stairs takes you down the bank past some very old, crumbling stairs and toward two shorefront structures, the newly patched boathouses belonging to the historic farm. A colourful sign at the bottom of the stairs advises caution: you are about to plunge the last few steps to the shore on a "natural path."

**Beach** What will bring you here primarily is your interest in the historically picturesque. The two boathouses sit atop log structures extending onto the rough boulder shore. There is little room to spread out your shore-going wares on this beach, though if you are determined to do so, you can find a pleasant enough spot on the patch of solid rock immediately to the left. You can also make your way along the 50 m or so of loose fist-sized rocks to the left, toward a more appealing rocky promontory and the tiny pebbly beach beside it.

**Suitability for children** Adventurous children can enjoy climbing over the lumps of rock and investigating the tidal pools for strange and catchable creatures. More timid little ones or those struggling to totter around on level surfaces won't be happy here.

**Suitability for groups** This is not the place to bring a group for a picnic or walk on the beach. If you have a bevy of historically minded friends, however, and they don't mind the awkward parking and walking, you can guarantee them an unusual shorefront experience.

**View** The pretty promontory to the left and the tip of Ferguson Cove to the south frame a clear view of the sequence of islands that begins north of Sidney and encompasses distant San Juan and nearby James.

**Winds, sun and shade** Morning is the time for sun. Thereafter, expect a lot of shade from the high, wooded bank behind you. Because you are in a cove, you will be a little protected from the winds that can whisk up Haro Strait, but you will be exposed to those from the east.

**Beachcombing** This is not the place to come if you are looking for a long walk with your iPod or iPoodle.

**Seclusion** You probably won't see a single, solitary soul while you are here. The spot is sufficiently hidden that few are even aware of its existence.

## 35

### ARTHUR DRIVE

**A rather functional approach to the centre of a sheltered, north-facing cove lined with houses**

**Location, signs and parking** Shortly after the beginning of this northern section of Lochside, approached from Mount Newton Cross Road, turn right onto James Island Road and first left onto Arthur Drive. Almost immediately you will see a matter-of-fact PUBLIC BEACH ACCESS sign, though it can be hidden in the bushes to the right along the path. Parking is easy along the shoulder but be careful not to block the chained service road that leads down the centre of the path.

**Path** Follow the well-beaten path along the right-hand side of the service road, between high hedges, past the chained gate and finally to a spiffy, concrete set of stairs. En route you will have observed that, like so many public access routes, this one has a double function, in this case manifest in a concrete structure with metal trap doors and a sign indicating a cable from shore.

**Beach** You will find yourself in the middle of the small, north-facing bay called Ferguson Cove. This bay may not match your ideal picture of a cozy, protected cove, since it is not enclosed by headlands. While the east end is formed by Turgoose Point protruding a couple of hundred metres from the main north–south shoreline, the western edge to the cove simply merges directly into that banked shoreline. The beach itself is a mixture of mostly gravel and rocks with some areas of coarse rock. At low tide it is possible to walk out to an intriguing rocky outcropping that at high tide looks like a decorative reef. Watch for the attractive picnic spot on the upper beach to the left of the access stairs.

**Suitability for children** Access is easy for children and the shoreline is safe, though, of course the water is cold except near the edge on an incoming tide. Choose a high tide for splashing, a low tide for exploring, but make sure you have solid water shoes.

**Suitability for groups** A small group can find enough parking and enough place to disperse along the beach—at low tide, anyway—that they won't be intruding into a quiet neighbourhood.

**View** The view is framed by the bushy, treed low bank around the entire bay and highlighted by Turgoose Point to the south.

**Winds, sun and shade** When a strong southeast or southwest wind is raising goosebumps among beachgoers at other spots accessible from Lochside, those who have chosen this spot can feel complacent that they are largely protected, particularly if they walk south a little distance. Sun lovers who like only afternoon outings will be disappointed by the amount of shade this beach can collect in the afternoon, although the shade mostly covers the area above the high-tide line.

**Beachcombing** It is easy, and tempting, to walk some distance, particularly at low tide—but only if you turn north. The shoreline around Turgoose Point becomes increasingly steep and tricky.

**Seclusion** Although there are houses surrounding the bay, you may well be the only visitors to the spot. Don't come here expecting to be isolated or unobserved, but don't expect, either, to feel you are intruding.

## 36 JAMES ISLAND ROAD—SAANICHTON BAY PUBLIC DOCK

An intriguing shorefront opportunity for crabbing at a public wharf

**Location, signs and parking** See the directions for Arthur Drive, but instead of turning onto Arthur Drive, keep going directly to the end of James Island Road. You will immediately notice the large parking lot to your right behind a chain-link fence—used by those who work on the privately owned James Island immediately across from this access spot. Other signs will limit areas of roadside parking, but as the gravel shoulder is wide, parking should not be difficult.

**Path** The path is actually a small, level, paved road leading a few steps to the beginning of the large, wide and railed wharf projecting a few dozen metres into the water. It is so easy to get a wonderful view over the water, and within such an easy distance of the car, that this is an excellent destination for those with difficulty walking or even in wheelchairs.

**Beach** There is no beach to speak of—this is a public wharf. The reason for coming here is to enjoy a wonderful view, especially in morning light, and either to observe others engaged in the fine sport of crabbing or to take part in a little crabbing yourself. The L-shaped dock has a lower dock, but crab fishermen seem to put out their traps and baited lines mostly from the upper dock. Here you will find lots of information about the two large edible species of crabs, rock crab and the much preferred Dungeness crab. The Department of Fisheries and Oceans has installed a permanent measuring device for making sure your (male only!) crabs are the legal size. If you do decide to try your luck, make sure you buy your licence and check limits (licences can be bought online at the Department of Oceans and Fisheries site).

**Suitability for children** Those children who love to do a little make-believe fishing or "help" their parents attempt to catch crabs could love this unusual spot. Not all children, of course, have such interests and temperaments. If you are planning to stay any length of time with a child, bring a child-sized life jacket/PFD for the obvious reasons, your peace of mind probably being the paramount one.

**Suitability for groups** A few friends or a family could enjoy a visit here, but it would be unfair to others to arrive with hordes.

**View** Even if you are not interested in the edible arthropods, a visit here is well justified. Especially on a sunny, still morning, the view is wonderful—and unusual for this stretch of coast. To the north you will see the almost block-like rocky shore of Turgoose Point and a decorative dead fir on the point itself, along with a less charming jetty. To the south, if you direct your view past the houses lining the treed bank, you will be rewarded with an excellent view of most of Saanichton Bay and the almost entirely unspoiled peninsula that ends in Cordova Spit.

**Winds, sun and shade** The spot can be windy—when wind is blowing from just about any direction. Likewise, of course, there isn't a morsel of shade to be had.

**Beachcombing** The shoreline itself is too steep and rugged for walking.

**Seclusion** This is a public dock, but it is usually quiet. Houses line the shore a short distance to the north and a slightly greater distance to the south, but the wharf is on the promontory of Turgoose Point, so you will experience some of the sensation of being on a small island.

## 37

### SAANICHTON BAY PARK

**Paved walkways through a lawn area with an estuary at one end and a gently curving bay at the other**

**Location, signs and parking** Nowhere could be simpler to find. Turn off Highway 17 at the traffic lights and follow Mount Newton Cross Road a short distance to where the main road curves off to the right. This leads directly to a First Nations reserve; it is not a public road. You will see a public access sign directing you to dip down the road on the left leading to a parking lot. The sign at the end of the parking lot reading NARROW WALKWAY, NO BIKES is the only clue that you are in the right place. You will also see one of the standard restrictions on overnight parking. About 10 cars can fit in the paved parking lot. Don't be surprised if the air there is redolent of *eau de sewage*, a scent associated with some very business-like outflow structures located on one side of the lot.

It is also possible to gain quick access to the park via Lancelot Lane to the north. Ironically, the path is clearly signposted from this northern approach, but the parking is considerably more limited.

**Path** A sign on the sea side of the parking lot identifies the beginning of a smooth and level walkway. The path winds its way almost 100 m along the edge of a small estuary behind a screen of trees on one side and, on the other, a phalanx of condominiums. Once the path has run the gauntlet of this residential block, it turns onto a raised promontory of trees and mowed grass. A sign on the branch to the right warns you to "use caution" on this "nature path." The caution that you are to use relates, no doubt, to the slippery dirt path that drops onto the rocky shore at the mouth of the estuary. The alternate path takes you back toward a residential area and, after a short distance, a broad, gravel path toward the shore. One sign here tells you that you are on municipal parkland; the other that you should show caution in the event of an earthquake and the tsunami that such an earthquake might cause, though presumably tsunami danger is equally high at several similar but unsignposted spots. This latter trail is by far the easier of the two approaches to the shore.

**Beach** This is one of those places along the east side of Saanich Peninsula that are charming at high or even a partially high tide. Visitors who arrive at low tide, however, will be forgiven for finding the shore charmless. Naturalists will be fascinated by the squelchy mud-and-rock flats that extend to the distant water line at low tide. Other visitors will not. The upper shore near the estuary is a mixture of pebbly patches and lumpy rock. A few places would make pleasant enough perching spots, but the slightly eroded bank and generally damp feeling to this end of the shore encourage more strolling than staying. The shore directly accessible from the second path is less varied, more consistently gravelly, but likewise more suitable for strolling.

**Suitability for children** This is the kind of place where you bring your children for a little mild diversion as you satisfy your own curiosity or take a stroll. You are unlikely to bring a child here just to play. At the same time, at high tide the eager water-loving child could find plenty of scope for imaginative and soggy fun.

**Suitability for groups** Small groups will find plenty of parking and plenty of space to stroll on the paths or upper shore. For picnicking, though, most groups would be happier elsewhere.

**View** At high tide and in sunny weather, the curving and tree-adorned shores of the estuary provide lots of changing, though confined, perspectives. Once you have emerged from the estuary, your view is primarily across Cordova Channel to James Island. The wooded peninsula to your right across Saanichton Bay is Cordova Spit, mostly First Nations reserve land, while that to your left is Turgoose Point.

**Winds, sun and shade** All winds are fairly muted here, particularly those from the west and north, and especially in the estuary part of the walk. Since the shoreline primarily faces north, the beach never feels sun-baked. At the same time, because there are no high banks and only scatterings of trees, all times of day in sunny weather produce patches of sun and shade.

**Beachcombing** Strolling is the main attraction of this unusual bit of shore. While walking is comfortable and varied along the upper shore, some will no doubt prefer the level and smooth paths.

**Seclusion** All approaches to this area could hardly be less secluded. You may feel you are in the front yard of a congested residential area. If you press on, past all of the residences, and if you keep to the shore rather than the paved paths, you can, in spite of everything, remove yourself from the suburban congestion and find considerable quiet and peace.

* **Also nearby** **Cordova Spit Park** is an undeveloped but dramatic piece of land clearly visible from Saanichton Bay Park. The spot, much prized by birders, can be reached only by walking north along the shore from Island View Beach, since it is separated from other public land by Tsawout First Nation Reserve land. Permission can occasionally be obtained to use the road through the reserve, but such access should not be expected or relied upon.

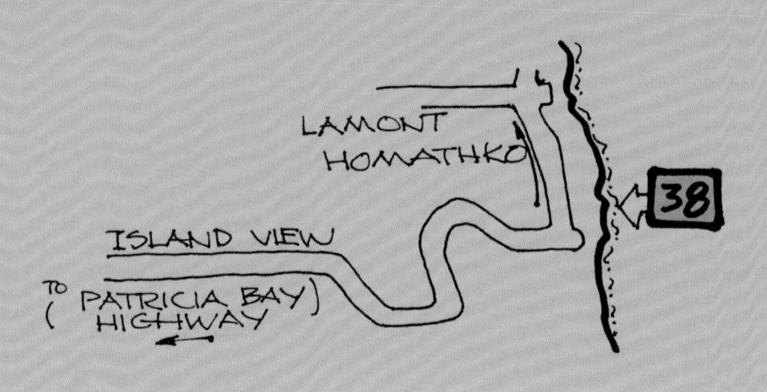

## 38

## ISLAND VIEW BEACH REGIONAL PARK

**A large park with full picnic facilities, a level sandy beach, launching ramp and dune walks**

**Location, signs and parking** Finding the turn off Patricia Bay Highway could hardly be easier. Both Island View Road and a huge sign for the park will start you on your way east through the low farming area of Saanich Peninsula. Two different routes can take you to the beach, but it is easiest to use the signposted route by following Island View Road through some crazy squiggles and then left onto Homathko Road. Large signs and a gigantic parking lot will welcome you to the spot. You may choose to carry on north along Homathko past a seasonal RV park to a second, larger parking lot, though most of the park's day-use facilities are close to the lot to the south. If you are planning to bring your Alsatian here for a romp, you should be aware of the sign with a slightly confusing message: "Dogs must be on a leash when passing through beach and picnic areas and are not allowed to stay. June 1 to September 15." Interpret that as you will. Those planning an evening here will likewise have to do a little interpretation of their own: the park's website will tell you that the park is open from "sunrise to sunset," but you will see a sign telling you that you will be towed away between 11 p.m. and 6 a.m.

**Path** This is a great place to bring those with unsteady or diminutive legs. A few level, easy steps can bring you from your car to a nesting spot on the sand amidst the sun-bleached logs. Alternately, if you want to begin your stay with a feast eaten at a picnic table, it is only a short distance through a level grassy area to a picnic table and, beyond that, washrooms. Since there are few picnic tables, however, don't expect one to be free. On the other hand, if you fear you may need shelter from drizzle or blistering UV rays, come to the beach fortified with the knowledge that there is a picnic shelter here.

**Beach** Island View Beach, completely out of sight and out of mind to those who shoot by on the Pat Bay Highway, is one of those special spots that, once discovered, can become first on anyone's list for a great place to spend a weekend afternoon. A huge area of soft, dry sand allows plenty of room for spreading out your family's fun gear. If you like to do so among logs, you will find a dense clutter of them to the right of the main parking area. In spite of the sandy character of the beach, flip-flops or crocs will be handy for getting to the water across some bands of small rocks. On the other hand, don't be surprised if you find the water much too bracing for more than a Nordic-style dip. You will have to go to one of the spots on the Saanich Inlet side of the peninsula if you want a less teeth-clenching swim.

**Suitability for children** For little children who are most likely to paddle near the water's edge, the otherwise bracing water will not be a problem—on an incoming tide, the water can get very pleasant. In fact, the beach is altogether the perfect spot for all of those activities a child expects to do at a beach. Building castles, playing with seashells, dashing through shallow water, kicking sand into the potato salad and the like are perfectly accomplished here.

**Suitability for groups** This is probably the best spot in the entire Victoria area for a large group picnic, but only if such a group is willing to eat not from tables but on the beach itself. The huge parking area and substantial area of dry sand well above summer high tides mean that there is always room for even the most fecund family's reunion.

**View** The park comes by its name honestly: the beach does, indeed, provide a view amply decorated with islands. The closest islands, to your left, are James, Sydney and D'Arcy (part of a park). Looking surprisingly close directly ahead—but on the other side of the US border—is San Juan Island and, if you could make them out, the smaller Henry, Guss and Low islands. On a clear day the trademark crest of Mount Baker rises in the background.

**Winds, sun and shade** A westerly can blow with unimpeded enthusiasm up Haro Strait, so you might want to consider forecasts before planning a major afternoon outing here. If your intention is to sunbathe or finish off a suspenseful novel, come assured that you can find significant shelter from these winds among the dense rows of beach logs. On the other hand, there is no shelter from the sun at any time of day, other than under the picnic shelter and a few trees set well back from the beach. Sunscreen, sun hats, sunglasses and the rest of your anti-sun arsenal should be part of your planning.

**Beachcombing** Those who want to stride out to drink in the sea air or work off an over-indulgent picnic will find this the perfect spot to do so. Walking to the north, however, will probably please more people than walking to the south, since to the south the beach narrows and steep sandy banks begin to rise above it. Be sensitive to the fact that to the north you will eventually come to First Nations reserve land. In either case, though, most will like to come when a mid to low tide exposes damp sand. Walking through powdery high-tide sand is really only easily done by camels.

**Seclusion** This is, indeed, a public park, so you can hardly expect privacy. Surprisingly, though, the park is rarely crowded and, more to the point, is surrounded by undeveloped land. Set out for a stroll along the beach and expect to be deliriously and deliciously alone!

* **Also nearby** If you are exploring the area, you might discover **Martindale Road** to the south (not on the accompanying map) and the completely undeveloped but slightly trampled path alongside a private fence at the road's end. Be careful: the path leads to the edge of a sheer sandy cliff—but an excellent view. On a windy day, don't be surprised if you see a hang-glider.

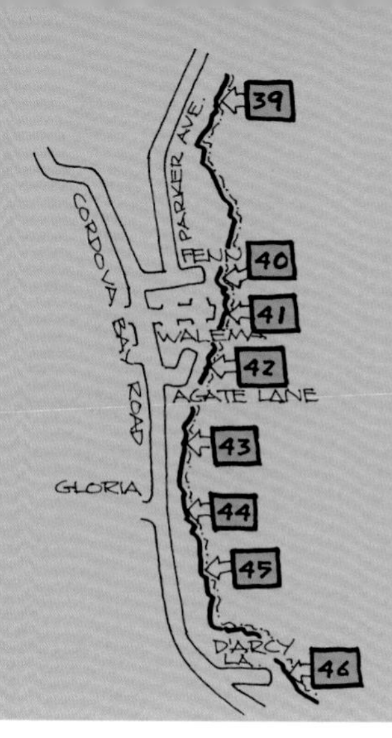

## 39

### PARKER PARK

A few steps to a quiet shore with long stretches of low-tide sand

**Location, signs and parking** From Cordova Bay Road, turn onto Fenn Avenue, opposite a school, and then swing to the left onto Parker Avenue. After about a kilometre along a residential street, you will see a large paved parking lot and a prominent painted wooden sign identifying this as Parker Park. Parker Park parking (to be said 10 times quickly) is plentiful. An additional Saanich sign identifies this as BEACH ACCESS. This may be a great place for your dog to bring you for a seaside romp, because it is one of the few big beaches in the area where both of you are allowed during summer months—and, apparently, where there are no leash restrictions. Do notice, however, that dog owners are "required"—the word is capitalized and underlined—to "remove excrement left by their dogs." Once you are on the beach, you are told that clams and their kin are contaminated and thus, reasonably, the area is closed to shellfish collecting.

**Path** The path leads directly from the end of the parking area down 28 wooden steps that might not be the sturdiest you've ever encountered.

At the bottom, you're still not at the beach, but, strangely, at the top of a 2 m-high concrete retaining wall. Take the path along the top of the wall behind a chain for a distance until a flight of 10 concrete steps brings you onto the shore.

**Beach** You arrive onto a sizable upper shore of loose, coarse sand at the bottom of the retaining wall. This retaining wall extends a long distance in either direction, giving a slightly odd character to the shore for those accustomed to—and looking for—a battery of weathered logs for nesting among or leaning against. On the other hand, except for a mid-beach strip of loose golf-ball-sized rocks, the beach provides sand, sand and more sand. The tide does not go out very far—most low tides will give you a strip of about 100 m from the top of the beach.

**Suitability for children** The beach isn't designer-perfect for kids. The lack of shade, toilets and protection from wind could induce parents or grandparents to choose another spot farther south into Cordova Bay. Otherwise, however, the wide open space to go crazy—dashing through shallow water, flinging Frisbees, fabricating unlikely sandcastles and the like—makes this a great place for children.

**Suitability for groups** Lots of parking and lots of room to spread out make this a good group destination. If the lack of facilities is not an issue, then your group—and particularly a group that wants to take advantage of the stretches of sand one way or another—could be purring-happy here.

**View** At this point you are in a shallow bay, so you have a fine perspective, especially at low tide, of the full sweep of gently curving shore, though it is lined with house after house after house. The view is generally open though embellished with distant views of Sidney and D'Arcy islands on the Canadian side of the border and, to the south, the graceful silhouette of Mount Douglas.

**Winds, sun and shade** Although not smacked directly by winds and protected somewhat from southwesterlies, this section is fairly exposed, like the rest of this coast. Think of shielding yourself from all of those UV rays, too, since there is no shade to be had.

**Beachcombing** This is one of *the* beachcombing beaches of all beach-combing beaches—with a couple of considerations. First, you really should come at low tide if you want to stride out on firm sand rather than slide around in the Kalahari of the upper beach. Second, even at low tide, several big strips of tidal pool require shoes that you don't mind getting wet, or, in cold weather, boots that keep out the water.

**Seclusion** A search for seclusion would not bring you here—though neither would a search for the opposite. Though you will see lots of people here on a hot summer's day, you won't find yourself in the middle of a throng all primed to admire your abs or skimpy swimsuit.

## 40

### FENN AVENUE

**A long flight of steps down a high bank to a secluded spot on a mixed shore**

**Location, signs and parking** Fenn Avenue is both a destination for those looking for a secluded access spot and a linking road for those exploring the coast north of here. Fenn is the northernmost shore access to Cordova Bay from Cordova Bay Road before the main road heads inland. Follow Fenn to the end, but note Parker Avenue on your left if you are intending to do more northerly exploring. You will see a SAANICH BEACH ACCESS sign welcoming you to the spot, but also another sign warning about making noise, disturbing others, dropping litter—or having fires. If you do want a fire, taking into consideration that they leave long-lasting scars on the beach, you can apparently apply for a permit.

**Path** From the end of the road, pause partway down the stairs to take in a beautifully tree-framed view of Mount Douglas. Then take a deep breath and continue down the impressive flight of 87 steps. Once on the beach, turn back and allow yourself to be impressed at the engineering effort that has gone into providing access to this hidden piece of shore.

**Beach** Unusually for the Cordova Bay area, the beach here doesn't often have logs among which to nestle. The final flight of steps drops down a little rocky bluff onto a strip of pebbles still exposed at most high tides, but head to either side if you are looking for a larger area of coarse sand on which to spread out your artistic, gastronomic or sun-absorbing wares. Low tide offers interesting diversions—rocky shelves with tidal pools on a generally mixed shore of different surfaces.

**Suitability for children** Think seriously, very seriously, of the 87 steps that bring you not only down to, but also up from, this beach. If you and your child can toss aside that consideration, then do expect amusements aplenty at this beach as long as they do not require long stretches of sand.

**Suitability for groups** If you are looking for an area with lots of space where you are not likely to disturb neighbours or be inspected by them, then this is a good candidate for a group, though you could hardly choose a worse place for such an activity as a wedding photo shoot. Because of the configuration of the shore, pursuing artistic endeavours and examining birds and shore life are better than at most other spots in the main sweep of Cordova Bay.

**View** Beautiful views can be found here because the bank is high and treed and the access brings you to the middle of an indented piece of shore surrounded by dramatic, rocky bluffs with weathered trees. From various spots on the stairs or the solid-rock upper shore, from high tide to low, you can find dozens of combinations of picturesque elements.

**Winds, sun and shade** Because this spot has headlands on either side, you will be partially protected from the winds blowing up and down the straits. Come during the first part of the day if you want the maximum sun, but the mid and lower parts of the beach are in the sun all day.

**Beachcombing** Go to one of the nearby access spots immediately south along Cordova Bay if you want to walk hand-in-hand without trying to balance or step around slippery bits. At low tide, however, you can explore lots of rocky outcroppings, tidal pools and gravelly little bays.

**Seclusion** Seclusion is one of the great attributes of this access. The high, wooded bank shields you from the surrounding houses—and them from you—except near the low-tide area. You can come here with your journal or your Johnny and expect few (human) distractions.

# 41

## WALEMA AVENUE

A flight of concrete steps to a mixed shore with tidal pools and rocks, coarse sand and logs

**Location, signs and parking** Walema Avenue crosses Cordova Bay Road and leads directly to the beach. If you are navigating with a GPS or even a good old-fashioned map, don't confuse this section of Walema with that west of Cordova Bay Road, approached from Santa Clara Avenue and completely detached from the section that you want. Once at the end of Walema, choose your parking spot carefully. You will find not just the usual instructions for where and when you cannot park, but also the warning that your car will be towed if you get it wrong. A more welcoming sign announces this to be, indeed, a beach access. Dog owners, be aware that your eager, panting companion isn't welcome here from the beginning of May until the end of August. As for your intentions to make noise, create a "disturbance" or drop litter, put those out of your head altogether or you will be fined 50 dollars.

**Path** From the end of the road a few steps bring you to a flight of more than 30 concrete steps, complete with handrail, leading down a bushy slope.

**Beach** The most striking feature of the immediate beach, is, alas, temporary: a much-weathered beach stump with a swing dangling from one of its roots high above. Having registered this charming embellishment, you will notice that you have arrived at the head of a tiny, bush-lined cove with an inviting area of loose, coarse sand and pebbles among a litter of beach logs. The lowest lumps of rock at the mid-tide and low-tide levels, with their tidal pools, are worth exploring.

**Suitability for children** Most children will probably prefer to go to those nearby access spots to the south that allow low-tide access to sandbars for running and digging. But for children who do find themselves here, this is a safe, interesting spot for considerable beach play—not least of all if the swing is still in place when they arrive.

**Suitability for groups** Although parking can require a minor feat of logistical genius, the beach itself provides plenty of space for even a large group to picnic, share stories or set out on a long walk.

**View** Walema arrives at the most convex bit of shore for several kilometres and, as a result, the most expansive view. You can see a considerable distance in both directions along the shore, including the whole sweep of Cordova Bay and Mount Douglas.

**Winds, sun and shade** If you huddle up among the logs where the shore tucks into the leafy bank surrounding the access steps, you can find a little protection from both wind and sun. Otherwise, you are fairly exposed to all the elements.

**Beachcombing** The shore is low and mostly level in both directions. To the north, however, rise a few minor sections of rock and the beach is generally rougher. If you want to be able to trot along with the wind in your hair, head south at a low tide.

**Seclusion** While the centre part of Cordova Bay provides little seclusion, here you will usually find something approximating privacy. Not only do most people go to the sandier version and lower-banked area farther south, but also the comparatively high, wooded banks here mean that the houses are well out of sight.

Walema Swing

## 42

### AGATE PARK

**A grassy park area with two picnic tables and easy access to the long sweep of Cordova Bay Beach**

**Location, signs and parking** Look for Agate Lane just north of that part of Cordova Bay Road where the road angles away from the sea. Agate Lane does not cross Cordova Bay Road but merely juts off toward the ocean for a short distance. It then turns sharply north and comes to an end at Agate Park, where a dozen or so cars can park in the large paved parking area. An official Saanich sign identifies this both as AGATE PARK and BEACH ACCESS. Other signs are a little more complicated. They will dampen your pent-up desires to throw litter around and make a lot of noise. Not here, friends. And looking for a place to bring your whippet for a race along the shore? Not here—at least not in summer. However, "summer" ends here at the end of August, unlike many beaches in Oak Bay, for example, where the no-dog summer goes until the end of September. An additional boon is that not only are you supplied with plastic bags for your dog's "excrement," but also a barrel in which to deposit it afterwards. A final sign tells you not to choose this beach if you need to collect shellfish for a bouillabaisse. They are contaminated.

**Path** This is one of the best places in Cordova Bay to bring those who have walking difficulty. The shore is low here and, although the path is about 30 m long, it is smooth and level through the grassy area and slopes gradually to the shore. En route through the treed area, you will find not just a park bench, but two picnic tables—the only park conveniences here. If you are looking for a park with washrooms, you will have to go elsewhere.

**Beach** The beach here is similar to most other beaches in Cordova Bay, as it curves gradually for kilometres southwards in a shallow bay. The upper beach is exactly the hodgepodge of beach logs and loose, coarse sand that makes for a perfect, if sometimes gritty, picnic spot and an even more perfect sunbathing spot. The tide does not go out very far, but the shore slopes gradually at low tide past an area of loose gravel toward sandy flats intermingled with tidal pools.

**Suitability for children** The easy approach and level, safe beach make Agate Park a great spot for high-energy children armed with kites, spades or skimboards. Be aware, though, that the water warms up only near the shore. Flip-flops or water shoes are also a good idea for navigating areas of gravel. You might want to weatherproof your child if you are planning more than a short visit. And, of course, be mindful that there are no washrooms.

**Suitability for groups** This is an excellent place for a wedding or large family photo shoot. In the afternoon or early evening, the light will allow you to take your photo with the curving shore and sea as your backdrop. Other groups will find lots of room to roam or spread out their beach wares. The easy parking amplifies all of these features.

**View** This is the northern end of a large, shallow bay. To the south you will see a sweeping shoreline and Mount Douglas. Turning toward the east, you will find that the vista is wide and open, punctuated by the low, distant outlines of Sidney and D'Arcy islands.

**Winds, sun and shade** This beach can get windy, especially with a southeast wind. If the wind becomes more than just a cooling breeze on a warm day, the area of logs can provide a cozy, protected shelter. On the other hand, if the sun is more than you want, you will have to retreat even farther, in this case up into the park area and the shade afforded by the few huge, spreading trees.

**Beachcombing** As long as you are not planning to walk with your dog in summer months, you will find this a great place for a long seaside stroll, especially if you head south. Come at low tide, when the level, hard sand is exposed in most places. The loose upper shore can make you feel a little like Lawrence of Arabia. And do wear shoes that you don't mind getting wet, since you will encounter tidal pools and patches of wet sand.

**Seclusion** There isn't a speck of seclusion to be found here. Houses on low, generally treeless, banks line the shore in both directions. On the other hand, since there are many different access spots near here and since the area is not generally well known, don't be surprised if there are few to appreciate your matching beach outfits.

# 43

## CORDOVA BAY ROAD

A park-like approach to a large area of sand and logs on a long, level beach

**Location, signs and parking** Where Cordova Bay Road runs close to the shore, look for McMorran's Beach House restaurant (now housing Charter's Restaurant) and the small park-like grassy area. Numerous cars can park in the designated slots abutting the sidewalk. Dog owners' alert: you will have to take Prunella elsewhere for her summertime sea air. Dogs are not allowed on the beach from May 1 to August 31, though after that magic date, not even a leash seems to be required. In addition, note the sign asserting two points. The first will hardly affect your planning, unless you are looking for a beach where you can engage in "noise and other disturbances," both prohibited. A beach fire, on the other hand, seems to be legal, as at many local beaches—but only if you have a fire permit and extinguish the fire by 11 p.m. The 11 p.m. conclusion to your festivities is unusually liberal, especially in the context of prohibitions in nearby North Saanich where you cannot even park near the beach after 9 p.m.!

**Path** A hi-tech and elegant concrete and stone staircase leads down 24 steps to the shore from the restaurant side of the park area. You run the gauntlet of signs as you walk down the stairs.

**Beach** The beach is scarred with the remains of several beach fires, but the fact that you are allowed fires tells you that this, indeed, is a perfect spot for all kinds of sandy social activities, including sandy picnics. A large area of level sand and bleached logs above the high tide extends in both directions from the bottom of the steps. Mid-beach are patches of fist-sized rocks and tidal pools; beyond, areas of sand extend to the low tide about 100 m out. If you come at low tide, this large and level shore invites activity—Frisbee throwing, kite flying, skimboarding and so on. As for high tide, if only the water were a little warmer...

**Suitability for children** With all of that sand, both of the wet and dry varieties, children should be blissfully happy constructing castles and kicking sand over sunbathing parents. Water shoes or flip-flops are a good idea, though, especially if you come at low tide, since getting over the rocky area can be a little... abrasive. If your child wants to splash—and all children do—remember that the water is warmest near the edge of an incoming tide.

**Suitability for groups** There is a reasonably large area for parking and an extremely large one for lounging, picnicking and wandering. As long as your family reunion isn't hell-bent on producing "noise and other disturbances" (whatever those might be), they should be welcome here.

**View** Although Cordova Bay is indeed a bay, as its name suggests, it is a very large, very slightly curving one. As a result, the house-lined shore fills your view to the south. The attractively contoured green lump at the head of the bay is Mount Douglas. Island spotters will be able to pick out the sandy cliffs at the south end of James Island as well as the tip of Sidney Island and D'Arcy Island.

**Winds, sun and shade** The shore receives some southeast winds, to which it runs roughly parallel. Westerlies, however, tend to skirt the shore. The sun, in contrast, has little to impede it. On a sunny day expect as much UV as can penetrate the various barricades of creams and clothes you can throw up against it.

**Beachcombing** As the many locals walking on the beach clearly demonstrate, this is a great place for long-distance striding—at least at low tide. You will get wet feet, however, so come prepared. Long-distance walking is also possible at high tide but, with the loose sand that lines much of the upper shore, you may find yourself slip-sliding away.

**Seclusion** This is a popular spot on a popular beach. To boot, the shore is generally low at this part of Cordova Bay—not so to the south—and packed with houses.

## 44

### GLORIA PLACE

**Extremely easy, level access to a long, level shore of mixed sand and pebbles**

**Location, signs and parking** Slightly north of Cordova Bay Park, where Cordova Bay Road runs close to the shore, watch for a SAANICH BEACH ACCESS sign near the GLORIA PLACE road sign. Since it is easy to miss this spot, looking for a bus stop and houses numbered 5056 and 5058 will help with your quest. On the sea side of the road you will see a barred gate with a telephone number to use if you need to get a vehicle onto the shore—presumably a need experienced only by official service vehicles.

Are you looking for a place to walk your dog or host a surprise birthday party? If the former, then note that you and your dog need to find another spot from May 1 to August 31. If the latter, then note that you need a "valid permit" to have a beach fire. It's hard to imagine that many would need to be reminded that "noise, disturbance and littering" are forbidden. Parking is a little awkward since you have to pull up along the curb on Cordova Bay Road, not the quietest road in the world.

**Path** The main reason for coming to this section of Cordova Bay rather than some of the other spots nearby is the ease of access. Those with walking difficulties or mounds of heavy paraphernalia for picnics or projects need take only a few steps to get directly onto the shore, down a gradually sloping, car-width track, part dirt, part concrete.

**Beach** Although this is a part of the great sandy sweep of Cordova Bay, the beach at this particular spot isn't quite as sandy as it is at some other points. Those looking to picnic or bask will find a large area of loose, coarse sand and pebbles, but the usual beach logs often appear only partway toward the waterline or to the right of the access spot near the exit of a small stream. The mid-beach can get a little slimy with a band of weed-covered small rocks, and the strip of low-tide sand isn't quite as wide or quickly revealed by low tides as at some other access spots.

**Suitability for children** At nearby Cordova Bay Park are the toilets that many parents need for their children. If you are not such a parent, you can come here with the expectation of finding a safe, level beach with lots of sand and sun. Be aware of the need for protection from the rocks underfoot and the sun overhead.

**Suitability for groups** Parking is a bit of a nuisance here, but otherwise even a fairly large group can spread out comfortably. The ease of access would make this a good spot for a wedding or family photo, if the awkward parking isn't an issue.

**View** The immediate shore in either direction could hardly be more crowded with cheek-by-jowl houses pressing as close to the ocean as bylaws allow. If you keep your eyes more or less forward, though, you will enjoy the sweep of view around the curve of Cordova Bay and north from Sidney Island to Mount Douglas in the south.

**Winds, sun and shade** You should come prepared for protection from wind and sun if you are planning to stay a while. Both can be in greater abundance than you might want.

**Beachcombing** Low tide over the patchily wet sandbars provides the firmest surface for long-distance exercise. Dog owners looking to bring their dogs here after Saanich's official end of summer will probably want to come early in the morning in the fall or in the afternoon in the spring to get the lowest tides.

**Seclusion** While this isn't a hugely popular destination for day use, the low, treeless bank, particularly to the south, and the press of houses makes seclusion a rather elusive notion at this access.

# 45

## CORDOVA BAY BEACH PARK

**A child-oriented park with playground, toilets and a long, level shore with large areas of low-tide sand**

**Location, signs and parking** Located more or less in the middle of Cordova Bay, the park sits right along the side of Cordova Bay Road, slides and teeter-totters in full view. You really can't miss it. A paved strip on the sea side of the road provides parking for a dozen or so cars. To the left of this area, past the drop of a small concrete wall, a SAANICH BEACH ACCESS sign will confirm your location. Like other spots in the area, this one forbids you and your hound from coming here from May through August. At the moment, the common sign requiring a valid fire permit for beach fires is absent—though the situation can change overnight.

**Path** The path is really a significantly sloping paved road, usually barred, curving through a heavily treed bank past a grassy area to the beachfront public toilets. A few concrete steps set into a mammoth concrete retaining wall bring you to the shore.

**Beach** The upper beach is a large area of loose, dry sand, though with a few pebble patches and a couple of beach fire scars. Like most other parts of the beach along Cordova Bay, this one has mysteriously few logs and is backed for a considerable distance in either direction by retaining walls of boulders or concrete. Partway down the gradually sloping beach is a band of sometimes slimy rocks and a large tidal pool. Even a moderately low tide reveals a wide stretch of sand to the waterline. Unusually, this part of the beach extends to a rocky reef a couple of hundred metres south.

**Suitability for children** The obvious pleasures of sand and water aplenty are complemented by the diversions of the playground and the conveniences of the washrooms. The next closest park as convenient for its facilities is Mount Douglas Park some distance to the south. Be prepared with protection from wind, sun and sharp rocks.

**Suitability for groups** The same facilities that make this a great spot for children make it also a good spot for groups. Just about any group, as long as it does not require more than half a dozen cars to bring it here, will find the room and the environment for a thoroughly enjoyable beach experience.

**View** You won't find a much more open view in the Victoria area than the one from the middle of Cordova Bay. Framed by Gordon Head in the south and the northern tip of Cordova Bay in the north, the horizon is embellished only by the low profiles of distant Sidney Island and San Juan Island; the other US islands and mountains are largely out of sight below the horizon.

**Winds, sun and shade** On the hottest of days you might want to picnic in the shadow of the trees in the lower park. On the windiest of days you can find a little shelter at the top of the shore. On the whole, though, come prepared to protect arms against both sunburn and goosebumps. Just in case.

**Beachcombing** It is for good reason that many come here for a long walk or jog. Shod against rough patches and pools, and arriving at low tide, you can put kilometres under your belt and sea air into your lungs. When the tide is not low, however, you can expect a little ungainly lurching through the softer and slimier parts of the shore.

**Seclusion** You could hardly find less seclusion. Even so, you should have no difficulty finding a spot to lay down a beach towel for a sun-baked doze.

## 46

### D'ARCY LANE

**A huge flight of stairs down a cliff face to the quiet end of Cordova Bay and its mixed shore of rock and sand**

**Location, signs and parking** The name says it all. D'Arcy Lane really isn't much more than a lane, at least in width. It heads off Cordova Bay Road where the road is high above the shore at the southern end of Cordova Bay. You will have a bit of a trick parking since you are not allowed to park at the constricted end of the lane. There is a little room on the shoulder, however. A short walk to the end of the lane brings you to a lovely natural patch of wild grass and a large Douglas-fir. Here you will see one of the SAANICH BEACH ACCESS signs as well as the common Saanich one warning against "noise, disturbance and litter" and stating the need for a fire permit for beach fires. Currently, no signs prohibit dogs coming here in summer months, possibly because the beach at this end is little used, possibly because getting some dogs down the mammoth flight of stairs seems sufficient discouragement.

**Path** When you have made your way down the flight of more than 70 steps, look back. You can then fully appreciate the masterpiece of engineering that has gone into placing onto a cliff face this now rather venerable flight of stairs.

**Beach** This shore is largely a continuation of the great sweep of beach that runs throughout Cordova Bay. It may not be quite as attractive to most beach explorers as nearby beaches, but it does have its own appeal. The giant staircase deposits you onto an interesting upper shore of loose pebbles among a scattering of large boulders—an almost Zen garden effect—and a pleasant spot to nestle with an edifying book. Lower down the shore you will see small boulders covered with barnacles, rockweed and sea lettuce. The section ends in a deep tidal pool extending a considerable distance in both directions. While low tide reveals a long stretch of sand, it is not obvious how you would get to this sand across the tidal pool without getting wet or walking a considerable distance in either direction.

**Suitability for children** A truly adventurous child, flexible in expectations, sturdy of limb and full of imagination, will be happy here. Plenty of climbing and exploring can be done, but little easy sand play.

**Suitability for groups** The atrociously difficult parking and remarkably long flight of stairs makes this a spot for only a group who wants a secluded and unusual chunk of shoreline to explore.

**View** From this far down Cordova Bay you can see James Island as well as Sidney Island and D'Arcy Island, presumably the source of D'Arcy Lane's name. The generally wide-open view is framed on your right by Gordon Head.

**Winds, sun and shade** You are more protected from wind here than at the popular spots farther north in Cordova Bay, though a southwesterly in particular can still be cooling. Depending on the time of year and how far you go down the shore, you can expect considerable late-afternoon shade from the wooded cliff behind.

**Beachcombing** Beachgoers can stride up and down the low-tide sand. Getting to this sand, however, is more easily done at Cordova Bay Park to the north or, less obviously, at Timber Lane to the south.

**Seclusion** The treed cliff behind you and the generally awkward beach in front of you virtually guarantee wonderful and possibly fruitful seclusion.

### * Also nearby

**A. Timber Lane** (not on the accompanying map), a short distance south from D'Arcy Lane, is very similar, but a little less attractive, with its higher proportion of broken rock. Parking is difficult.

**B. Mount Douglas Park** (not on the accompanying map) is too much a landmark to require detailed information here. Those who are approaching the park for the first time, though, might want to know that the park is a huge one and, for many, is primarily of interest for the many paths leading up the "mountain" to some wonderful views. On the shore side of the park, though, across Cordova Bay Road, are washrooms and a long, sloping path to the shore. The beach has some sand to one side, but is mostly rounded rocks. The view is northwards toward the tip of Saanich Peninsula.

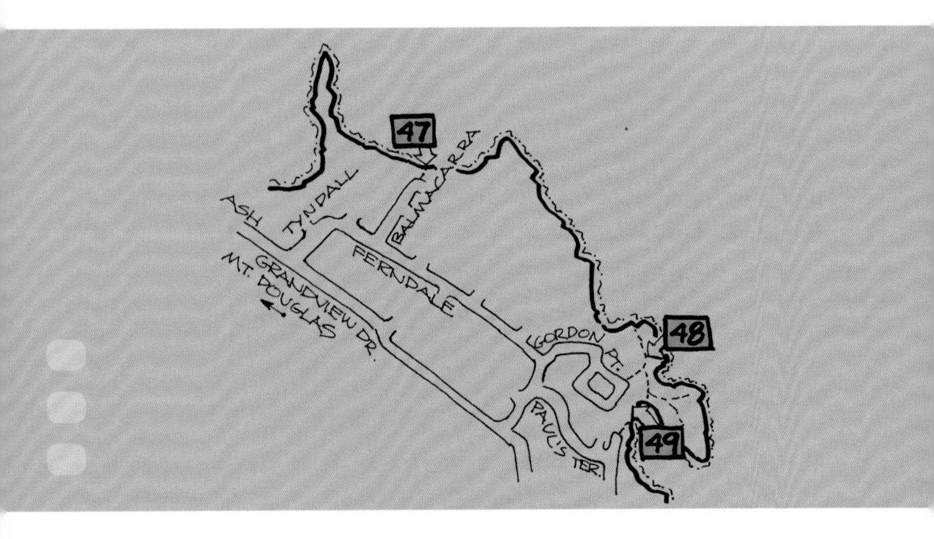

# 47

## BALMACARRA ROAD

An elaborate aluminum staircase down a high, wooded bank to the pebble shore of north-facing Margaret Bay

**Location, signs and parking** Brace yourself for some advanced navigation. East of Mount Douglas Park, a scenic drive (marked as such on most maps) begins at Ash and continues down Ferndale, which is reached by turning up Tyndall and then right onto Ferndale. If you come from the south, Ferndale winds north from Gordon Head and then turns west. Balmacarra Road leads directly from Ferndale toward the shore of Gordon Point. Where the road takes a sharp turn right you will see a SAANICH BEACH ACCESS sign and a smaller sign saying "dog owners are required to remove excrement"—adding, lest there be any embarrassing confusion, "left by their dogs." Partway to the shore is a sign forbidding fires, so you and your marshmallows should go elsewhere. A tiny green sign points toward the Gordon Head Coastal Greenway. If you are interested in linking your visit to Balmacarra's beach—and two other beaches described in this book—with this greenway, you can find a map at the Saanich Municipality website. Go to www.gov.saanich.bc.ca/ and click on "Residential" and "Parks."

**Path** A broad, level dirt track leads through balsam, fir and maple to the edge of the bank. From there, a huge, complex aluminum staircase heads down some 40 or so steps in several zigzagging flights to the shore.

**Beach** You will arrive in the middle of Margaret Bay, a shallow, curving shore almost a kilometre long. Although you can't appreciate the fact from the beach, Cormorant Point on your left is actually a narrow headland that forms a dramatic knifepoint separating Cordova Bay from Margaret Bay. While the considerable upper beach is composed of loose, dry pebbles and a few beach logs, most of its length is overhung with trees, a good indication of how protected the bay is. It is really at mid to high tide, and during the morning, that the beach is at its most attractive. The mid-beach is covered by a band of large seaweed-and-barnacle-covered rocks and boulders. The very low-tide area is soft, wet sand and algae.

**Suitability for children** You probably don't want to hunt out this area for your children, if only because Mount Douglas Park and Arbutus Cove Park are nearby and much more obviously suited to them. The beach is safe, though, and at high tide, gentle on little feet. Still, think about the stairs, mid-beach rocks and shady afternoons before you go too far in your beach plans.

**Suitability for groups** If you're looking for a generic beach for your group, go to nearby Mount Douglas Park or Arbutus Cove. If, however, you're looking for an unusual experience on a generally unexplored piece of coast, come here with the expectation of finding lots of space. A group walking the greenway mapped out by Saanich Municipality could well include this spot in their itinerary.

**View** The view is fairly confined since you are in the middle of a small, deeply inset bay, framed by Cormorant Point on your left and Gordon Head on your right. The uplifting view past the treed banks include James and Sidney islands and, on a clear day, that volcanic shape you just might recognize.

**Winds, sun and shade** With little wind at any time of day and no sun on the upper shore in the afternoon, this shore presents a combination of elements requiring some careful planning.

**Beachcombing** Any beach walker worth his or her mettle will instinctively want to walk around the curve of the bay in either direction. Stay away when high tides narrow the foreshore, or you might be forced awkwardly up and under the overhanging trees.

**Seclusion** The high, wooded bank puts you at a considerable distance from the houses above—and their sightlines.

## 48 GLENCOE COVE KWATSECH PARK—NORTH

**A historically interesting area of exposed, sun-bleached bare bluffs surrounding bays of fine pebbles**

**Location, signs and parking** The north part of the park is linked by footpaths to the southern part, where you will find two other beaches and a separate set of approach roads. For the northern approach, first be aware that some maps, inaccurately, show Gordon Point Drive connecting directly to Shore Way and, to boot, label the park just "Glencoe Cove Park." Along the well-signposted scenic drive, find the eastern section of Ferndale, from which Gordon Point Drive curves through a new housing development down to a small parking area and large sign with the name of the park. A paved area provides parking for six cars. Other signs will tell you that beach fires are forbidden. Dog owners might want to tune into the fact that this is one of the few large park areas in the district where dogs are allowed in summer. Here you will also want to study a map of the park's intersecting trails and three different beaches, along with interesting historical information about the First Nations people who once lived here.

**Path** While paths connect to other parts of the park to the southeast, to get to the nearest beach, follow the path leading left for about 100 m through an area of low bush and scattered Garry oaks. A set of 40 stairs takes you down a slightly bushy bank to the shore.

**Beach** The stairs bring you to the right-hand side of a fine, pebbly beach about 100 m long. Unusually, the pebbles extend far down the beach almost to the low-tide line, except for the odd boulder. Lots of beach logs line the upper beach and provide plenty of areas to spread out picnic goods or sunbathing accoutrements. The right side of the beach is the widest and merges into an area of low headlands of solid rock and the rest of the park. The other end of the beach, in contrast, is backed by increasingly high, wooded banks and, ultimately, cliffs lined with houses.

**Suitability for children** If your children will be happy with a beach where there is no sand, you can take them here. The rounded bluffs and large, usually empty, pebbly beach provide lots of space and variety for children who want to roam and explore or, at mid to high tide, get much wetter than their parents probably want. The water, of course, is icy beyond knee depth.

**Suitability for groups** Now if only there were washrooms... Aside from that lack, this is the perfect spot for a group of three or four cars' worth of beachgoers. Space abounds in this little-used park, as do diversions. If you are looking for a dramatic background for a wedding or family photo shoot, then investigate the plenitude of options close to the parking lot, but you will probably want to stay on the bluffs. Be mindful, though, that the parking area provides room for only half a dozen cars and parking along the curbed side of the road could be an issue.

**View** From the bluffs, your view will be magnificently airy and exposed as you look north toward the San Juan Islands and east toward the barely visible mountains leading into Puget Sound. The view from the beach is much more confined, but likewise cries out to be photographed or sketched, with its intricate arrangement of reef, bluff, cliff and sweeping pebbly beach.

**Winds, sun and shade** The exposed bluffs are in both sun and wind as long as there are sun and wind, though the spot is most exposed to a southeast wind. For significant shelter from either, go down to the beach where shade starts to creep across the upper beach from late morning and expands during the course of the day.

**Beachcombing** This is the perfect area for a varied walk. Combine strolling along the pebbly beach with climbing over the generally easy headlands and along the intersecting trails to the southern beach.

**Seclusion** The spot seems to be little known and little used. Not only that, but there are plenty of little coves and nooks in the rocky headlands where you can find a spot to be magnificently alone.

## 49 GLENCOE COVE KWATSECH PARK—SOUTH

**A separate approach to the south end of the park and a south-facing pebbly beach surrounded by bluffs**

**Location, signs and parking** Don't trust any maps that show Gordon Point Drive linking to Shore Way. To reach this part of Glencoe Cove Kwatsech Park, find your way first to where Ferndale turns north from Grandview. While you turn onto Gordon Point Drive for the northern access to the park, for the southern access, turn down Paul's Terrace and, at the T-junction, left onto Shore Way. Look for a prominent wooden sign with the name of the park and a SAANICH BEACH ACCESS sign at the head of a gravel track. The paved parking area can hold several cars, a significant asset because the adjoining streets are curbed. You will see one of the Saanich signs warning you about noise, disturbance and litter and telling you to pick up your dog's excrement—though take note, eager dog-and-owner couples: Saanich does not prohibit your use of the park in the summer months.

**Path** The short, level path toward the shore is really a far-too-functional service drive that takes you past a utility building. Take the right track for quick access to the beach, the left track for longer access to the bluffs. Just under 40 steps takes you down a bushy slope onto the shore.

**Beach** The path drops you into the middle of a short beach at the head of a deeply inset bay buttressed by outcroppings of bare rock. The upper shore is lined with more than enough logs bleaching in the sun for anyone's beaching needs. Backing the shore is a bank of low bushes, mostly willows, tucked well back from the area. A few patches of coarse sand mingle with pebbles just below the high-tide line, but at the low-tide line, about 20 m down a gradually sloping shore, the mostly pebble upper shore gives way to slightly larger gravel and occasional rocks. Look for another, smaller and much rockier beach in a little cove below the bluffs between this beach and the north beach (see the description for the north approach to the park).

**Suitability for children** Most children will be happiest here at mid to high tide if they are intent on creating as much watery havoc as possible. Low tide, predictably, reveals more in the way of crabs and sea stars. Older children would probably enjoy this beach more than younger children would, particularly if they are the sort who like running over tangles of logs and climbing around inviting rocky headlands. Keep in mind that even though this is a large park, there are no toilets or picnic tables.

**Suitability for groups** Although the parking lot isn't huge, the park itself provides plenty of room for a group to disperse through the park or to spread out a sumptuous—or frugal—picnic on the generally very quiet beach.

**View** From the beach your view is almost entirely enclosed by shoreline, with a headland on your left and, a couple of kilometres away to the right, the base of the peninsula that turns into Ten Mile Point. Walk along the bluffs, however, and you will find your view open and airy, especially if you look north and east toward the San Juan Islands and Puget Sound.

**Winds, sun and shade** No other beach between Sidney and the south shore of Ten Mile Point is as much of a sun trap as this one. Take care that you are not done to a crisp in no time, particularly if you come in the early afternoon. On the other hand, the beach can be well air-conditioned by a southeast or even southwest wind. In addition, you can take your beach things and your business to the north beach, just over 100 m away through the central part of the park. On the exposed bluffs, as you might expect, not only will you find barely a blade of living organism, but you will also find as much sun and wind as there is to be had.

**Beachcombing** Beachcombing is not really an option here. However, it would be criminal to come to the park and spend all of your time on the beach without spending half an hour exploring the bluffs. Head east and you will cross a narrow neck out to a promontory extending well into the ocean. Head northwest and you will eventually come to the north beach. Do, however, wear something a little sturdier than flip-flops if you are going to wander the bluffs on this beach outing.

**Seclusion** This is a large public park in a densely populated area. Nevertheless, if you prefer seclusion to an audience, you can easily find it. Not only can you zero in on a spot totally out of sight of the subdivision behind, but you can also expect few other beachgoers to blunder into your lair.

* **Also nearby** **Gordon Head Road** (on next map) is shown on some maps as having a shore access at its northern end, and to some extent this is true. If you want to find a shore with a high-point view of the Glencoe Cove peninsula and San Juan Island, park a short distance back on the road. Make your way through a rough track down a rocky, bushy slope until you reach an open area and see the solid-rock bluffs dropping steeply toward the shore. And voila—your view!

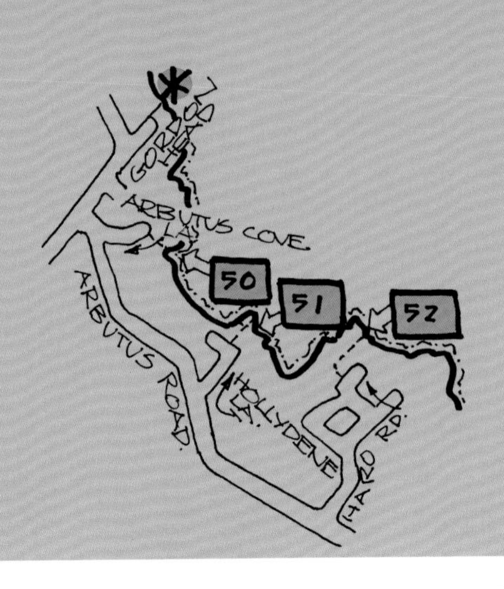

## 50

### ARBUTUS COVE PARK

**A large park of lawns and high views with access down a long flight of stairs to the north shore of Arbutus Cove**

**Location, signs and parking** Arbutus Cove Lane branches off from Gordon Head Road midway between the intersections where Arbutus Road meets Gordon Head Road and Gordon Head Road meets Ferndale. Arbutus Cove Lane leads a short distance to the entrance of Arbutus Cove, a Saanich park. This park begins as a manicured area of lawns and parking with a paved and curbed turnaround area. One sign warns that you can park your car only between the surprisingly generous hours of 6 a.m. and 11 p.m., or it will be towed. As for your plans to roast a few s'mores over a burning cedar log, note that not only are beach fires forbidden, but also the prohibition is "strictly enforced." Another sign, in rather small print for such a big park, reminds you that you are not to create noise, disturbance or litter. If you are interested in long-distance walking, study the detailed map sign showing how you can connect to the various trails and greenways in the area.

**Path** Before descending to the beach to the right of the parking area, you may want to walk down the sloping grassy area toward the shore.

While you can't get to the water here, you can get a pretty view through a lattice of Garry oaks. To get onto the shore itself, return to the parking area and take the path to the long flight of stairs to the shore.

**Beach** You will find yourself at the north end of a sweeping sand-and-pebble beach about 200 m long. The northern end is considerably less popular than the southern end, in large part because the southern end has a broad band of low-tide sand. At the northern end the trees hang over the shore, but leave room for picnicking.

**Suitability for children** This is a great beach for children though the flight of steps is long and most young'ins will want to dash toward the central part of the sandy shore. The shore is gradually sloping and safe. Keep in mind that there are no toilets at either park.

**Suitability for groups** There is enough parking and more than enough beach area for a group to spread out—depending, as always, on the group's chief goals for coming to the beach.

**View** As you walk down the beach, the view changes. At the base of the stairs, to the left is a point that somewhat restricts your view. Generally, though, you will look down the graceful curve of the sandy shore and the wooded point at the south end of the beach. The open waters of Haro Strait and the far distant San Juan Island form the centre of the view.

**Winds, sun and shade** Compared to Hollydene, its sister park, Arbutus Cove is much sunnier in the afternoon but also more exposed to the most common winds. Even by early afternoon, though, it is possible to find shade—if that is what you're after—on the uppermost part of the beach.

**Beachcombing** Few are the visitors who do not, instinctively, walk the length of the curving bay—and back again. If you want to walk much farther, however, examine the sign near the car park for links to the whole greenway trail system—linking shore access spots but often away from the shore.

**Seclusion** The bay is a popular destination for beach lovers, but Hollydene Park at the other end generally attracts more visitors. On the beach itself you will be grateful not to be under the inspection of the suburban housing development, nor to have to inspect them yourself.

## 51

### HOLLYDENE PARK

**A well-hidden park at the south end of Arbutus Cove and with a largely sandy beach**

**Location, signs and parking** Some maps identify this as Finnerty Park, but at the park itself the signs identify it as Hollydene Park. Arbutus Road, the main artery through this part of Cadboro Bay, is also part of the well-signposted scenic drive. Hollydene Place leads off Arbutus Road between Gordon Head and Finnerty roads. The area at the end of the road can be a little congested on a sunny day, when the six officially designated parking spots are full. It is usually possible, however, to find a place on the side of the road nearby. You will see a SAANICH PARKS sign with the word "Hollydene" squeezed onto the top of the sign. You will also see signs with various prohibitions about littering, creating disturbances and fires—the latter prohibition reinforced by a second, larger and more vehement sign. Another private sign warns you about mistaking a private entrance for the park path.

**Path** Make sure you head down the broad, level dirt track to the left of the chain-link fence and high hedge. The path is quite long—more than 50 m—and passes through an area of fir, Garry oak, arbutus and hawthorn. Eventually, it brings you to the head of a long flight of stairs. About 50 steps will bring you down to the shore.

**Beach** You will find yourself among a litter of barnacle-covered boulders at the base of the high, treed bank. Only a few feet from this area, however, is a long stretch of sand and logs, exactly the kind of place to settle down with a few delectables and beach-going paraphernalia. The tide goes out several dozen metres here, revealing lots of sand dotted with a few large boulders and tidal pools. Those who want to explore the whole park, however, rather than just stay on the sand, will want to scramble beyond the junction of the main trail and stairs down a rough trail and onto the exposed headland of solid rock—and great views.

**Suitability for children** Bring spades and buckets, Frisbees and a swimsuit or change of clothes when your rambunctious child accompanies you here. Expect lots of sand to fly and lots of water to make its way onto your child's clothes, even in cool weather. This is the kind of beach most children will tear gleefully around on before returning to their parents laid out in the sand like beached seals. There are no toilets.

**Suitability for groups** Finding a place to park is the biggest problem for groups. Arbutus Cove Park at the other end of the beach is much better. The beach itself has lots of space for wandering and loitering.

**View** From the bottom of the access steps, the view is entirely of the curve of the bay and the overhanging trees. From the promontory at the end of the access path, however, the view is much more extensive, looking north toward distant San Juan Island and across the broad stretches of Haro Strait.

**Winds, sun and shade** In cool or middling weather, the lack of afternoon sunshine is the real fly in the ointment of this otherwise gorgeous beach. You could move farther along the beach to increase the amount of afternoon sun, but you just might be exposing yourself to more wind. The moral? Check weather and wind predictions and consider coming in the early part of the day when the protected upper shore still has lots of sun.

**Beachcombing** Except for the little bit of adventurous climbing around the promontory at the head of the access trail, your walking will be limited to strolling up and down the beach. The state of the tide will significantly affect the nature of your beach walking.

**Seclusion** On a sunny day, expect to find fellow beach-lovers in the sandy area or strolling along the beach. Don't, however, anticipate many. The difficult parking and relative obscurity of the beach keep away the crowds.

## 52

### HARO PLACE

A long, level walk along a leafy lane to an exposed area of sun-baked bluffs and a steep drop to the waterline

**Location, signs and parking** Queen Alexandra Centre for Children's Health on Arbutus Road is the prominent landmark for locating the Haro Road access. The road you are after runs down the south side of the centre's grounds, winds and goes through some slightly confusing configurations, and turns left just before Monarch Place near the end. Your destination is clearly marked by a SAANICH BEACH ACCESS sign. A smaller, official-looking sign cites the various bylaws against the kind of abusive behaviour you are not likely to engage in. Parking along the side of the road is comparatively easy, though be mindful of driveways.

**Path** The walk to the shore is one of the pleasures of this hidden access route. The leafy path through Garry oak, arbutus and Douglas-fir resembles a curving country lane, notwithstanding the chain-link fence on one side. After about 100 m you will come to a pretty scattering of small Garry oaks and, beyond that, an easily negotiable area of exposed solid rock with only a little wild grass, oceanspray and (evil) broom. Although the situation will doubtless change soon, at present a barbed wire bit of fence around the private land has been pushed down, and a track leads through to a large plywood gazebo and wooden walkway to private land. These are not part of the public access.

**Beach** This is the place to come for an isolated and uninterrupted opportunity to choose a viewing spot, and not the place to come for easy access to the waterline. Those who want to poke around the water's edge can make their way down the lumps of irregular rock. The shore can be negotiated in both directions for a more welcoming beach, particularly a pebbly section to your right with two tiny islets reachable at low tide.

**Suitability for children** Few children will want to join any adult who wants to sit and absorb the view and sea air. The opportunities for much beach play are too scant to justify bringing a child here.

**Suitability for groups** Unless you have a special purpose linked to coming to this spot, there is no point in guiding a group to an area with such limited parking and shore area.

**View** Because the access spot arrives on a slightly elevated area of solid rock facing north, and because the shoreline is largely convex here, you will have a wonderfully open and expansive view. On your left is the distant promontory of Glencoe Cove Kwatsech Park. The view sweeps past the expanse of Haro Strait and to the northern shore of Ten Mile Point.

**Winds, sun and shade** Most prevailing winds come from slightly behind you, but you will be well buffeted by a strong northwest or southeast wind on this exposed shore. The sun will be at your back during the course of the afternoon, but there is little shade at any point in the day.

**Beachcombing** Consider the lane-like path to be the best walking. This is not a place for strolling along the shore!

**Seclusion** The spot itself is prominent, but so quiet and so out of the way that you should be undisturbed if you come hand-in-hand and in quest of some removal from the rest of the world.

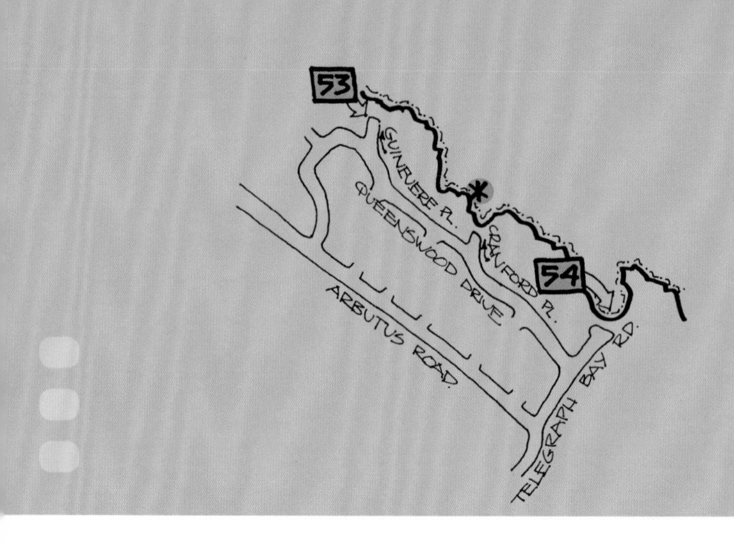

## 53

### GUINEVERE PLACE

**A good spot for car picnicking, with a view toward the San Juan Islands**

**Location, signs and parking** Since the roads in this area are narrow and winding, you will have to drive carefully. Queenswood Drive is more or less a loop off Arbutus, its southeast end connecting via Telegraph Bay Road. Guinevere Place, in turn, is a tiny stub off Queenswood, concluding in a parking spot right near the shore. Look for a Saanich BEACH ACCESS sign partly hidden in the bushes. One sign indicates that the end of the road is a tow-away zone, but you can squeeze along the shoulder of the approaching roads.

**Path** The path to the shore itself is short, but a little rough and largely undeveloped. Those unsteady on their feet will need assistance or may prefer to make this a spot just for a car picnic, though you can't park and leave your car here. The park bench under a large fir immediately to the left of the short path, however, is even better as an intermediate spot to sit while you ponder the view or enjoy a little salty solitude.

**Beach** The shore, composed almost entirely of boulders, does not make for easy picnicking or anything very much. The tide does not go out very far here, so you can pick your way to the waterline, but you will have to be careful of the slippery rocks at low tide. If sunbathing is part of your plan, this is not the best spot to choose.

**Suitability for children** Sure-footed children desperate to get out of the car and romp a bit will no doubt be happy enough. They probably won't be happily engaged for very long, though, so plan to sit and read the newspaper, not a novel, while they explore the rocky shore.

**Suitability for groups** The spot is too small and the range of options too limited for a group to come here.

**View** It is really the view that will bring you here. The set of reefs slightly to the left and the islands overlapping each other on the horizon constitute a beautiful combination of scenic elements. You may be able to pick out Sidney Island, D'Arcy Island and Little D'Arcy Island on the Canadian side of the border, and, to your right, Henry Island and the much larger San Juan Island in the United States.

**Winds, sun and shade** The shore is heavily forested in this area and the access spot faces north. The result is that you will be mostly in shade for most of the day. Southeast winds, even when they are stirring up a fuss a short distance away, leave this shore largely untouched.

**Beachcombing** The amount of rough shore exposed at even a low tide makes this the kind of beach where your walking will mostly be limited to poking around the rocks.

**Seclusion** Although the whole area is dotted with houses, this is an extremely quiet and rarely visited area. Arrive alone and you are likely to leave alone as well.

* **Also nearby** A PUBLIC ACCESS sign at the corner of Queenswood and Cranford Place indicates access to the shore via **Cranford Place**. The path to the shore is a little rough, but passable. You will arrive at the base of a small cove with views to the north. The shore itself has a few patches of gravel but is mostly large boulders, especially toward the low-tide line.

## 54

### TELEGRAPH BAY

A protected sandy cove with rocky headlands, good for launching kayaks

**Location, signs and parking** Arbutus Road crosses Telegraph Bay Road, which begins to the south at Cadboro Bay Road. Telegraph Bay Road shoots off north for about a kilometre toward the shore of Telegraph Bay. Look for a PUBLIC BEACH ACCESS sign on the corner with Queenswood. The very end of the road brings you to a large, level area for 20 or 30 cars parked in a circle and a large sign clearly identifying the spot.

**Path** A few steps take you from your car and onto the shore. Those with walking difficulties or those toting vast amounts of paraphernalia for barbecuing a hotdog or painting a masterpiece will be pleased with the proximity of the beach and the ease of walking to it. This is a good spot to launch kayaks, not only because the parking is close and the approach to the beach so easy, but also because the tide does not go out nearly as far here as at some beaches with similar features.

**Beach** As the name suggests, this is a cove—and thus a small, deeply inset bit of shore. You will find a short stretch of fine, level sand protected by a high, rocky headland on your right and, on the left, abutted by a high stretch of rocky shore leading toward the more exposed coast. Though only the width of three houses, this is a great socializing beach, as the few firepits in the sand signify. You will find lots of soft sand above the high-tide level on which to doze away an afternoon or ponder your next chess move.

**Suitability for children** This is an excellent spot for children who want to fling sand about or splash energetically in protected water. The beach isn't huge, but free-spirited children can test their latest skimboard skills or throw a Frisbee.

**Suitability for groups** Two or three families or a voracious bridge club are about the right size to be best accommodated here. They should arrive with no assumptions of coming across the picnic tables and other facilities a Proper Park will provide.

**View** Since the cove opens to the northwest and is really a narrow slot in the rocky coast, the view is necessarily limited. Do not expect a wide sweep of ocean view, but do expect to be charmed by the sense of coziness with the high, rocky shore looming on your left over the open waters beyond.

**Winds, sun and shade** When a strong southeast wind is brewing, you will find odd eddies and gusts bustling their way into the cove a little but blowing largely offshore. No such protection is provided from the sun on a hot day, however. Come prepared to be done to a turn—or to bring the necessaries to avoid being even mildly roasted.

**Beachcombing** This is a small beach. You can't climb comfortably over the rocky bluffs on either side, so it is best to stay where you are.

**Seclusion** With little visual barrier between the beach and the three houses immediately behind the shore, you will be very much in full view. Nevertheless, the beach feels public, so you won't feel that you are invading private space.

Telegraph Bay

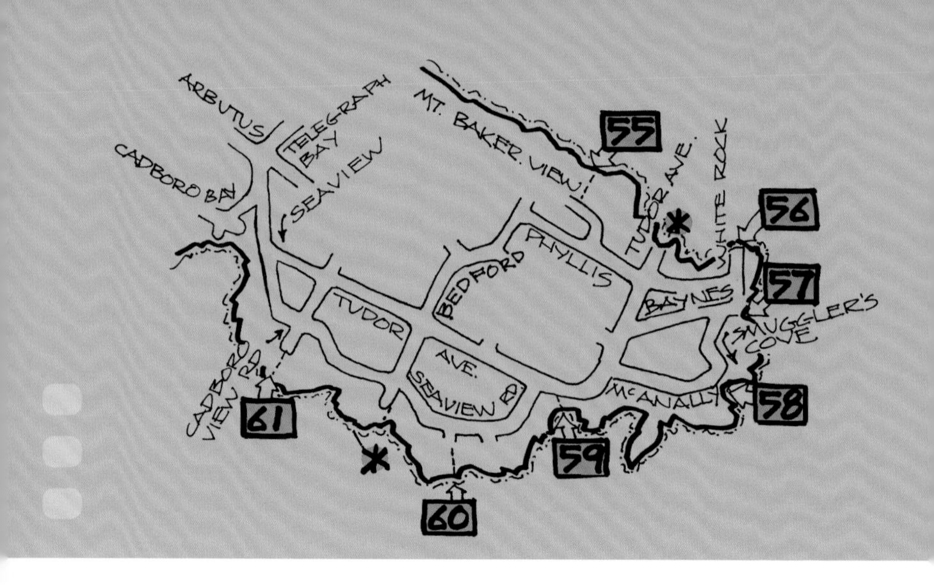

## 55

### MOUNT BAKER VIEW ROAD

**A slightly awkward, undeveloped access to a distinctive, sun-baked rocky bluff dropping steeply to the waterline**

**Location, signs and parking** Although the roads on a map of the Ten Mile Point peninsula seem to meander only a bit on a map, don't be surprised if you feel in something of a maze. The roads are narrow and the whole area hilly, dominated by Prevost Hill. From Telegraph Bay Road, turn onto Seaview Road until you reach Tudor Avenue, on the left. Follow Tudor, the main artery of Ten Mile Point, almost to its end and turn onto Phyllis Street, the last road on the left. Turn right onto Mount Baker View Road and once it has curved left keep your eyes open for a narrow gap between houses. This is your destination, but you will have to be a little inventive about finding a parking spot on this narrow and congested street.

**Path** Two sets of steps, the first 18 and the second 10, lead down a narrow dirt path between houses. Once you have reached the grassy rock bluffs, you may need to use some adventurous footwork, depending on how close to the edge of the bluffs and how close to the water's edge you wish to go.

**Beach** You will find no beach. Instead, you will find yourself on a large area of high, exposed, sun-baked rock. While it is possible to wander around this area a little, it is unlikely that you will want to navigate to the water's edge—though the shore drops off steeply here and could yield something for the intrepid fisherman. There are comfortable spots to settle on this elevated viewpoint, though, if you want to sit quietly in the sun with an iPod or thermos.

**Suitability for children** You could hardly choose a less likely spot for even the most cooperative child to spend more than a few minutes. Nearby Telegraph Bay is vastly preferable.

**Suitability for groups** A group of exactly two people is the maximum size for an outing here!

**View** It is, of course, all in the name. This road is called Mount Baker View for a reason, as are several other roads along the southern coast of the island. Quite apart from the (nearly) extinct volcano, though, the view is given particular depth by the elevation. You can primarily see the various islands spreading from James Island on your left to the large and imposing San Juan Island on your right, across the US border. The promontory on your immediate right is, according to marine charts, Ten Mile Point, though some maps insist that it is Cadboro Point and put Ten Mile Point by Maynard Cove.

**Winds, sun and shade** If there is wind, you will feel it. If there is sun, you will be soaking it up. This spot could hardly be more exposed to all of the elements!

**Beachcombing** Read the Beach description and abandon all thoughts of taking more than a few steps.

**Seclusion** On your approach here you may feel, uncomfortably, that you are invading a closed neighbourhood. That feeling will only partly fade as you make your way down the bluffs since it is difficult to get far away from the picture windows of the houses behind you.

* **Also nearby** **Tudor Avenue**, which begins inauspiciously inland off Seaview Road, is the main artery through this area. It ends in a small parking area with several signs, including a BEACH ACCESS sign.

Fifteen stairs take you down a wooded bank into a tiny cove of mixed gravel flanked by solid rock on either side and backed by overhanging willows. The upper beach has a welcoming expanse of fine pebbles. Except in the morning, the spot is fairly shadowy. The view, toward San Juan Island, is limited but pleasant. While the beach has no houses immediately behind it or to the left, once you move down the beach you might feel yourself under the full inspection of a phalanx of houses to your right.

## 56

### WHITE ROCK STREET

**An excellent spot for a car picnic with lots of parking and views toward the San Juans over an exposed area of rocky bluffs**

**Location, signs and parking** If you are doing a tour of Ten Mile Point's highly distinctive spots, you are clearly willing to make your way through the labyrinth of narrow, hilly roads. While you can approach White Rock Street from a few directions, if you are coming directly from the outside world, it is easiest to turn onto Tudor from Seaview, off Telegraph Bay Road, and follow it almost to the end. A right turn onto Baynes Road will take you the short distance to White Rock Street. Here you will see an unusually large paved turnaround area with lots of parking. In fact, this is one of those spots with generous parking hours: the overnight parking limitation doesn't start until midnight and ends at 6 a.m. Compare that to the 9 p.m. to 7 a.m. limit almost everywhere else in North Saanich.

**Path** A few steps will take you from your car to an exposed area of rocky bluffs where a park bench invites contemplation, but bring folding chairs, picnic baskets and the like for a full feast in comfort.

**Beach** The comparatively even rock bluffs make for easy blundering away from the water. The closer you get to the water's edge, in general, the steeper the shore gets. The rocks drop off almost immediately into deep water, though, so those with casting rods might find this a productive spot for a little afternoon's fishing. Expect to see scuba divers here taking advantage of the easy approach to deep water.

**Suitability for children** Bring your children here if your intention is to picnic on the sunny bluffs. Don't bring them here if you expect them to defuse hyperactivity by splashing in the water: the rocks are awkwardly steep near the water's edge.

**Suitability for groups** Two or three cars' worth of like-minded picnickers will find enough space to spread out their potluck provender or prop up their painting materials. There are no facilities, however, and the area is very much exposed to the elements—every last one of them.

**View** The view encompasses not just Mount Baker—on a clear day—but also the islands off Sidney to the north and east and across the US border to the much larger San Juan Island.

**Winds, sun and shade** You would be hard-pressed to find a spot more the shorefront equivalent of Wuthering Heights, though there are a few competitors along the south coast farther into Victoria. The spot is in full sun and full wind as long as there is sun and wind.

**Beachcombing** Come to this spot to wander a little, perhaps, especially on the bluffs around Ten Mile Point, called Cadboro Point on some maps. Don't expect, however, to go far, since the area of bare rock narrows once you have rounded the point.

**Seclusion** You will be fully exposed to the sightlines of the neighbours—as well as any other visitors to the spot. The turnaround area is so large and open, however, that you will not feel, as you might at nearby Mount Baker View Road, as if you are intruding into a neighbourhood.

## 57

### BAYNES ROAD

A good spot for car picnicking in a bright little cove with views of Baynes Channel

**Location, signs and parking** The directions for getting here are a little more straightforward than for some other spots on Ten Mile Point. Take Tudor Avenue from Seaview via Telegraph Bay Road almost to its northeastern end, then turn right onto Baynes Road and follow it until following it any farther would land you up to your gills in the water. You could park at the very end of the road, but the space is limited so you might have to find a spot on the broad, grassy shoulder.

**Path** Not only is your car parked at a road's end that almost has you in the water, but the parking area is also level and open to the ocean. A storm will bring its pelting rain and howling wind to you while you remain in your car enjoying the wild waves and your shrimp-on-a-bagel lunch. A large pine to your left and an odd little hillock in front cramp your view a little, but only a little. Even though the shore is only a few steps away, it can be a struggle to get down the rock bank—not least of all because the uppermost shore is thick with jagged boulders and logs. If you are sure-footed, you may find this a viable spot for launching a pair of kayaks. The area is fairly cramped, however, so you're probably better off taking your kayaks to nearby McAnally Road.

**Beach** The access brings you to the right side of a tiny cove with a few offshore rocks to the left and an exposed area of bluffs to the right. The upper shore of pretty, polished pebbles is welcoming, but seems unusually effective at collecting dense tangles of beach logs. The lower shore is a mixture of angular boulders and outcroppings of solid rock. Since there is a house immediately above the attractive retaining wall to your left, picnickers or sunbathers will probably feel most comfortable immediately below the access point. Others, however, might prefer to make their way along the rocky bluffs to the right, being careful not to intrude on the house there, even though it is well set back from the bluffs.

**Suitability for children** There isn't much room in this cozy little spot for children to romp. The small beach, however, is sheltered and gradual. For the duration of a picnic, at least, or as long as it takes for a parent to read a few chapters of a sizzling romance, a few children could easily enjoy making watery havoc and climbing around on the rocky bluffs.

**Suitability for groups** The area is too confined to bring more than a few friends or family members.

**View** Because you are in a small cove, your view is largely framed by the bluffs on either side. Mostly you will be looking far across the open water north of Baynes Channel, but walking around the bluff will bring into view the tiny, aptly named Strongtide Island and the convoluted Chatham Islands immediately behind. Because the currents rush through Baynes Channel at speeds of up to 6 knots (11 km) per hour, expect lots of seabirds feeding on churned-up morsels as well as small boats either whisking or labouring past, depending on their direction.

**Winds, sun and shade** Essentially east-facing, the little cove is sunniest during the first half of the day. During summer, however, because there is no tree cover, shade is scarce throughout the day, except up against the rocks in late afternoon. The amount of wind you get depends on how much you want to take shelter at the top of the cove or along the bluffs.

**Beachcombing** This is a spot for a little exploring and rock climbing or beachside contemplation, not for a long walk.

**Seclusion** You might feel a little wedged in among houses. They are configured in such a higgledy-piggledy way, though, that you won't be facing a phalanx of local eyes the instant you step out of your car. In any case, the spot is generally quiet.

## 58

### MCANALLY ROAD—SMUGGLER'S COVE ROAD

**A small, nearly circular cove with a pebbly beach good for launching kayaks**

**Location, signs and parking** Follow Tudor Avenue from Seaview and Telegraph Bay Road for about a kilometre and then turn right onto McAnally Road. You won't have to look hard for the beach access since the residential road virtually runs onto the small beach of Maynard Cove, just before the road bends into Smuggler's Cove Road. The locals know Maynard Cove as Smuggler's Cove. This beach, probably the most popular in the area, is also one of the few without a BEACH ACCESS sign. The signs that you do see alert you to the access, but they are also a little odd. One, besides prohibiting high-volume antisocial behaviour, tells you that you need a permit for a beach fire, while another, immediately below, tells you that you may never (in any circumstance?) have a beach fire.

It is easy for several cars to pull over onto the wide shoulder, though you might also face competition for the few spots because some kayaking businesses occasionally use the spot. If you have a kayak yourself, avoid the temptation to park close to the beach since, as one sign tells you, the closest spot is an "emergency access."

**Path** This is about as easy an approach to a beach as you are going to find anywhere. You can virtually drive onto the fine, pebbly upper shore. It's a perfect spot for those with walking difficulties or those freighted with complicated beaching equipment.

**Beach** Although Maynard Cove is nearly circular, the beach makes up only about half of its circumference. From the access spot in the middle of the beach you can obviously go in either direction, but many will prefer to go left, where a bushy bank provides considerable screening from the house behind. In addition, this end of the beach offers a few convenient beach logs, a better view through the cove's entrance and the full effects of the afternoon sun. Although the upper beach is mostly pebbly, sand lovers will be pleased to find a tiny section of coarse sand on which to settle their sun-screened limbs. The shore shelves off fairly quickly so kayakers don't need to worry about tides when launching their pleasure craft.

**Suitability for children** This is a good, safe place for a romp and splash, in close proximity of the familymobile. It is a warm spot on an otherwise cool day, but the water is icy. Be watchful if your child is playing in the water, as the shore slopes down quite quickly. And plan carefully, as there are no washrooms.

**Suitability for groups** A family or a set of double-daters can be easily accommodated here. For much more than that, the parking is too limited and the beach too small.

**View** Don't expect a sweeping vista. Do, however, enjoy the prettily framed views of the distant Olympic Mountains punctuated by tiny Jemmy Jones Island and behind it, the Chain Islets. In early morning or late afternoon, when the angle of the sun throws the contours on the horizon into relief, your view is at its best. Unfortunately, from the beach you will not quite be able to see a tiny, picturesque islet just around the corner to your right.

**Winds, sun and shade** A southeast wind can blow directly into the bay, so check the forecast if you're looking for a sun-bake on a cool, sunny day. Otherwise, the cove is well protected from the blusters and breezes out in the straits—but not from a roasting sun.

**Beachcombing** The houses are set far enough back to give some beach space for manoeuvering. If you're into a bit of clambering over rocky headlands, and if you keep below the high-tide line, you could make your way out of the cove to view the pretty cluster of reefs and islets just around the corner. In general, though, you're better off staying where you are and enjoying the view.

**Seclusion** The little beach is surprisingly private considering that it is smack in the middle of one of the most desirable morsels of real estate in Victoria. You will be aware of the three houses overlooking the beach, but the buffer of willows and the size and irregularity of the properties mean that only one large house at the east end of the beach is positioned to inspect your every move.

## 59

### TUDOR AVENUE

**A few concrete steps past a garden area and two benches onto a pocket beach**

**Location, signs and parking** You can't miss it, as they say—at least if you can find your way onto Tudor Avenue from Cadboro Bay Road. Tudor Avenue ploughs straight ahead for several blocks and suddenly makes a sharp left. Just before the curve, keep your eyes right and you will instantly spot an open area of lawn and trimmed shrubs with water beyond. Parking here is a bit of a trick since there is only one good pull-off spot on a street that can be surprisingly busy. You will see a BEACH ACCESS sign right at the curve in the road, but the shoulder is very narrow there because of a barricade of wooden posts.

**Path** Someone has decided to make the best of an iffy arrangement by placing two park benches atop a plainly functional concrete structure. From here you can choose to drink your fill of the view or descend to the shore. Don't be distracted by the concrete stairs that curve down and in front of the concrete structure, since they go nowhere—at least for a beachgoer. Instead, cast your eyes far to the left. Almost hidden by a willow is a staircase with 21 concrete steps that do lead to the shore.

**Beach** The beach is tiny and beautiful. This cove is actually a kind of "covette" set into another, not much larger, cove. The upper beach, among a scattering of beach logs, is fine, pretty pebbles and coarse sand. Here you can set out your suntanning emollients or prop yourself up with a supermarket tabloid, but not much more. If you are feeling adventurous, at low tide you can make your way around to Ten Mile Point or wade out to the tiny islands.

**Suitability for children** Don't bring children to this small beach if they are genetically engineered to dash and romp. If, however, they are being fed peanut butter sandwiches, or if they enjoy exploiting the resources of a pebbly beach and their own imagination, they could easily while away an hour or two at this safe, pretty spot.

**Suitability for groups** A group of two is about as many as you will want to bring here, though, to be fair, a family could picnic or a few friends could have a great gossip-in-the-sun session.

**View** The view is charming rather than expansive. A few offshore rocks and reefs, the Chain Islets and, in the distance, the Olympic Mountains populate the picture. Depending on where you are along the cove, your view may be limited by the rocky bluffs on either side.

**Winds, sun and shade** This spot is sheltered from nearly all wind, though a strong southeast blow can import enough rushing breezes to raise gooseflesh on a cool day. On the other hand, the afternoon sun hits the shore more or less directly without benefit of shade. If you are not prepared, expect to be done to a turn, or slightly more.

**Beachcombing** Because of the big gap between shorefront houses on either side of this spot, and especially to the right, you could climb over the miniature rocky headlands a little, especially if you were willing to stay below the high-tide line. Generally, though, you should feel content merely to savour the cozy pleasures of this tiny spot.

**Seclusion** Though houses are thick in the area, none overlooks the extensive area immediately above the shore. In any case, the lots are sufficiently large and their configuration sufficiently irregular that you just might feel deliciously alone in your little hidden cove.

## 60

### SEAVIEW ROAD

**A short, level path through woods to low, rocky bluffs and a great view across Cadboro Bay**

**Location, signs and parking** Seaview Road leaves Telegraph Bay Road and winds along the southern shore of Ten Mile Point. In some places the gravel shoulder of the road is wide enough that you can park comfortably. Look for a wooden post numbered 2929 and a SAANICH BEACH ACCESS sign pointing you down a paved lane heading toward the water. The sign is visible only if you are approaching from Cadboro Bay. In addition, you might swear on a stack of local maps that you are trespassing down a private drive—but press on.

**Path** The largely level path crosses a little wooden bridge, a bit slippery when wet. The path then winds gently for 40 or 50 m through a pretty wooded strip past a clearing where locals evidently store dinghies.

**Beach** The trail emerges onto a sun-baked area of solid rock. Unlike the rocky shore along most of Ten Mile Point, though, this one is comparatively smooth, level and easy to make your way across. The shore has collected quite the pick-up sticks of beach logs, of possible use as seats or tables. Toward the low-tide line the rock is covered with weeds: if you are going to explore a little, be aware that the rocks can be slippery.

**Suitability for children** This is the place to come for your thoughts to play freely, not your children. Some children may be happy for a while on the rocks, particularly at high tide when they can easily reach the water. Most children would rather be elsewhere, though; try the nearby beach at Cadboro Bay.

**Suitability for groups** Don't bring more than one or two others with you. Even better, bring only your own thoughts, camera, sketchpad or latest Elvis bio.

**View** The view is both attractive and unusual. Only one other access from Seaview Road looks out over similar features. What makes the view from here attractive is its combination of elements: a small island immediately offshore to the right, the wooded shore of northern Oak Bay, the Chain Islets and, of course, the distant Olympic Mountains.

**Winds, sun and shade** If a strong southeast wind is blowing, you will have a lot of sailboats to watch scudding to and fro. You will also have to hold onto your hat, in spite of the slight shelter from the small island just offshore. Even a westerly will be more than a little fresh here, though not quite as direct. While you are cooling off from the wind, however, you will be heating up from the sun. For the entire middle part of the day, nothing impedes a single photon's worth of sunshine from hitting this spot.

**Beachcombing** You can stumble your way along the shore a considerable distance in either direction, since the rocky outcroppings are level and low in this area. Those who are interested in substantial beach walking can drive the 15 minutes north to Cordova Bay or the 5 minutes to nearby Cadboro Bay.

**Seclusion** Although houses line the waterfront here, the bushes immediately behind and on the bank afford you a surprising amount of privacy. In addition, don't expect to have to share the most comfortable part of the shore with any other visitor.

* **Also nearby** A Saanich sign clearly labels the **Bedford beach access** where Bedford Road forms a T-junction with Seaview Road. A whole city-sized lot is set aside for the access. However, only an undeveloped little path winds its way over lumps and bumps of rocky outcroppings and oaks. The solid-rock shore is not high, but drops fairly steeply to the water. A tiny islet decorates the view across Cadboro Bay, and the area behind the shore is attractively wild, but the beach does not lend itself to more than a brief visit.

## 61

### CADBORO VIEW ROAD

**An open grassy area with a park bench looking over a rough rock area toward the Royal Victoria Yacht Club and Cadboro Bay Beach**

**Location, signs and parking** Once you are on Seaview Road from Telegraph Bay Road, you can stay on the narrow, winding Seaview to approach Cadboro View Road closest to the coast, or turn onto Tudor from Seaview and Cadboro View will shortly appear to the right, a block north of Seaview. This latter approach allows you to choose one of several parking spots on the shoulder of the road leading toward the shore, should there be any congestion. In fact, you cannot park near the end of Cadboro View Road without facing a battery of signs warning that this is a tow-away zone. Once here, you can see right to the end of the road and beyond it into the briny deep—indeed, you've found the beach access.

**Path** From the end of the road, a few steps lead through a grassy road-width area to a park bench well situated to maximize the view and minimize the winds. En route, unfortunately, you will have to pass a grimly functional set of green metal structures and run the gauntlet of two high wooden fences. Although you can't park at the end of the road, on a stormy day you could stop here a short while and appreciate the view without leaving your car.

**Beach** The shore here is made up of dark, rugged rock. Some of the rock is flat and rounded, particularly to the right, and you can find a spot close to the water's edge to sit and drink in the view and the sunshine. It is also possible, but not particularly inviting, to make your way to the water's edge down a kind of groove in the rocks angling forward. As the presence of kelp bobbing just offshore suggests, the shore drops off quickly here. It levels out at a depth of about 4 m, though, so this is not a promising spot for fishermen to nab their supper.

**Suitability for children** You could entice your children here with promises of treats and keep them happy while you feed them. You might also have children endowed with the sureness of foot and strength of imagination to leap about on the rocks, fending off pirates and alien spacecraft. Don't, however, expect most children to be happy here for long.

**Suitability for groups** A car-sized group with a specific purpose such as looking for double-crested cormorants or watching a sailboat race could be grateful that this access spot exists. Take a large group to nearby Cadboro Bay Park.

**View** Since the Royal Victoria Yacht Club is directly across Cadboro Bay from you, a windy day will provide wonderful views of sailboats of all sizes picturesquely gliding back and forth. The Olympic Mountains, of course, provide a wonderful backdrop to the sails, though they are backlit in the middle part of the day. Because this spot on the shore is generally convex, you also have a wonderful view for some distance down the rocky coast.

**Winds, sun and shade** The same southerly winds that drive the sailboats back and forth will blow your sunhat off your head. Like most other spots on the south coast of Ten Mile Point, this one allows you to be simultaneously baked by the sun and cooled by the wind.

**Beachcombing** If you want to poke around the low-tide line, you're better off heading to your right than to your left since a Riviera-style series of concrete patios descends from the house on the left well down the shore. In any case, of course, you should stay below the high-tide line. If you have a yen to walk or jog, the beach at nearby Cadboro Bay gives you lots of opportunity to break into a full gallop.

**Seclusion** This is probably the least secluded spot on Ten Mile Point. Don't expect anything approximating a private moment.

Cadboro Bay

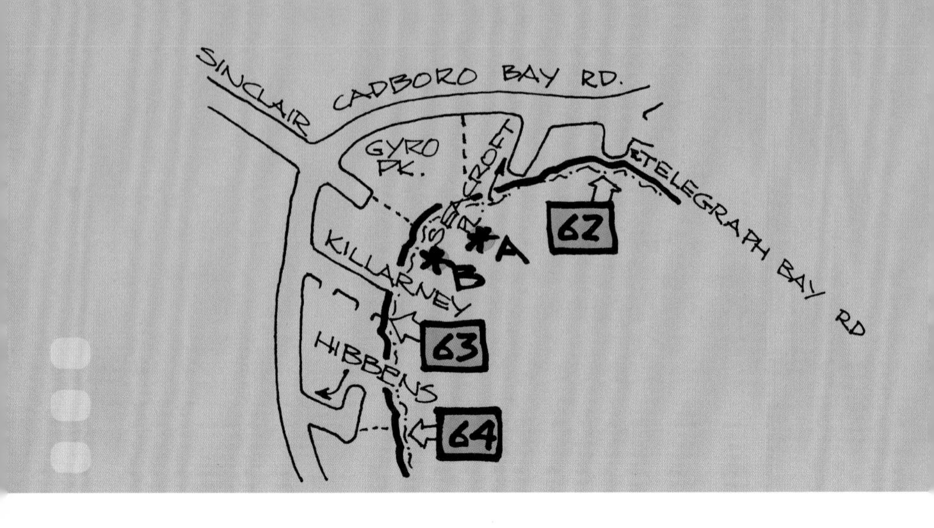

## 62 TELEGRAPH BAY ROAD—SOUTH

**A small access to the north end of Cadboro Bay beach, with the ambience of a sandy neighbourhood beach rather than a large public park**

**Location, signs and parking** At the point where Cadboro Bay Road curves toward the northeast and before it turns into Telegraph Bay Road, a spur off Telegraph Bay Road juts south and heads directly down a slight hill a short distance to the clearly visible shore of Cadboro Bay. Be careful, though, since the road sign seems to be pointing toward Tudor Avenue, which at this point is not a through road. Seven or eight cars can park either along the shoulder or at the end of the paved area.

You will be greeted by a battery of signs at the end of this paved area, the most vehement and extensive ones concerning dog "excrement." Not only the usual plastic bags are provided for dispatching your dog's "excrement," but also a garbage container in the form of an insalubrious-looking barrel. Before you bring your beach-loving retriever, though, check the Killarney Road entry for more, rather complicated, restrictions on your pooch at the Cadboro Bay beach. Two other signs at this Telegraph Bay Road access insist on the prohibition of beach fires, one of them threatening transgressors with a fine. And, if you are planning to bring your kazoo to serenade your beloved, beware: "noise, disturbance and litter" are "prohibited." You will have to use your imagination to decide what a disturbance might entail or what level of noise will get you a fine.

**Path** Having hissed at your children to be quiet, you can scoop up your armfuls of beach paraphernalia and make your way the few steps down a kind of asphalt track. In fact, one of the advantages of coming to this back door to Cadboro Bay's beach rather than the main public entrance is that you can drive so close to the shore. There is a park bench at the end of the paved area, though it's hard to imagine wanting to stop here rather than on the sandy beach. Do be careful on the paved path, though, since sand and pebbles on the sloping path can make it treacherously slippery. Experience speaks.

**Beach** Anyone who knows Cadboro Bay beach knows what the beach is like here. They know the area of dry, sugary sand among rows of beach logs; they know the stretches of level, hard sand extending to the low tide line. The beach ends a short distance to the left of the access spot, coming to a dramatic conclusion at a high, rocky bluff of firs and oaks projecting into the water. The only really unpleasant feature of the beach at this end is the hideous concrete drain-water outlet and the section of oozing sand it seems to be responsible for.

**Suitability for children** The single disadvantage of coming to this access rather than the main one is the absence of big park facilities—playground, washrooms and picnic tables. Otherwise, this is the perfect beach for virtually every beachy activity a child can undertake. Everything from flying uncooperative kites, falling off skimboards, building ruinous castles and so on—all will be on the menu.

**Suitability for groups** Although there is limited parking and none of the picnic tables that a group might want, even a large group can find plenty of space to spread out. The proximity of parking to the beach, too, makes this a good spot for capturing a visual record of a wedding party or family reunion—though you will have to come late in the afternoon if you wish to avoid backlighting.

**View** The high, wooded bluffs immediately to your left frame the view. Across the bay, the water is dotted with hundreds of sailboats, some of them anchored in the protected waters there, some of them moored in the yacht club, some of them obligingly gliding back and forth.

**Winds, sun and shade** You will be slightly sheltered from a strong southeasterly wind, but only slightly. A westerly, however, is significantly tamed here. At virtually any time of day you and yours will be in full sun and, if the breeze is cool, not quite realize how much you are burning. Plan accordingly.

**Beachcombing** If you have a yearning to saunter decoratively, stride manfully or run pell-mell by the water's edge, this is the place to do it. You can go for well over 1 kilometre toward the far end of the beach. You will, however, find that at the distant, more protected part of the beach, the sand turns to gravel and then, farther along, begins to get a little muddy.

**Seclusion** Houses line the shore here. If you head to the right when you reach the beach, where the upper beach is much more suitable for nestling, anyway, you should not feel as if you are nigh on trespassing.

*** Also nearby**

**A. Cadboro-Gyro Park**, one of the best-known beach spots in the area, probably needs no description. This approach to the long, sandy beach is the most convenient access for large groups and children, with its playground, toilets and large parking lot.

**B.** Opposite house number **3888 on Cadboro Bay Road** is a grassy lot with a paved walk leading to Cadboro Bay beach. Parking is difficult along the busy road where there is no shoulder, so most visitors to the beach will be better off at the Telegraph Bay Road access or Cadboro-Gyro Park.

## 63

### KILLARNEY ROAD

A residential cul-de-sac and a short flight of stairs to the central section of Cadboro Bay beach

**Location, signs and parking** From Cadboro Bay Road turn down Killarney on the southwest side of the main Cadboro-Gyro Park beach and simply follow it to its end. You are not allowed to park at the very end of the road, but can usually find a spot on the shoulder near the end. Dog owners' alert: be careful to read the slightly complicated list of regulations posted here. The simplified version: from September to May you can use the whole beach if Brutus is on a leash, but you must stay away from the playground at Cadboro-Gyro Park and the far west end of the beach. During the summer these rules apply only to the morning "before 9 a.m.," though presumably to the late evening as well. During the middle part of the day, "after 9 a.m." (until when?), you and your soulmate must take your romping and sniffing elsewhere.

**Path** This access is not quite as convenient as the spur off Telegraph Bay Road for getting awkward armfuls of beach goods or children onto the beach, but nearly so. Nine concrete stairs a few steps from your car deposit you onto the beach.

**Beach** This section of beach is preferable to that in front of the park only for its ease of access and comparative quietness. It does lack the beach logs that many like to use as all-purpose beach furniture, and it also lacks a stretch of unbroken sand. A wide band of egg-sized gravel covers the middle of the beach, so be sure to bring water shoes or flip-flops for getting to the water's edge.

**Suitability for children** As long as your children don't mind making the trek to the toilets at Cadboro-Gyro Park, they should be happy here doing all the running and sand-throwing that they are instinctively programmed to do. The beach is level, the gravel fairly easy to cross and the sand plentiful.

**Suitability for groups** Like the Telegraph Bay Road spur access, this is a good one for a photo shoot with a family group or small wedding party since you can get to the shore so conveniently and don't need to worry overmuch about passersby eager to ogle any and all wedding parties. The large area of dry sand allows plenty of space for your friends or family to spread out their picnic or sunbathing gear.

**View** From this spot, Ten Mile Point largely encloses the view on the one side and Spurn Head on the other. Lacking the beauty of rugged shoreline, it is nevertheless a picturesque take on the dozens of sailboats that anchor at this end of the bay and sail decoratively in and out of the nearby Royal Victoria Yacht Club.

**Winds, sun and shade** This part of the bay is considerably more protected from both wind and waves than the end accessible from the south end of Telegraph Bay Road. On a hot day, it can become very hot, not least of all because there is not an iota of shade throughout the day.

**Beachcombing** If you would like a romp or stroll, you will probably be happier heading to your left since the sand in that direction becomes harder and more consistently free of rocks.

**Seclusion** Cheek-by-jowl houses line the shore, without benefit of much bank or shorefront trees. Few visitors use this access spot, though, certainly in comparison to that at the south end of Telegraph Bay Road or, of course, Cadboro-Gyro Park.

# 64

## HIBBENS CLOSE

**A bank-top view of the southwest end of Cadboro Bay and a long flight of stairs to the shore**

**Location, signs and parking** Hibbens Close is a short, L-shaped dead-end road nipping off Cadboro Bay Road north of the Royal Victoria Yacht Club. You will immediately identify the access spot by the clearly visible large, park-like area with a cluster of signs, a park bench and the railings of the staircase to the beach. The two signs concern fires and dogs. If you are looking for a spot for a marshmallow roast, go elsewhere. The ban against beach fires is "strictly enforced" here. As for your dog's desire to sniff at clamshells, note that you must have her on a leash and, from May 1 to August 30, can come only before 9 a.m. Another sign—NO PARKING—is more problematic for most hopeful beachgoers since there isn't any shoulder along the adjoining roads. Still, the road is wide and quiet enough that you can go a short distance past the access lawn area to find a discreet spot.

**Path** A level, asphalt path takes you 20 m to a park bench. Beside the bench descends an impressive set of no fewer than 75 wooden stairs.

**Beach** With all the effort that has gone into the meticulously prepared approach to the shore, you might expect something a little more attractive than you will find—particularly at low tide. Immediately in front of the access spot the sand is squelchy and largely covered with green sea lettuce dotted with barnacle-covered rocks. The upper edge of the beach is a little more conducive to barefooted beach-going, but even there the sand is dampish right up to the edge of the bushes. On both sides of the access point, however, there are lots of beach logs and enough dry sand that, especially when the tide is largely in, you can spend a pleasant time.

**Suitability for children** Given the 75 steps, the lack of facilities and the nearby alternative of a full-on child-friendly beach at the Cadboro-Gyro Park, few parents would choose to bring their children here.

**Suitability for groups** A small group could park here, and a larger group could find room to disperse themselves along the beach. Otherwise there seems little reason why groups would choose this spot.

**View** It is really the unusual view that most recommends this spot to beach explorers. The view from the park bench overlooking the sailboat-dotted sweep of the bay and, beyond, the picturesquely convoluted shore of Ten Mile Point can be seen from no other spot. And if you like looking at sailboats, you will enjoy the forest of them that sail against the backdrop of the wooded southern shores of Ten Mile Point.

**Winds, sun and shade** This is one of the most protected bits of beach you will find in the area—hence the slimy nature of the lower shore. This is the only access spot in Cadboro Bay where you can get much protection from the baking afternoon sun, particularly to the right. Likewise, come here when most of the coast is being buffeted by winds blowing up Haro Strait and you will feel only occasional riffles.

**Beachcombing** This is a good place to begin a stroll of a few kilometres along the upper shore toward the far end of the bay. You could build in a visit to a coffee shop in Cadboro Bay Village. You will probably want to keep to the high-tide area of the beach, though, until you have gone a few hundred metres and the shore becomes more pleasant underfoot.

**Seclusion** You may well be the only one on this part of the shore. Moreover, because of the high, wooded banks, you will feel under almost no inspection.

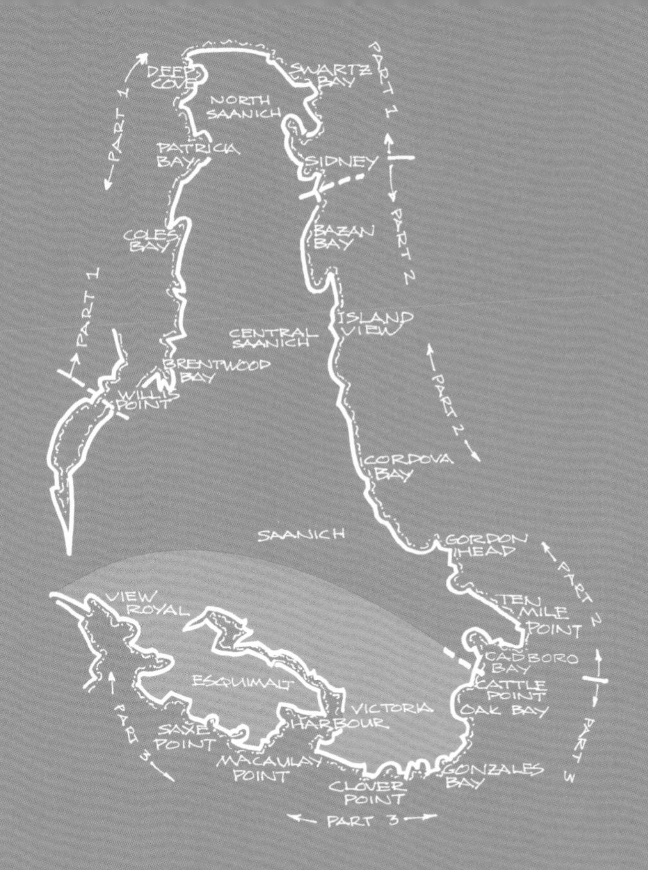


# PART 3 Oak Bay to View Royal

ALONG THE SOUTHEASTERN SHORES OF Vancouver Island, the prettified world of rose gardens and gabled Victoriana is dramatically juxtaposed with a bleak coast of rugged coves and headlands. This, the most cultivated and citified area on the Island, opens upon beaches exposed to the wild north Pacific storms and upon the best views of magnificent mountains and craggy reefs.

Also striking is that a scenic marine drive, marked on many street maps, runs along much of the coastline. This route is as familiar to every visitor to and resident of Victoria as the Parliament Buildings. It may seem unnecessary to provide information on access to hidden beaches along such a well-known shorefront. Such is the complexity of the shoreline, however, that tiny pocket beaches and obscure coves can be discovered even in areas that seem entirely public and obvious. The coastal route from Oak Bay to Beacon Hill, for example, through the most visited areas of Victoria, has its very own secret gems.

The western side of Victoria's Inner Harbour, beginning immediately south of the Johnson Street bridge, has long seemed the coast of another world—that is, until condominium developments brought it into the urban fold. Now, the shorefront walk from Songhees through Vic West and all the way to West Bay in Esquimalt is teaming with joggers, strollers and ecstatic dogs.

Even so, within this area and beyond, far into deepest Esquimalt, the shoreline bristles with surprises. Exposed to the south and west, this stretch of coast not only has splendid views down the Strait of Juan de Fuca and toward the sunsets, but also the kinds of bare headlands and pebbly coves that make for a real sense of discovery. Probably least known and farthest off most Victorians' radar is View Royal. Although you will need good map-reading skills to make your way through the narrow, hilly streets in View Royal, you can expect some surprisingly beautiful and well-developed routes to shorefront spots that make you realize that for waterfront beauty, the whole Victoria region is hard to beat.

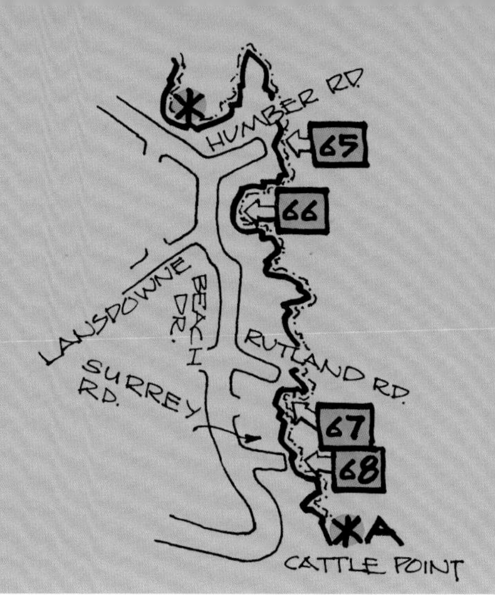

## 65

### HUMBER ROAD

**A hidden cove with a pebbly upper beach and view of Baynes Channel**

**Location, signs and parking** You will find Humber Road immediately south of the Royal Victoria Yacht Club on Beach Drive. A short distance toward the water brings you to the end of a large flowery turnaround and, frustratingly, a sign telling you that you cannot park in the turnaround. You can, however, park along the curb a little farther back on Humber. Another sign informs you that you are outside the gates of the palatial Consulate of St. Kitts and Nevis. You will see no other signs prodding you or restricting you at this intriguing little access spot.

**Path** An open, grassy area at the end of the turnaround leads past a grimly functional set of utilities to five or six concrete steps built into the small retaining wall.

**Beach** From these steps you will find yourself in the middle of a tiny cove. A low tide will completely empty the cove, revealing patches of boulder and solid rock near its mouth. Farther up the shore is a mysterious little wall of concrete and rock jutting toward the water line. For most of the shore, a strip of fine pebbles and beach logs lines the upper beach, backed by metre-high retaining walls of the two residences abutting the cove.

**Suitability for children** If your primary purpose is to find a pretty, sheltered beach spot to while away an hour or so, then your child companion might find diversion in the form of squidgy low-tide creatures or high-tide water. Not many parents, however, will choose this confined spot if their main purpose is to entertain a child.

**Suitability for groups** A family or a besotted couple could be happy here, but no more.

**View** The view seems almost cramped by the enclosing ends of the cove, but the result is charming. You will have the sense of looking through a portal from a hidden spot onto the watery world beyond: Cadboro Point, Baynes Channel and the low profile of Jemmy Jones Island and the northern Chatham Islands.

**Winds, sun and shade** This is a great spot to come if you want to nestle down with a book on a day when the wind is too cool for your taste and you want to absorb a little sunshine. Be aware, though, that by early afternoon the right side of the cove is entirely in shade, so you will have to move in front of the retaining wall of the house to your left.

**Beachcombing** You might feel tempted to poke around the low-tide rocks a little, but otherwise you can expect to take no more than a few steps from your perching spot.

**Seclusion** Don't be surprised if you are entirely alone here. You will feel as secluded as you are likely to be anywhere nearby. From certain positions in the cove you will neither see the two residences nor be seen by them.

* **Also nearby** **Loon Bay Park** is a grassy area opposite Exeter Road on Beach Drive. From the sea side of the lawn area, a gap in the bushes and a few steps lead down onto the shore, largely overhung with bushes. The surface is quite muddy, so few would want more than a quick look at this spot beside the Royal Victoria Yacht Club.

## 66

### LANSDOWNE ROAD

A few steps off a grassy area to a miniature world of reefs, pebble beaches and islets

**Location, signs and parking** Anyone who knows Lansdowne Road will have a hard time thinking of it in terms of beach access. In fact, what you are looking for is a small, rectangular, white and green sign saying PUBLIC BEACH ACCESS at the junction of Lansdowne Road and Beach Drive. You will see a 10 m-wide grass area with a convenient water fountain and a break in the curb allowing vehicles to drive onto the grassy area. What is not clear is whether private vehicles are expected to park in this grassy area or whether it is intended for service vehicles. No signs clarify the uncertainty.

**Path** From the left side of the grassy area a level dirt path leads between the fence of a house and a thicket of bushes to a grassy bluff with a few Garry oaks on the bank side. From here a few concrete steps lead to the shore.

**Beach** The steps bring you to a foreshore of lumpy solid rock, dropping a little awkwardly to the tidal zone. You could find a spot here to sit and enjoy the view, but it has to be confessed that this part of the shore is not very welcoming for those who want to linger. The most fascinating aspect of this spot is the shore in either direction. On the right, a small pebble-lined isthmus groomed with the park-like gardens of the residents leads out to a picturesque rocky knoll called The Naze, named after a headland on the coast of Essex popular with migrating birds. To the left, low tide exposes a pebbly spit connected to a miniature islet with a few bushes and rounded-rock shore. Farther to the left you will see another solid-rock section leading onto the circular shore of a pebbly Spoon Bay about 100 m long and thence to Skegness, another rocky promontory. At this point, you cannot help being charmed by the complex interplay of curves, bumps, pebbly shores and rocky knolls. The shore in front of the access would be more welcoming if it were more comfortable, but you can find a pleasant spot to your left either on the upper shore or out on the spit and islet.

**Suitability for children** You probably don't want to leave a child alone here while you get absorbed in a murder mystery. A supervised and fairly adventurous child or two, though, can have lots of fun simply because the shore is so diverse.

**Suitability for groups** This beach is too limited for more than a family or a few friends.

**View** The chief attraction of the spot really is visual. Photographers and sketchers will come away with dozens of different views, each one a different combination of elements. Lovers of wide, open views, however, will feel a little stymied since all of the reefs and knolls frame a fairly narrow portal onto Cadboro Point, Jemmy Jones and the Chatham Islands beyond.

**Winds, sun and shade** Come during the first part of the day if you want a lot of sun on the access part of the shore. The shore in front of the houses to the left remains in sun well into the afternoon as, of course, does the little islet-like rocky promontory. Expect to be hot on a hot day, although some breezes could stir a few pages of your book.

**Beachcombing** The whole shoreline around Spoon Bay can be walked. You will probably enjoy it most when the tide is not high, so you can distance yourself from the shorefront houses—most of them perched well back into large gardens and fronted by small retaining walls.

**Seclusion** You will likely not escape from the feeling that you are in a residential neighbourhood. Nevertheless, you could be pleasantly surprised to find yourself secluded on this side of the hidden door that has brought you to this charming spot.

## 67

### RUTLAND ROAD

**A small, hidden cove with a sunny, pebble-and-log upper beach framed by low, rocky headlands**

**Location, signs and parking** Rutland crosses Beach Drive a short distance north of Uplands Park and Cattle Point. Without the aid of telltale signs, drive the 100 m or so down Rutland and find a parking spot along the edge of the paved area. Avoid running afoul of the driveways that feed into this area.

**Path** At the end of the paved turnaround area you will see a red, diamond-shaped metal post preventing cars from entering the small, grassy, treed area at the end of the road. This is your path. Through this area, a short, unkempt dirt path, complemented by some sinister-looking utilities, leads to the edge of a bank. Eight weather-worn concrete stairs lead to the shore beside a concrete structure evidently designed to hold a drainpipe in place. Those with walking difficulties will find this an easy way to the shore but should be mindful that these stairs, unusually, have no handrail.

**Beach** Nestled up into the overhanging bushes is a phalanx of weathered logs and a few very large boulders. Immediately below and intermingled with the rock and logs, though, are several patches of dry, fine pebbles, exactly the kind of shore most suitable for putting down a beach towel or opening up plastic containers of Greek salad and chicken legs.

Farther down the beach and all the way to the waterline, the shore is covered with small, barnacle-encrusted rocks mixed with larger boulders. Beyond that, the shore shelves off gradually into the waters of the small, deeply inset Funnel Cove, almost entirely cut off from the open sea by long, low, rocky promontories and a series of reefs. Unfortunately, the mid-beach is subject to influxes of greenish seaweed that decides to rot in situ. If you were to launch a kayak here or at nearby Cattle Point, you would enjoy exploring the tangle of reefs and islets beyond the edges of this cove. If you happened to bring a wetsuit, this would be a fascinating place to explore with mask and snorkel.

**Suitability for children** As long as your children aren't the most unstable of toddlers or don't expect sand, they will find much to amuse them at this little beachy retreat—particularly if the mid-beach is free of sea algae when you come. Assuming you set up a home base with drinks and sun-protection equipment, most children will poke about for rock crabs, sea stars and sculpins to their hearts' content. Much beyond ankle-depth, however, the water is icy.

**Suitability for groups** A matched set of lovebirds or a family equipped with refreshments and protective materials can spend a happy hour or two here, but the space is too small for more than that.

**View** You can get glimpses of the southern Chain Islets here and the northern part of the Olympic Mountains fading into distant Puget Sound. Otherwise, your view is almost entirely limited to the pleasantly rocky foreshore of the little cove.

**Winds, sun and shade** Because the cove faces southeast and is surrounded by only low bush and rock, it is in full sun well into the afternoon. Expect a sun-baked picnic on a hot day. On the other hand, a southeast wind funnels more or less directly into the bay, so check your forecast for how much cooling off you want.

**Beachcombing** The solid-rock shore is rough, though not steep, and slippery near the low-tide mark. Though you will want to watch how you place your feet, you would probably enjoy making your way to either or both of the headlands (equipped with a camera) to view the interesting hodgepodge of reefs and rocks slightly offshore.

**Seclusion** Astound yourself and your beloved by coming to a spot where you will be virtually unseen and, most likely, alone!

## 68

### SURREY ROAD

**A flight of concrete steps to a cove with a pebbly upper shore and view to the northeast**

**Location, signs and parking** Surrey Road is immediately north of Cattle Point, just outside of Uplands Park. Drive the very short distance to the end of Surrey Road and swing around before the road morphs into the driveway of a house. You will see a small grassy area separated from the road by a few large boulders. A glimpse through the barricade of thimbleberry bushes at the end of the grassy area will reassure you—in the complete absence of any posted sign—that you have come to the right place—the shore of Flotsam Cove.

**Path** A few steps to the edge of the grassy area will take you to a flight of just over 20 concrete steps leading directly to the shore.

**Beach** The beach of Flotsam Cove is about 30 or 40 m long, covered with fine pebbles and lined by a muddle of beach logs. The mid-beach, sometimes subject to dead and malodorous sea lettuce, slopes gradually to patches of larger boulders and the finer subtidal zone. Low but steep solid-rock promontories frame the cove on either side. The beach is backed by scrubby brush near the access area and, to the left, by a series of garden terraces from the house sharing the end of the beach.

**Suitability for children** A fairly high tide will likely keep most children happiest. At such a tide they can choose between climbing over their sunbathing parents or splashing in the somewhat frigid water of Flotsam Cove. Climbing over logs and making driftwood boats to assault with pebbles are, of course, always within a child's repertoire.

**Suitability for groups** There is enough space for a car or two's worth of sea-loving folk, but no more.

**View** The view is similar to that at the cove off Rutland Road immediately north, but more open, more directed toward the whole Chatham Island group and more decorated with a string of small reefs and rocks almost closing off the bay.

**Winds, sun and shade** Morning is the time to come if you want full sun, late afternoon if you want full shade. During the middle part of the day the shade at the south end of the beach gradually spreads farther along the beach. Although strong southeasterly winds curl around the headland and cool off the beach, the bay is generally sheltered from most winds. A hot day can be baking hot.

**Beachcombing** Although the promontories on either side of the bay are low, the rock drops almost vertically below the high-tide mark. Going anywhere very far is more or less out of the question.

**Seclusion** While you share the bay with three houses, all three are set back among gardens, trees and promontories in such a way that you will only glimpse them. For the most part you can simply enjoy a quiet time in a pretty little bay.

*** Also nearby**

**A. Cattle Point** is probably harder to miss than just about any other shorefront spot in the Victoria area. Kayakers in particular might note the point's two convenient launching ramps. Lovers of views, walkers and picnickers will all seek out this astoundingly beautiful shore.

**B. Willows Beach Park**, along with **The Esplanade**, a street running above the beach, vies with Cattle Point for popularity. Anyone who loves a beautiful, long, sandy beach with lots of convenient facilities will quickly single out this central spot in Oak Bay. Easy to approach, just off the marine waterfront route along Beach Drive via several different side streets, the beach and the street suit all ages and all walking abilities.

Surrey Road

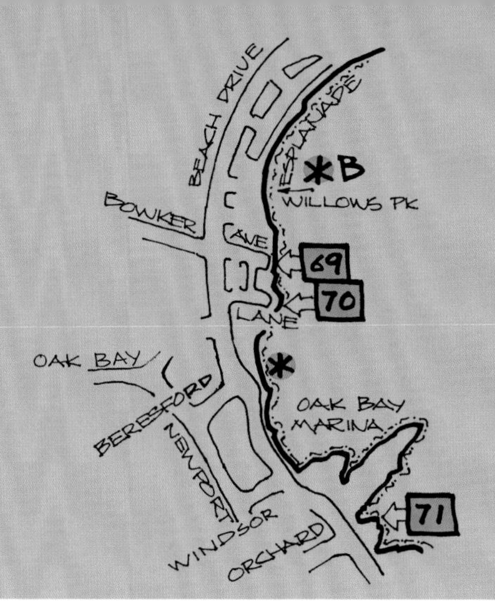

## 69

### BOWKER AVENUE

Level access to dune-like sand and grass at the southern end of Willows Beach

**Location, signs and parking** Bowker Avenue cuts across Beach Drive two blocks south of Willows Beach Park. It ends just past Bowker Place, a street parallel to the beach. It is possible to squeeze in along the edges of the road in spite of the high hedge and fence on the other. If these spots happen to be full, as can happen on a hot summer's day, you can usually find a place to park a little farther away. Although none of the signs tells you that this is a public beach access, they are happy to impose some restrictions on your visit. While you cannot park overnight, because this is Oak Bay, the restricted period doesn't start until midnight. Dog walkers cannot choose this spot during the summer months, May to September, inclusive—though there seem to be no leash restrictions thereafter. Predictably, beach fires are never permitted, and, in addition, "loud music volumes [are] prohibited," presumably from car stereos rather than ukulele players. Cyclists looking for a seaside route are told not to use the path that begins here.

**Path** You can virtually drive onto the beach. The path is then only a few steps through a level field of tall, wild grass. Bring all your sun-protection gear, kites, buckets and spades, as they are easily toted to the shore or retrieved from the car.

**Beach** This beach is the southern end of the beautiful, long stretch of Willows Beach proper. You will arrive at a large area of fine, white sand among a clutter of beach logs, as you would on the main beach. Some beachgoers prefer this access to the main part of the beach because of two features. First, at low tide the sand gives way to a section of rocks and reefs just offshore, in front and to your right, enhancing the view and making for an interesting bit of exploring. Second, the large area of almost dune-like sand and grass above the main line of the beach allows you to tuck well back out of the strongest breezes on a day when the wind is raising too many goosebumps for comfort.

**Suitability for children** Aside from the lack of toilets or picnic tables, this section of beach has all of the pleasures and attractions of the main sandy beach to the north.

**Suitability for groups** Because this Bowker access has a distinctive feel to it and is separated from the busy public part of Willows Beach by a few blocks' worth of houses, a family group or club might want to come here for a picnic. Don't forget the limitations on parking and the lack of facilities, however. A wedding or family photo shoot could be perfect on this beach—and the background of your photo would be much more interesting than that gained from the main beach.

**View** From this slight promontory you will see the full, fine sweep of Willows Beach, Cattle Point, Chatham and Discovery islands, and just in front of the Oak Bay Marina to your right, Mary Tod Island. From this angle, however, the Olympics are tucked out of sight.

**Winds, sun and shade** On a hot day, you might find that there is less breeze and more sun than you consider ideal; on a cool day, you will feel the advantages of the spot. If you need to find shade, it is to be had at Willows Beach Park a few blocks north, but also along the upper shore a short walk to your right.

**Beachcombing** Many will find this the perfect spot to begin a walk since this is the southern terminus of the paved shorefront path. If you are looking to jog decoratively and barefootedly at the water's edge, don't come at high tide when all of the hard, wet sand is covered, or you will soon be lurching and struggling through the Sahara-like conditions of the sandy upper shore.

**Seclusion** Don't expect anything approaching seclusion here—except, of course, on a glowering winter's day when you might want to choose this spot to give yourself and your four-legged friend a few lungfuls of fresh salt air.

## 70

### LANE STREET

A simple access to a shoreline of sand and logs on the upper beach and rocky shoals on the lower beach

**Location, signs and parking** Between Oak Bay Marina and Willows Beach Park, turn off Lane Street from Beach Drive and head straight toward the shore. Look for parking here or around the corner of this quiet street and Bowker Place. Although the spot is not labelled as a beach access, you will have no difficulty seeing what looks like a service track leading a short distance to the beach. The only sign is one put in place, doubtless, by some exasperated locals. According to the sign, "pedestrians on the beach" will find "no street access" if they turn right here once they reach the beach. There is a lot of truth to the warning—the shoreline to the south becomes narrow and steep, thus tempting beach walkers to nip through a level bit of private lawn. However, at low tide it is physically possible, though awkward, to walk to the access just south of Glenlyon-Norfolk School and return via Beach Drive.

**Path** Approach the shore between a high hedge on one side and a fence, almost as high, on the other. A short section of level, partially paved service road brings you past some low, charmless metallic utilities and to the shoreline.

**Beach** Even though Lane Street is only one block south of the Bowker Avenue access, the beach is distinctly different. From here, the long sweep of unbroken sand that is Willows Beach is completely out of sight. The upper shore is backed by houses with retaining walls, either of boulders, on the right, or concrete, on the left—not inviting for those who want to feast on sandwiches or sunshine. Farther down, the shore provides some pleasant areas of loose, dry sand and beach grass. The most distinctive elements of the beach, however, are the areas of low, shelving rock, a few prominent boulders and the low-tide reefs, all of which are conducive to finding the kind of low-tide creatures not to be found at the long, sandy beach to the north.

**Suitability for children** Most children, of course, will prefer to go the sandy beach where they can scamper or skimboard. Some children, though, will enjoy the diversified, level shore, and parents will enjoy its relative safety. Water shoes are a must.

**Suitability for groups** The area is comparatively small and the houses are comparatively close. Two or three cars' worth of visitors can be accommodated here, but they should choose this spot over one of the spots immediately north only if there is something about the character of this shore that they prefer.

**View** Since the shore here faces largely southeast, the view is dominated by the Chatham Islands, Discovery Island and Mary Tod Island, interlaced with the masts and stays of the sailboats in Oak Bay Marina.

**Winds, sun and shade** A southeast wind is a little muffled by Turkey Head, the point of land beyond the marina, but the wind will hit the shore more or less directly. Unlike most spots to the north that offer little protection from the sun, this one provides a patch of afternoon shade under a large overhanging tree slightly to the left of the access spot.

**Beachcombing** Don't head south unless you don't mind walking only a short distance. Do, however, consider this a good starting point for a long stroll, saunter or romp accompanied by iPod or soulmate. Head to your left and you will soon be able to choose between the beachfront promenade of Esplanade Street and the stretch of sand that will allow you to go all the way to Cattle Point.

**Seclusion** This spot is not the least bit secluded, either from neighbouring houses or from other visitors. Come in marginal weather for a shorefront walk, however, and you may be alone with just a few others of your foul-weather ilk.

* **Also nearby** **Haynes Park** seems largely indistinguishable from the other park-like areas along the roadside running through this sedate but crowded part of Oak Bay north of the Oak Bay Marina. Be aware, though, that this little park provides an easy access to the small section of pleasant shoreline just south of Glenlyon-Norfolk School on Beach Drive. It is at the base of Oak Bay Avenue as the crow flies—but not as you drive. To get to this beach from Oak Bay Avenue, angle to the right on Oak Bay when you can no longer go straight, and you will be on Newport Avenue. Take the first left, Beresford Street. Haynes Park is across Beach Drive at the end of Beresford.

## 71

**BEACH DRIVE—ORCHARD AVENUE**

**Two side-by-side pocket beaches immediately below Beach Drive**

**Location, signs and parking** Twin beaches along Beach Drive, separated by a small promontory, are certainly among the least "secret" in this book. They deserve singling out, though, since the vast number of sightseers who wander up and down this busy section of Beach Drive seem rarely to stop here. If you are coming from the south, take notice when you pass Satellite Street and perk up even more where the road passes immediately by a small cove. From Oak Bay Avenue, take Newport Avenue where it angles right, then turn left onto Windsor Street and right onto Beach Drive. Oak Bay Marina is your landmark and, again, once you have passed it, Beach Drive comes close to the shore. Pull into the paved parking area between the two little coves. There is room here for eight cars and a few advisory signs, one, of course, telling you that you may not park overnight.

**Path** Those with walking difficulties or wishing to enjoy a car picnic in stormy weather will find this an excellent option. Picnic tables on a flat, grassy area immediately off the car park make life easy for those whose life otherwise is not. A few steps also lead toward the beach, including a ramp near the house numbered 1247. Two or three kayaks could be launched here without too much of a struggle.

**Beach** Few features distinguish the two beaches from each other, though the one closer to the marina is a little smaller. Both slope fairly steeply and thus do not reveal huge areas of shore at low tide. Both are lined with bleached logs among pebbles and give way to larger rocks farther down the shore. While picnickers might choose the tables by the parking lot, both beaches, in fact, make good spots to spread out your designer sandwiches and carrot sticks. In your headlong rush to get onto the shore, don't overlook the interesting rocky promontory between the two beaches, particularly if you have come equipped with a camera, binoculars or sketchpad.

**Suitability for children** While not ideally suited to the hyperactive and sand-loving child, this is a safe and sheltered spot for children who like to climb over patches of solid rock and poke around a shoreline, getting wetter than their parents would like.

**Suitability for groups** The promontory is an excellent spot for a family or wedding photo shoot. Come in late afternoon when the sun is well behind you. Otherwise, two or three cars' worth of friends or family members could set up camp here for an hour or two of chat and seaside sun. In general, though, the proximity of the road and the size of these small beaches do not make this a good spot for groups.

**View** The view is best from the promontory, of course, though the parking areas and buildings of Oak Bay Marina are in full view from here. The rest of your view is a wonderful hodgepodge of overlapping reefs and islets and, in the distance to your right, the open waters of the straits. If you like to know exactly what you're looking at, and love Proper Nouns, you might be able to pick out (from left to right) Mary Tod Island, Emily Islet, Harris Island and Mayor Channel behind, leading to the Chain Islets. Beyond, and separated by Plumper Passage, you should be able to distinguish the low contours of Chatham Islands and Discovery Island, the southernmost of these, terminating in Commodore Point.

**Winds, sun and shade** The first half of the day is the sunniest, though in the summer the sun is high enough that, even with it behind you, it will burn you to a crisp if you are not careful. On a sunny day, when breezes cool the surrounding area, both beaches can be more than a little warm, given that they—the promontory less so—are protected from most wind.

**Beachcombing** Almost everyone who visits the spot wants, no, *needs* to do a little exploring not just of the two beaches, but also the solid-rock lumps and bumps between. If you yearn for a long-distance beach walk or jog, keep in mind that you are but a short distance from Willows Beach.

**Seclusion** You are right beside a busy but generally sedate road. To the south, a house overlooks the beach. Both beaches are well used by those who live in the apartment buildings across the road. Put all this together and be prepared to find little seclusion—though also be prepared to be pleasantly surprised if you are more or less alone.

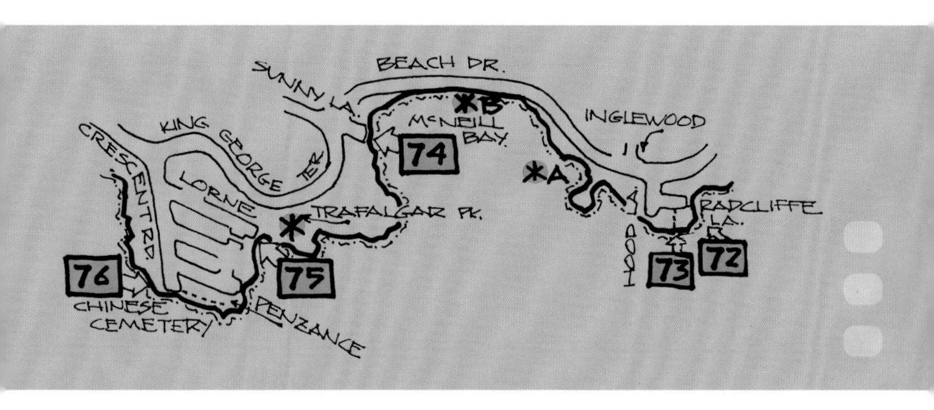

## 72

### RADCLIFFE LANE—EAST

**A small, pebbly cove with rocky outcroppings, immediately next to Victoria Golf Course**

**Location, signs and parking** This truly "secret" spot on the east side of McMicking Point is, in fact, only a short distance from the well-beaten sightseers' route of Beach Drive. Using the Victoria Golf Club as your landmark from one direction and McNeill Bay from the other, look for tiny Hood Lane. After only a few metres down this narrow road, turn left onto Radcliffe Lane and, after three houses, look for a surprisingly generous gravel parking area with a telltale path and two signs, one restricting your time to two hours, the other reminding you that there is no parking at all between midnight and 6 a.m. In fact, because this is a "lane," as the name tells you, it is probably best to use this parking area and walk the short distance to the end of the lane. You could also park right at the end of the lane if you are careful not to block access to driveways.

**Path** Pass another path to the right on your way to the end of Radcliffe, which is described in the next entry, leading to the south shore of McMicking Point. The path to the east-facing shore, at the end of the Radcliffe, is really a gently sloping road with a swath of gravel and grass between the low wooden fences of the neighbouring houses. Obviously put in place to provide access for service vehicles to the concrete and metal structures between you and the shore, the path makes the going easy for anyone with walking difficulties.

**Beach** The beach is a striking mixture of elements. The upper beach is a kind of crazy quilt of fine pebbles amid tangles of beach logs and driftwood. Prettiest at mid to high tide, the shore nevertheless makes for varied exploring at low tide when several little reefs can be easily reached. The configuration of the beach is a bit odd. The access strip brings you to the west end of the pebbly strip that stretches directly away from you in front of two houses and ends with a low outcropping—and the manicured golf greens of Victoria Golf Club. Although the whole length of the beach is enticing, you will probably feel most comfortable with your lunchables and readables at the end of the beach immediately below the access.

**Suitability for children** Like most other pebbly beaches in this area, this one is safe and welcoming for children who have imagination, patience or an appetite. If they can be tempted to make forts among the driftwood or set sail to driftwood pirate ships, for example, they will find lots to do while their parents engage in more languid pleasures. If, however, you want lots of space and lots of sand, go to nearby Gonzales Bay where you will find both—along with toilets and a battery of picnic tables.

**Suitability for groups** The spot is perfect for a small family picnic or a double date—but not much more.

**View** While the view is restricted to about 90 degrees, the irregular but low rocky outcroppings in both directions make for a prettily varied scene. Trial Island is partly visible to one side, but largely hidden if you are sitting among the pebbles.

**Winds, sun and shade** Since the beach itself faces more or less south, expect lots of sun on a sunny day and lots of wind on a windy day. If, however, there is a westerly battering the nearby access on the side of this point farther to the south, you can find a little refuge here since the rocky shore to your right actually faces east. On the other hand, if you see a gorgeous sunset forming and cannot view it fully, don't forget that half a block away another access strip allows you a splendid view of sunsets.

**Beachcombing** You could do a little curious prodding around low-tide rocks and pools. Otherwise, this is a beach for remaining deliciously, decadently static, soaking up sun and sensations.

**Seclusion** Be set to be surprised. You are surrounded by houses—and yet are not near any of them or, more to the point, not all that near their sightlines. You might feel a little intrusive if you stray too far from the end of the beach below the access path, but if you stay on the beach you can plan on peace and quiet—at least until your two-hour parking limit runs out!

# 73

## RADCLIFFE LANE—MCMICKING POINT

**A gorse-covered, bleak headland hidden from all but beach explorers**

**Location, signs and parking** This access point, on the southern shore of McMicking Point, is reached the same way as the previous one. From tiny Hood Lane, off Beach Drive, turn left onto Radcliffe Lane. If you use the same parking area and begin the same walk toward the end of the lane described in the previous entry, you will see a path going off to the right.

**Path** From the beginning you will sense that you are not on one of the most used public access routes in the area. With an adventurous spirit thoroughly charged, though, press ahead through a path that can be nearly overgrown at times onto a rough and wild, low promontory bristling with gorse. If this is your first encounter with gorse, you will quickly understand why it is not considered a desirable invasive species. About 20 m or so through the brush will bring you to what you might arbitrarily decide is the shore.

**Beach** This is one of those startling spots around Victoria where the contrast between the cozy, civilized, residential world and the bleakly rugged could hardly be more striking. This is not a spot for the faint of heart. Even on a hot, still summer day you can witness the power of the currents surging through Enterprise Channel immediately in front of you. The expansive area of rock outcroppings has a few clusters of logs and is crossed near the low-tide line by an unsightly long concrete structure (probably part of the sewage outfall system that once flowed into Enterprise Channel and that now empties off Clover Point). Bring your binoculars, camera or even a good book and find the perfect spot on this rocky promontory of McMicking Point.

**Suitability for children** An older child with a truly adventurous spirit or a lot of patience might be happy accompanying a determined parent. This is not the place to choose, however, if your primary purpose is to bring beachfront pleasure to your heir.

**Suitability for groups** McMicking Point could suit a plucky set of friends with a desire for an unusual experience or an unusual view to photograph. Bring them in the middle of a westerly storm, or in time for the sunset, and they may well judge the experience to be unforgettable.

**View** The proximity to Enterprise Channel and the northern tip of the Trial Islands give this spot its character. The many hidden rocks of the channel, the thick kelp beds, the strong currents and the standing waves they sometimes produce, and, not least of all, the boats that struggle or surge through the narrow gap—depending on the size of their motor—make this a fascinating place to spend an hour or two. From here you also have an intriguing view of Harling Point, the location of the Chinese Cemetery, to your right and, to your left, Gonzales Point.

**Winds, sun and shade** This is a spot for experiencing the elements. From dawn to dusk on a clear day you will be in sun; in any wind except a northwesterly, which blows offshore here, your coat will whip around you.

**Beachcombing** It is actually possible to explore the rocky shore—particularly interesting at low tide—for 100 m or so in each direction, but you will have to be sure of foot and willing to take your time.

Radcliffe Lane
McMicking Point

**Seclusion** Five houses huddle together at the back of the promontory and fix their gaze out to sea—and on you as well. However, they are well set back, especially in the middle of the promontory, so you won't feel you are in their front gardens.

*** Also nearby**

**A.** Near a house numbered 572 Beach Drive, a short distance west of Inglewood Place, is **Kitty Islet**, a wonderful little bit of rock and beach in full view of the scenic drive, but not visited nearly enough. A few cars can park in the small area at the west end of the thick bushy area along the road. Across a strip of land bounded by a beach on either side rises the little rocky promontory. There is even a picnic table on this promontory to entice passersby to this magical little spot—with, to boot, an interesting view of the often surging narrows between here and the Trial Islands.

**B.** The scenic marine drive runs along the shore of **McNeill Bay**. At a few spots, concrete steps take you down to the beach for shore walking and a good chance to get close to the briny deep. If you want to walk along the beach, be sure to choose low tide since at high tide the water laps cheerfully up against the retaining wall. During a southeast storm life can get fairly tumultuous here!

## 74

## SUNNY LANE

**A candidate for the "most secret" beach in the area, a small, pebbly cove with a low-tide reef, well hidden from the scenic route**

**Location, signs and parking** From the part of the scenic drive that is called King George Terrace, at the west end of McNeill Bay, Sunny Lane goes a very short distance toward the shore and grinds to a halt. Because this tiny road really is, as the name suggests, only a lane, you might do best to park on King George Terrace and walk the short distance down Sunny Lane. If, however, you are driving a small car (Humvee owners take note), you could squeeze onto the shoulder of Sunny Lane itself, up against a retaining wall.

**Path** After a short interlude under wild cherries, the path begins its descent to the shore. The first dozen steps, constructed of planks holding up dirt and gravel, are a little treacherous in wet weather—particularly with no helpful handrail. The last nine steps to the beach are concrete, however, and much more solid, even though they, too, have no handrail.

**Beach** This gravelly little cove extends only the length of the four houses overlooking it. A small, rocky promontory defines one end while the other simply merges into an area of steeper, rocky shore. The upper beach is surprisingly expansive, with a large area of fine, polished pebbles well above most high tides. A distinctive feature of the beach is a reef toward the east end, easily accessible at low tide—an obvious destination for a bit of low-tide exploration. The sloping beach and cove-like shape of this shoreline attract a fine clutter of bleached sea logs along the upper shore.

**Suitability for children** If the stairs aren't too much of a hurdle for accident-prone toddlers, once children reach this protected beach they cannot go far astray or come a cropper. You can, with peace of mind, watch your child amble about and get up to watery mischief. Most children will be happiest, though, with either a short visit or one embellished with snacks or a full-blown picnic.

**Suitability for groups** Take your group elsewhere. The parking is too limited and the little beach too much a part of a neighbourhood for any group to go unnoticed.

**View** Although the little cove is actually in McNeill Bay, you cannot see the main sweep of the bay because of the rocky point at the end of the cove. You do have a pretty view of McMicking Point, directly across the bay, Enterprise Channel and the Trial Islands. The point at the west end of McNeill Bay prevents your seeing much out to the straits, so on the whole, your view is not wide open.

**Winds, sun and shade** During the morning and early afternoon on a sunny day, the beach is in full sun. By early afternoon, however, the high bank to your right and the trees that line it cast considerable shade on that end of the beach. This end of the shore is also most protected from winds—the same winds that can blow straight into McNeill Bay and invert a fair few umbrellas there.

**Beachcombing** Aside from strolling up and down the short beach, you won't find it easy to stretch your legs here. You could explore the low-tide rocks, though, and the critters that make their home on the reef at the north end of the cove.

**Seclusion** The bank is high and leafy, so you won't feel you've blundered onto a private stretch of shore. At the same time, be prepared to feel under inspection from the multi-storey apartments that crowd forward onto the shore to your right.

## 75

### LORNE TERRACE

**A pebbly cove tucked between the high bluffs below Trafalgar Park and the Chinese Cemetery at Harling Point**

**Location, signs and parking** Crescent Road is the part of the scenic drive behind Gonzales Bay, but it turns sharply off the scenic route at the point where the scenic route turns into King George Terrace. Immediately after Crescent Road turns toward the shore, turn left onto the extremely narrow Lorne Terrace and follow it to its end. To the left of a high hedge you will see parking for two or three cars and two signs, one prohibiting beach fires, the other telling you, generously, that only between midnight and 6 a.m. are you not to park.

**Path** A paved path through a little patch of grass takes you to a slightly weather-beaten set of almost 40 concrete stairs down a bushy bank to the shore. En route, notice two other paths on your left, one leading uphill toward the Trafalgar Park parking area, another leading through the thick bushes parallel to the cliffy shore.

**Beach** You will find yourself on a little beach about 40 m long and ending in a cluster of reefs immediately offshore. A few logs litter the pebbly beach, more or less decoratively, creating a welcoming shore for those who want to sprawl, picnic or ponder. A steep, almost cliffy outcropping of rock rises to the left of your entry point and leads directly ahead to a distinctive headland. Out of your sight, above you, it leads to Trafalgar Park, a large area of bleak rock between you and the marine drive high above. Partly because of the angle of the shore, and partly because the beach is so neatly tucked into a high, bushy bank on one side and the barren rocks on the other, you will truly feel you are in a miniature, hidden world. You could easily forget that part of the beach is visible from the Trafalgar Park roadside viewing point high above and behind you. Be warned!

**Suitability for children** The beach is child-friendly, especially after an enticing picnic when most children will be happy throwing rocks, looking for magic white pebbles, getting wet and wetter, and so on. An active child's yearning for long-distance romping will be constrained here, though.

**Suitability for groups** Two cars' worth of friends or families could have a wonderfully self-contained picnic here, cozily tucked away from the outside world. More than that, though, would not be a good idea.

**View** The view is almost the opposite from that to be had at nearby Crescent Road or Harling Point. The perspective here is not about open space but enclosed, picturesque rock—cliffs to the left; reefs, shoals and lumps of the Trial Islands almost entirely filling the centre; and reefs and bluffs to the right.

**Winds, sun and shade** Since the beach faces southeast, the very earliest part of the morning and late afternoon are a little shady. The rest of the day is full of sun. A southeast wind blows directly ashore, but there is considerable protection from all other winds.

**Beachcombing** Everyone will want to stroll down the short length of the beach and examine the low-tide line. The restless and adventurous will climb around the headland on your right toward Harling Point, while only those who enjoy rock climbing will try negotiating the steep rock on your left.

**Seclusion** This spot is not secluded. In fact, it is at the edge of a compact little neighbourhood. Nevertheless, you are almost guaranteed that wonderful feeling of seclusion because of the arrangement of steep, rocky shore, wooded bank and houses well placed behind the bank.

* **Also nearby** **Trafalgar Park** may look like a seaside park on maps, and technically it is, but as far as most visitors are concerned, it is a familiar roadside viewpoint high on the exposed rocky bluffs of King George Terrace with a good view of the Trial Islands. Two openings in the guardrail provide access to steeply descending paths over the bare rock bluffs. The one to the right, after a sequence of dirt track and stone stairs, leads to the same pebbly beach accessible from Lorne Terrace.

## 76

## CRESCENT ROAD—CHINESE CEMETERY

**A historically fascinating approach to a large area of exposed, rocky headland**

**Location, signs and parking** Road naming here is a little... odd. Crescent Road forms part of the scenic route but, without your noticing, flows into Hollywood Crescent at one end and King George Terrace on the other. You are looking for the bit of Crescent Road that shoots off the scenic drive portion and ends at the shoreline with the fascinatingly historic Chinese Cemetery on your left. Watch for the adequate parallel parking area on a broad gravel shoulder. The most prominent sign you will see reads, "Due to restoration of the cemetery please keep dogs and bikes off site." A welcome interpretative sign also provides some historical and biological information. If you want to park at the opposite end of the cemetery, immediately below the scrub-covered bluff, you can turn off Crescent onto Penzance Road and follow it to a roadside parking spot.

**Path** From the end of Crescent Road, only a few steps lead down to large, rounded boulders and solid rock underfoot, and, unfortunately, a gruesome drainage edifice. In foul weather—or a blazing winter sunset—this is quite a good place to car picnic. From the end of the road you can get an excellent view of the goings-on of the straits. If you don't want to walk on the shelf of rock, aim for the user-made track of dirt leading around the end of the cemetery fence, through the wild grass and low scrub, to the rounded hump of windblown Harling Point.

**Beach** At a glance, the rocky outcropping that makes up most of the shore might seem uninviting. On closer inspection, though, you will see that low tide reveals plenty of varied rock terrain, a lot of it not as difficult to explore as first glance might suggest. Just before Harling Point, in fact, is a large, mostly flat area of tidal pools and little crevices full of interesting intertidal shore life. Immediately offshore a few reefs add variety to the convoluted shoreline. The most remarkable feature of the beach, apart from artistic installations that can sometimes be found here, is Harpoon Rock, a large boulder deposited by a glacier ("harpoon" being a translation of the Songhees name for the point). According to Songhees legend, the transformer Haylas changed a seal hunter into this striking, vaguely humanoid rock. If you have a strong imagination... Geographically, the spot is likewise interesting, since the rock is an "erratic," a stone carried by glaciers a great distance from its point of origin. Many of the scars in the rock are apparently the marks of these glaciers.

**Suitability for children** If you have a toddler or a child looking to splash on a sandy beach, go elsewhere—possibly the beach at nearby Gonzales Bay. If, however, you have a child eager to rollick, explore, run along trails, poke around in tidal pools and the like, then this is an excellent place for an hour or so of energy-releasing.

**Suitability for groups** Don't be surprised if you see a group of painters or walkers—both can, not infrequently, be spotted here. Although no park facilities exist, there is the space for roaming, and even parking, that groups require. A group picnic could be a little awkward, though, despite a solid-rock shore level enough in places to be accommodating.

**View** The view is one of the main reasons for coming here. The historic shorefront cemetery frames much of what you see, adding to the striking atmosphere of the whole area. From a viewpoint on the highest part of Harling Point, your eye sweeps across a broad expanse of horizon. To one side you can see as far as Clover Point, to the other McNeill Bay, McMicking Point and Trial Islands. The backdrop of the Olympic Mountains completes the spectacle, of course.

**Winds, sun and shade** Like most other bits of shore in this area, this one is well suited to the romantic temperament and the lover of storms. Come here when the wind is howling and savour every dramatic gust. Likewise, come with protection from the sun—and just about every other element—since there isn't a morsel of shelter to be had. In fact, you may be surprised less that the brush on Harling Point is stunted than that it survives at all.

**Beachcombing** Come with sturdy shoes, maybe a walking stick and lots of curiosity.

**Seclusion** Although the Chinese Cemetery is quite well known as a local feature, rarely more than a few people at a time visit it. The shore is bleak and does not readily join up with the main routes. You will always find space enough to be alone with the cry of the gulls and the crash of the waves.

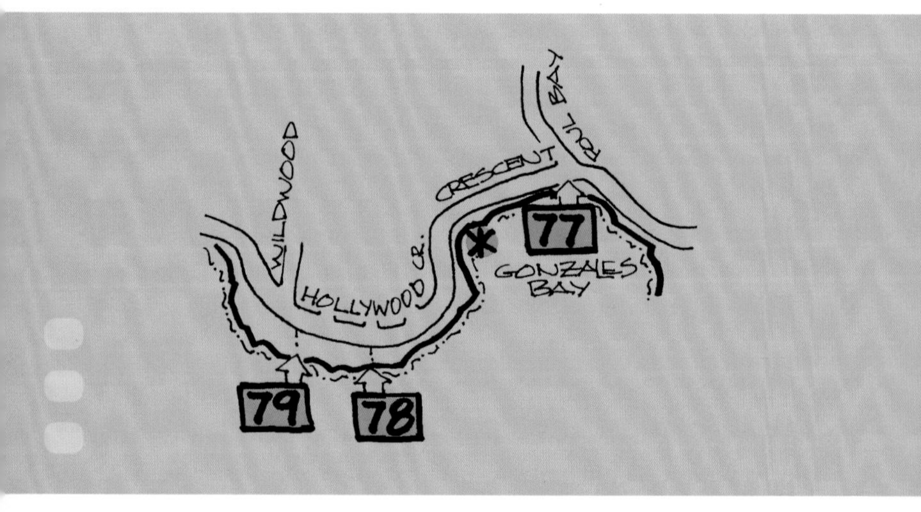

## 77

### FOUL BAY ROAD—GONZALES BAY

**A quiet and little-used approach to the fine, white sands of Gonzales Beach**

**Location, signs and parking** Most visitors to the park and beach of Gonzales Bay understandably go to the southwest end of the beach where they find plentiful parking, washrooms and a comparatively easy approach to the shore, all part of a park. This approach, at the opposite end of the sandy part of Gonzales Bay, can be found by following Foul Bay Road, just after it crosses Crescent Road and the scenic drive, to its southern terminus. Here you will find a parking lot, well off the road, and two signs of special significance. Dog owners will be particularly interested in the PAWS IN THE PARKS sign hilariously illustrated with a mournful basset (is there any other sort?). It provides a map revealing where you and your adrenalin-filled Yorky can run off leash in Victoria—but not during the summer months. Another sign prohibits beach fires.

**Path** You need to gird your loins for a bit of a hike to the beach or, more exactly, a bit of a hike up from the beach once you are thoroughly covered with sand. A long flight of 43 concrete steps descends over a sequence of three landings—each with its terraced strips of grass and picnic table.

**Beach** This beach stands a good chance of winning the medal for the most beautiful beach around Victoria. Deeply inset, and framed by a rocky promontory on either side, Gonzales Bay possesses for half its shore a sweeping curve of fine, white sand and an unusually wide strip of dry sand and logs. This access spot brings you to the east end of the sandy section, where at low tide a sandspit connects the beach to a set of rocky reefs emerging dramatically from the middle of the bay.

**Suitability for children** If you can overlook the monumental flight of stairs between you and your funmobile and the lack of washrooms at this end of the beach, you may well put this at the top of your list of child-perfect beaches. Do come at low tide, though, when your children can run and shriek for long distances. They can find large areas of wet sand to build castles and throw Frisbees, and almost equally large areas of dry sand in which to roll. Check the notes on wind and sun, though, before choosing your time. Remember that the water is warm only near the edge of an incoming afternoon tide. If your child ventures much deeper into the otherwise enticing water, be prepared to improvise a hypothermia treatment.

**Suitability for groups** As for children, so for groups. While you might want to take your clan reunion to the park at the other end of the beach, any medium-sized group, including a kindergarten class or a seniors rambling club, could come to this spot with a good chance they will find the parking, picnicking space and beach play area that make for a good group site.

**View** For those photographers and sketchers who prefer a view with lots of promontories, rocks, overlapping curves and the like to wide open vistas, this approach to Gonzales Bay has it all.

**Winds, sun and shade** Winds from both the southeast and southwest blow more or less directly into the bay, but are not nearly as strong here as they are on the exposed coast on either side. Morning is a little shady, but by late morning and through the afternoon you will be in more or less full sun. There is reprieve, though: on the three terraced areas behind the beach, huge leafy trees overhang grassy slopes.

**Beachcombing** Come at low tide so that you can fully appreciate the space on the beach. At low tide you can also walk out to the reefs—though be prepared to get wet feet since the low-tide sand has many tidal pools.

**Seclusion** The only time you will be secluded here is during the winter. Most visitors, though, use the park at the other end of the sandy strip, so you will never feel cramped or part of a crowd. If you want to parade your studio tan, go to the other end of the beach.

* **Also nearby** **Gonzales Beach Park** has all of the facilities required of a beach park. It is well signposted a short distance to the west of the Foul Bay approach.

# 78

## HOLLYWOOD CRESCENT

**An unlikely approach between shorefront houses to a solid-rock shelf on the promontory between Gonzales Bay and Ross Bay**

**Location, signs and parking** It is easy to miss this access point, even when you know approximately where it is. As you drive along Hollywood Crescent, the section of the shorefront scenic drive between Gonzales Bay and Ross Bay, look for a house numbered 1807. If your observation skills are honed, you will catch sight of what looks like a paved drive flanked by houses and leading to the brink of a cliff. This is what you're after! You will have to park along the curb of Hollywood Crescent and walk down the paved drive until you see a functional-looking little sign saying NO PARKING, NO DUMPING and, a little reluctantly, PUBLIC ACCESS.

**Path** Your path begins as a few wide concrete steps and becomes a flight of 20 wooden stairs—and a convenient site for a photo shoot. Be a little careful on these stairs since they are set close to the ground and weeds can grow through them, partially covering the stairs. The steps end on a kind of concrete platform built right into the solid rock, surrounded by a railing.

**Beach** If you also visit the other access spot on Hollywood Crescent, you may be surprised at how the shorefront compares. Here the rock of the upper shore is much more gently rounded, sometimes so smooth as to have a gleaming polish in bright sunshine. The almost level areas of rock just above the high-tide line give way to an increasingly steep and rough lower shore. On this lower shore you will find lots of interesting tidal pools and intertidal critters. The thick kelp beds just below the low-tide line give a distinctive character to the shore as well. Although most will find this spot appropriate for an intriguing but short visit, those who wish to linger to absorb the sunshine and view will find several areas where they can sit comfortably.

**Suitability for children** With the full facilities and sandy beach of Gonzales Beach Park so close by, there is no obvious reason to bring a child here, unless your child is a cooperative companion for your own explorations of this unusual spot.

**Suitability for groups** The parking is much too restricted for more than a few friends or a single family.

**View** The spot provides an unfamiliar perspective on familiar landmarks. With Clover Point just out of sight around the headland to your right, your view will be directed to the low, bleak promontory called Harling Point, the striking location of the Chinese Cemetery. Beyond the point you can see Templar Rock and the low profile of the main Trial Island with its light at Staines Point. Beyond, of course, is the magnificent sweep of the Strait of Juan de Fuca and the Olympic Mountains.

**Winds, sun and shade** This is a great place to visit when the elements are at their most furious. Nothing protects this shore from the full blast of storms sweeping up the strait, although the rare northeasterly storm will blow offshore. Likewise, the sun is partly behind you during the morning and full frontal on a sunny afternoon.

**Beachcombing** Do not come here to stretch your legs. The shore is too limited and awkward for that. You don't have to be a rock climber, though, to enjoy exploring the shore for a short distance on either side of the access stairs.

**Seclusion** Almost no one visits this spot because, presumably, almost no one outside of the immediate area knows that it exists. Even though the shore seems deserted, none of the houses here has significant shorefront vegetation, and most are built far forward onto the rock shore and held aloft by high retaining walls. Their backyard view will likely include you.

## 79

### WILDWOOD AVENUE

A flight of shallow concrete steps to a wide, rugged shoreline on a promontory

**Location, signs and parking** Hollywood Crescent winds through a congested neighbourhood between Ross Bay and Gonzales Bay. Opposite Wildwood Avenue you will find a paved access strip between houses with two telltale signs. One tells you that "overnight parking and sleeping" is forbidden, another that you must keep your pooch on a leash and clean up her "deposits." A couple of cars could park here, but in a pinch, more could squeeze along the side of Hollywood Crescent.

**Path** A set of about 40 concrete steps—awkwardly shallow—brings you to a railed concrete landing before a few more steps deposit you onto the shore.

**Beach** A bit of the shore could actually pass muster as a beach, if by that you mean a tiny section of pebbles on which a blanket could be spread and on which a sunhat could be donned. This section is to be found to the immediate left of the access area and, a little oddly, at the base of a giant retaining wall belonging to the residence immediately above it. Otherwise, the shore is really a large exposed area of solid rock, lined with a few beach logs, and dotted, near the low-tide line, with a few small tidal pools. Unusually thick kelp beds line the rocks, saying something about the richness of the nutrients in the water.

**Suitability for children** To enjoy this shore, a child will have to be good at jumping around jungle gyms or else interested in the watery goings-on of hermit crabs, sea stars and the like.

**Suitability for groups** Only a small group with a particular interest in the view would want to come to this more or less inaccessible and unknown rocky promontory.

**View** From this promontory you will see Clover Point on one side and Harling Point on the other, with Templar Rock, offshore reefs and the southern tip of Trial Island all punctuating the scene. The magnificent backdrop of the Olympic Mountains, of course, amplifies the beauty of the view.

**Winds, sun and shade** Come here during a westerly storm and you'll experience as much sound and fury as you're going to experience anywhere along these shores. There is no protection from any of the elements, in fact. On the rare hot and still day the spot can seem sun-baked in spite of the cool air off the icy currents that run past the coast.

**Beachcombing** If you are well shod and like this kind of thing, you can join your adventurous child in exploring the challenging rocky shore for some distance, but don't expect to go very far, very fast.

**Seclusion** Few trees shield you from the many houses built about as far forward as they can be, even to the edge of monumental retaining walls. Every move you make can be observed—unless, that is, you find a nook in the rock or retreat with your diary and sunscreen to the pebbly bit of beach to the left of the access spot.

**★ Also nearby**

**A.** The shore stretching from Ross Bay to the end of **Dallas Road** epitomizes the incomparable Victoria waterfront: Clover Point, Finlayson Point, Holland Point Park, Beacon Hill Park, Ogden Point Breakwater. Any and every tourist and citizen of Victoria has—or should be ashamed if they haven't—visited this strip of scenic splendour so often that they should have it burned into their sensibility forever.

**B.** The waterfront strip on the south shore of Victoria's **Inner Harbour**, from Fisherman's Wharf Park to Laurel Point Park, is only slightly less well known than the Dallas Road shorefront. It is such a natural extension of the tourist route, however, that it needs only the briefest mention.

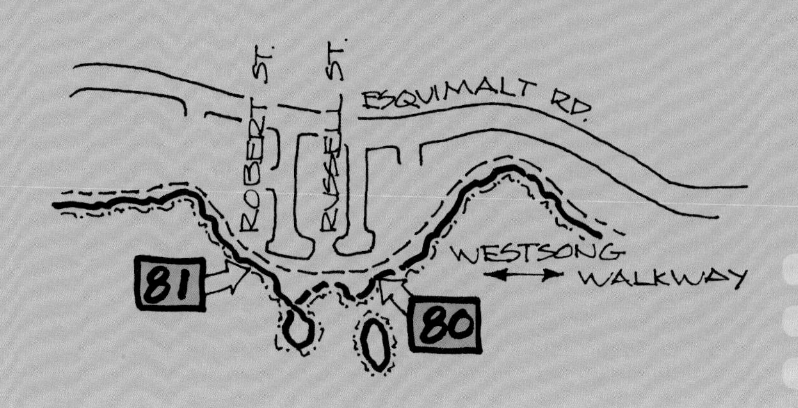

## 80

### RUSSELL STREET

**A tiny, flat promontory and ramp, good for kayaks, giving access to Victoria Harbour**

**Location, signs and parking** In Vic West, on the west side of the Inner Harbour, Russell Street is one of many streets running north to south off Esquimalt Road and giving access to the walkway that stretches between Songhees and West Bay. For those not interested in the walkway, the shore at the foot of Russell Street makes an intriguing destination—especially for those looking for a spot to launch a kayak. While some of the signs here will probably not affect your planning (prohibiting, for example, skateboarding!), the one telling you about the 3-hour parking limit may well be relevant if you are planning to kayak from here. Dog walkers must bring a leash and plastic bags, but can apparently come here year round. There is plenty of parking in the small lot, but if it happens to be full you will find similar arrangements at the end of Robert Street and Mary Street on either side of Russell.

**Path** Head to your left out of the parking area for a gradually sloping path to the esplanade. Farther along another gradually sloping path brings you first to a promontory and, in turn, down a few steps to the concrete ramp reaching almost to low tide.

**Beach** If you are looking for an unusual place for a picnic, this is a good spot to choose for the two options it affords. First, you will find a picnic table splendidly located on a small grassy promontory. Second, around this promontory you may find comfortable spots on the gradually sloping solid-rock upper shore. Those with a kayak on their roof rack, though, will have only one thing on their mind. At the lowest tide, the ramp is overgrown with rockweed and drops off a little steeply, but can be managed with a little deftness.

**Suitability for children** Without the lure of a cookie-rich picnic to tempt them, most children will not be all that thrilled about coming to this very limited spot. There is little space for them to do much and there are plenty of slippery rocks on which to come to grief.

**Suitability for groups** A small group could be satisfied with picnicking or capturing the fascinating view through one medium or another. The only other group that is suitable is one looking for a distinctive background for a wedding or family photo shoot. Easy parking and well-groomed paths make the spot perfect for such a group.

**View** It really is the view—starting with the fine stand of arbutus by the parking area and continuing around the whole complex shoreline—that should put this high on anyone's list of key places to visit. Coffin Island to the right, thus named by early settlers since First Nations people used this as a burial site, and Colville Island in the centre, add bleak, decorative touches in the foreground, completely out of sync with the rest of the urbanized view beyond.

**Winds, sun and shade** Except for a little shade by the parking area, the spot provides virtually no protection from wind or sun, especially not on the little promontory with the picnic bench.

**Beachcombing** Don't come here to expect a beach walk, though if you have sturdy shoes and the green algae isn't too thick on the low-tide rocks, you will enjoy making your way out to two sets of reefs and islets on your right. Otherwise, of course, you can use this as the starting point for a long walk along the shorefront esplanade.

**Seclusion** Even in dodgy weather the shorefront walk is well used. The thickets of apartments and condominiums in this high-rent area guarantee that though the crowds won't be madding, they will be plentiful.

* **Also nearby** Slightly off the radar for some Victorians and visitors, but nevertheless hugely popular, is the **Westsong Walkway**, a shorefront esplanade that starts at Songhees Point just south of the Johnston Street Bridge and goes all the way to West Bay in Esquimalt. Also called the Songhees Walkway, it passes through Rainbow Park, Lime Bay Park and Barnard Park and then takes on the name of West Bay Walkway or Promenade, the division in names from Songhees to West Bay dating to the days when the paths had not yet been connected. Almost every street running north to south in the Victoria West and West Bay neighbourhoods gives access to this walkway.

## 81

### ROBERT STREET—RAINBOW PARK

One of two adjacent approaches to the shorefront and its walkway between Songhees and West Bay

**Location, signs and parking** Most of the north-to-south streets in this area give you access to the shorefront path that runs all the way between Songhees Point and West Bay Marina. Rainbow Park lies between Robert and Russell streets (see previous access point). If you are not interested in the walkway but only in getting to an interesting bit of shore, come to the end of Robert Street off Esquimalt Road, then turn left onto Milne Street with its well-defined parking area. You will also see a sign for Rainbow Park. Be careful not to do a separate GPS computer search for either Milne Street or Rainbow Park. On some maps Milne Street is inaccurately shown as connecting through to Russell Street. On the other hand, if you do a search for Rainbow Park you will be sent to a different Rainbow Park in Saanich. The signs bristling on various posts are too many to list here, but the most relevant one restricts your visiting time to three hours—probably more than enough, considering the size of the shore. You can bring your eager dog here for a walk winter or summer but most obey leash restrictions and, of course, clean up "deposits."

**Path** Concrete paths take you down gentle slopes—past, be it noted, a drinking fountain—to the level concrete walkway. For those with walking difficulties, this approach to the walkway is easy, but walking on the shore itself is considerably more challenging. For access to the shore, turn right and you will find a short flight of concrete steps.

**Beach** The shore is interestingly configured, with a generally steep beach linked at low tide to the tiny islets that make up Coffin Island, once a First Nations burial site. To your right, the shore dips into a deep little bay. The real point in coming to this spot and treating it as not just a part of the well-known walkway, but a little-known and little-used access spot, is making your way at low tide out to the weathered islets. Here you can climb around a little and find a charming nook to remove yourself from the joggers and strollers along the walkway. The gravelly shore itself could be usable as well, but is often covered with green algae—its growth encouraged, perhaps, by the run-off from lawn fertilizers used in the manicured gardens of the area.

**Suitability for children** Children could well enjoy the feeling of exploring the tiny islets, but only for a short time and with a patient parent. This is not the place to bring a child who wants to play freely.

**Suitability for groups** If you have a small group strolling the walkway, you might want to treat them to this detour. It is hard to imagine, however, making this small spot the destination for more than two or three friends or a family.

**View** The chief attractions of the spot are its view and the novelty of its perspective on a familiar scene. The prettily convoluted shoreline of the east side of the harbour is in the foreground. Closing in on the shoreline from all sides is the heavily urbanized but charming world of the Inner Harbour, including the Coho, on its way to or from Port Angeles. Because you are a little offshore, too, you can enjoy an unusual view back on the whole foreshore area.

**Winds, sun and shade** There is no protection from any of the elements here, especially if you sit for some time on the most accessible islet.

**Beachcombing** Walkers will, of course, use the walkway and not attempt to go very far along the shore. Nevertheless, if you head toward the Russell Street access, a short distance east, you could walk on the shore itself.

**Seclusion** This is one of the busiest and most visible spots in the whole Victoria area—but don't be surprised if you are alone on the islet.

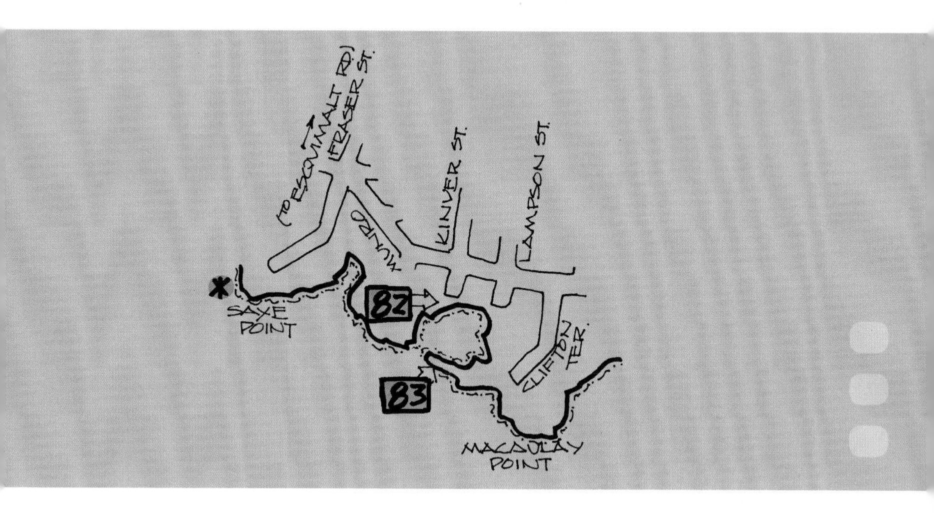

## 82 FLEMING BAY—MACAULAY POINT PARK

A protected boat launch area with shorefront trails leading to the exposed, sun-bleached bluffs of Macaulay Point

**Location, signs and parking** Macaulay Point Park and its beach on the east side of Fleming Bay is one of the few large parks in this book—included because it is far away from well-beaten paths. The ocean side part of the park outside Fleming Bay, in particular, seems to be known by few. Locating the park is easy: simply follow Lampson Street from Esquimalt Road all the way to its end at Munro Street. South of Munro you will find a spacious parking area, washrooms and offices of the Esquimalt Anglers and the Coast Guard. This is obviously a good place to launch kayaks.

Signs alert you to the dangers of rock climbing on the cliffs immediately beyond the parking area—if you are a rock climber, make note to return here when you are kitted out. If you are a dog walker, note the (biologically accurate) visual prompt for cleaning up after the dog, and the sign restricting dogs to leashes but only on the first part of the path ahead. Here is a chance for your hyperactive golden retriever to go cheerfully berserk. One final sign tells you that the park is open only from dawn to dusk.

If you want quick access to the wild part of Macaulay Point, away from Fleming Bay, without having to walk through the busy and developed area around Fleming Bay, you can use Clifton Terrace, one street east from Lampson along Munro. This approach is a little bizarre, since you will be driving beside a high chain-link fence barricading the National Defence land to your left. In addition, parking is restricted at the end of Clifton Terrace.

**Path** The first part of the path from the Lampson Street parking area is level, good for those with difficulty walking but with a desire to stroll next to the water. To the left of the boat launch area, the path curves along a concrete esplanade around one side of the large bay. Farther along, the path changes significantly, with far too many options to list here. Suffice it to say that you can walk out along the long breakwater at the mouth of Fleming Bay or head off for a long, airy walk along the exposed, low bluffs of Macaulay Point, looking out to the Strait of Juan de Fuca.

**Beach** Those looking for a sandy beach on which to picnic or sprawl will find by an area called Buxton Green a curving shore of soft, dry sand at the end of the esplanade inside the bay. If you are such a person, though, you will probably want to come when the beach is prettiest, at a fairly high tide, since low tide reveals long flats of unattractive slime. The shoreline on the other side of the breakwater is also accessible to beach explorers, but only those who enjoy a scramble over lumpy protrusions of solid rock. Some gorgeous little nooks on this long stretch of irregular shoreline outside Fleming Bay invite nestling with a magazine, a pair of binoculars or a cluttered head needing sorting out. Macaulay Point itself, facing the Strait of Juan de Fuca, presents a long area of fairly smooth rock extending well out from the grassy bluffs, appealing for those who like to sit and relax.

**Suitability for children** The washrooms and romping areas in Macaulay Point Park are compelling features for a child-centric afternoon by the shore. You can provide your child with the most conventional sort of shorefront play by choosing a sunny afternoon when the tide is fairly high and bringing child, towel, bucket and spade to the section of sandy shore at the esplanade. A shady morning at low tide? Probably not.

**Suitability for groups** This is a great place for groups to walk, sketch or bird, and a reasonably good place for a large group to picnic. Lots of parking, lots of space and lots of varied shoreline make for a great group experience.

**View** The views are as diverse as the geography is complex. In general, though, you can expect to linger over the enclosed views of Fleming Bay itself, and from atop Macaulay Point, the expansive views down the Strait of Juan de Fuca terminating in the tapering range of the Olympic Mountains. If you continue to the east end of the park, you will have intriguing views not just of Harrison Island lighthouse, but across the various headlands of Esquimalt Harbour to the right and over to the Ogden Point wharves and breakwater.

**Winds, sun and shade** A good reason exists for the sparse vegetation on Macaulay Point. If there is wind, then it's blowing here. If there is sun, then it's shining here. Think of this as a kind of shorefront Wuthering Heights. Come prepared to savour nature at its most elemental.

**Beachcombing** This is a great area for lots of walking, but most of it will be above the shore rather than on the shore, except when you are poking through tidal pools.

**Seclusion** While Fleming Beach is busy and public, Macaulay Point Park is not. Few people come to the park, not just because this end of Esquimalt isn't well known, but also because the park is wedged in between the ocean and a huge chunk of National Defence property. Even on a hot summer's day, expect the crowds here to be a tiny fraction of those on the well-known areas around the Victoria waterfront.

# 83

## KINVER STREET

**A shorefront patch of grass with park benches and a view of the sheltered waters of Fleming Bay**

**Location, signs and parking** The two most likely approaches to Fleming Beach are either along Munro Street, if you are heading east from Saxe Point Park direction, or down Lampson and onto Munro, if you are coming from anywhere else. In either case you will see Kinver Street leading directly to an open, grassy area where there is plenty of parking. No signs, at present, tell you what you must and mustn't do, so you will have to fall back on common sense.

**Path** There is no path to speak of because there is no beach to speak of. In fact, this is a good place to come with those who have difficulty walking and want the comfort of a bench seat right beside the ocean.

**Beach** This is one place where your mastery of the tide tables is essential. Read the introduction to this book if you've skipped it in your rush to get to the beach. If you come at low tide, you will wonder why you bothered to come at all. It would be the peculiar sensibility that would find much pleasure in the slimy expanse of broken rock and decaying concrete or would be induced to defy the sign warning you to keep off because of the danger of the "storm sewer outfall." If you come at high tide, however, and are planning only to sprawl on the grass or perch on one of the benches, then you can have a pleasant and protected shorefront experience.

**Suitability for children** As a favour for those children who have any energy at all, drive the extra block to Fleming Beach and its path to Macaulay Point Park. One strategy might be to come here for a picnic on the grass, since the spot would be conveniently close to a car full of awkward Tupperware containers and drink bottles, before moving onto the neighbouring park for a romp.

**Suitability for groups** There is room for a few cars' worth of folk in search of a grassy spot on which to picnic or sketch, but make sure the group's intentions match limited shorefront options.

**View** Do not come here if you are looking for an untrammelled view of distant horizons and open seas. In fact, don't come here if you want any sort of normal sea view. This is a view of a bay almost entirely closed off from the open waters by a long breakwater. Some will find the scene fascinating; others will be bored.

**Winds, sun and shade** There is plenty of sun and wind all day, though the afternoon is the sunniest when the sun has swung around to the front.

**Beachcombing** Look at the notes in the Beach section and take your walking legs elsewhere.

**Seclusion** This is a highly developed area with lots of houses overlooking one end of the bay, but it is not generally a busy one.

* **Also nearby** **Saxe Point Park** is probably not well known to all Victorians, but certainly is much loved by Esquimalt residents. The biggest and most dramatically beautiful park in the area, it combines several kilometres of walkways with groomed gardens, deep forest paths, viewpoints from exposed bluffs, small pebbly coves and the usual big-park facilities. Dog owners in particular might note that one area of the park is given over to off-leash dog use.

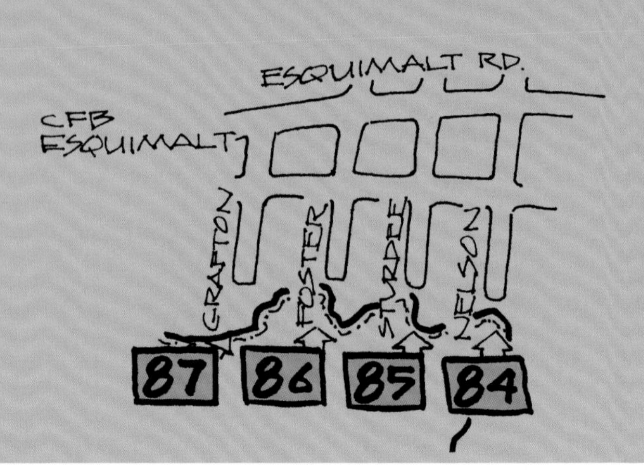

## 84

### NELSON STREET

**An elaborate sequence of cedar stairs leading to a viewing terrace overlooking the end of a small cove**

**Location, signs and parking** Depending on which direction you approach Nelson Street from, it is the first or fourth of four streets at the west end of Esquimalt, each of which ends with an access to a small cove. The parking at the end of Nelson is not easy, but it is a little less restricted here than along the similar streets to those nearby access spots. At present, no signs place restrictions on the use of the area, so visitors will have to dig deep into their reserve of good old-fashioned consideration for others.

**Path** The path is the reason for coming to the spot—that, at least, and the sequence of views. From the end of the paved turnaround the handrails of the first flight of cedar stairs are clearly visible. From here, prepare to be amazed and charmed by the sequence of stairs, platforms and bridges that bring you to a semicircular, railed deck complete with park bench. En route you will have passed another bench. A chain-link fence on one end of the platform makes it assertively clear that you are not to use the private bit of shore beyond to get down onto the beach itself.

**Beach** No easy access to the shore exists, though it is only a short vertical distance below the end of the stairs and it is possible to scramble down. The beach is probably at its prettiest at mid to high tide, when the intricate shoreline is most highlighted and when the low-tide area of weed-covered rock is submerged. The upper beach of pebbles is only a few metres wide and backed by a low wall of natural rock. On either side of the cove, vertical walls of solid rock are overhung with some natural vegetation and some garden trees.

**Suitability for children** A compliant child, or one susceptible to bribes or threats, might accompany an adult or matched set of parents for a snack or quiet visit on the platform. Obviously, however, you would not choose this spot if pleasing your child is your first priority.

**Suitability for groups** Three or four people, at most, can be comfortable here. Really, though, there is very, very little space.

**View** Along with the wonderfully elaborate set of stairs, the view of the charming little craggy cove and its glimpses of the distant shores of Colwood and Albert Head makes this a "must" spot for anyone who wants to explore Victoria's unusual accesses.

**Winds, sun and shade** Since it is the view you're after, come when the view is best and you are most inclined to rest. That means not just high tide, but afternoon, when the cove is flooded with light, or even better, perhaps, evening, when you might be lucky to have a ringside seat on a glorious sunset. Westerlies can blow directly into the cove, but they do so only appreciably when they are strong enough to kick up a few whitecaps farther out.

**Beachcombing** There is no beachcombing. None.

**Seclusion** You will be well within the sightlines of neighbouring houses, but their main windows are directed out to sea, not toward the head of the cove where you will be spending your quiet half-hour. Don't expect to be secluded, of course, but at least you will not feel exposed to direct observation.

# 85

## STURDEE STREET

**A long flight of concrete steps to a deeply cleft cove with morning shade and afternoon sun**

**Location, signs and parking** Sturdee Street leaves Esquimalt Road three blocks before the National Defence Dockyard property and leads directly to a paved turnaround. Although the situation can change quickly, at present, no signs indicate this to be public access, as it so clearly is—and no signs provide other restrictions or advice. Parking can be an issue, so be careful to check the restrictions on residential parking.

**Path** From the road itself, a few steps take you past a park bench to the beginning of a long flight of more than 30 concrete steps in three stages down a wooded bank. The last step onto the fairly steep section of solid rock can be a little tricky, so be careful.

**Beach** Like the two nearby access spots in either direction, this one is at the end of a tiny cove. In this case, however, the cove is more like a long cleft deep into the steeply sloping rock of the shore. The upper beach of fine pebbles is often littered with small pieces of driftwood and is backed by a concrete retaining wall under the bushy bank. If the pebbly section is more or less clear of debris and rotting seaweed it can be inviting. Otherwise... not. Low tide exposes a considerable strip of increasingly rocky and weed-covered shore buttressed on either side by the steep shore. Come at mid to high tide in the afternoon for the prettiest take on the beach. At low tide in the morning it can seem dark and slimy.

**Suitability for children** Like the other three spots in this short strip of four similar access spots, this one is much, much too restricted for children who want to romp or rollick. A child or two could, however, be fed into compliance while parents bask or read.

**Suitability for groups** As with children, so for groups. This is a tiny cove with restricted parking and houses that crowd in all around. Go to Saxe

Point Park nearby or include this as part of a walking tour through the neighbourhood, as some walking groups do.

**View** From the bench or partway down the steps, the view over the layers of projecting bluffs toward Saxe Point cries out to be photographed or emblazoned into your memory. From the tiny beach, you might find the view to be charmingly framed by the high, rocky shore, or more restricted than your senses crave.

**Winds, sun and shade** The cove is deep enough to provide considerable shelter from most winds, though westerlies blowing up the Strait of Juan de Fuca can provide a considerable cooling effect—and gratefully so on a hot afternoon when the sun bakes the pebbly beach. In the morning the beach is almost entirely in shade and can seem a little dank and uninviting.

**Beachcombing** You can do a little low-tide investigation of the local sea star and crab populations, especially in the section to the left of the cove. Other than that, do not come here with the expectation of taking more than a few steps from your munching or meditating spot.

**Seclusion** Only a few locals use the spot, so the chances are that on a warm afternoon you could spend an hour here without seeing a single soul. Even better, the houses on either side are set back among the trees in such a way that you will feel you have made an escape into a hidden cove rather than forced your way into someone's front yard. At the same time, be fully aware that you are coming to a spot immediately adjoining a densely populated neighbourhood.

## 86

### FOSTER STREET

**A charming set of brick steps leading to a tiny, pebbly cove with a porthole-like view**

**Location, signs and parking** Foster Road leads directly toward the water from the end of Esquimalt Road two blocks before the dockyard at Canadian Forces Base Esquimalt. Parking is a huge issue here since much of Foster Road bristles with signs telling you that parking is for residents only. To visit this tiny, charming spot, you are probably best off parking a few blocks away and including it in a walking exploration of nearby beach spots. Visit Grafton Street in one direction and Nelson and Sturdee in the other. The only other sign is of an anchor painted onto a low concrete wall.

**Path** Anyone who has been to some of the tiny village coves of Devon and Cornwall might find striking resemblances to this miniature, manicured spot. A carefully crafted little wall with a crafted little bench leads to a crafted set of curving, little brick-lined steps to a crafted little shore-top path—and the entirely natural, little bit of beach.

**Beach** The path deposits you onto a bit of solid rock underfoot and a few beach logs. Immediately below you will see a few metres of pebbly beach, dropping down another few metres to a weed-covered lower beach of larger rocks. The end of the cove is overhung on your left with a dramatic little bluff of sheer rock—and, more or less, the front yard of the neighbouring house.

**Suitability for children** If you have a child who is happy to stay put and be amused within a tiny area of pebbles and, at high tide, nearby water, then you could come here with a book, an iPod or a half-hour of empty time. Most children, of course, do not fit such a description.

**Suitability for groups** Include this, as some local groups do, as part of a morning's walk or, possibly, as the destination for a miniature picnic. Otherwise, don't forget nearby Saxe Point Park and its extensive facilities.

**View** Some might find the view, like the cove itself, a little cramped. Others will be charmed by the very narrowness of the porthole-like view past the rocky cliffs on either side of the beach. Lovers of the broad and open vistas will prefer to gaze from the bench at the top of the path.

**Winds, sun and shade** Wind from a westerly can funnel directly into the cove, but is softened considerably. Morning, even on a hot day, can seem a little shady and damp. By mid morning and throughout the afternoon, however, this shore on a still, sunny day can vary from warm right through to blistering.

**Beachcombing** You would be hard-pressed to find a spot with less beach to comb.

**Seclusion** Paradoxically, this is both private and public. Although the spot is right at the edge of a neighbourhood, and houses perch on the promontories on either side of the little cove, you and just one significant other can experience considerable seclusion. All it takes is one stranger and that sense of seclusion will evaporate.

Foster Street

# 87

## GRAFTON STREET—DENNISTON PARK

A groomed entrance to an unusual concrete walkway built into the side of a steep, craggy shore

**Location, signs and parking** One of several roads leading south from Esquimalt Road toward the shore, Grafton Street is the last public road you encounter before the National Defence Dockyard. Two short blocks take you to a prettified and manicured turnaround area ornamented with a spanking sign bearing the name of the park.

**Path** A wide, paved path takes you through a less kempt grassy bluff with a picnic table and picturesque rock outcroppings and seems to disappear into the area of jagged shore. At this point you will realize that your destination is the path, and not the shore itself. You might feel a little like a character in a James Bond film as the narrow, heavily weathered concrete walkway leads to a chain-link gate—but do press on, since the gate is open and a sign on the gate reassures you that the walkway beyond is still public access. The walkway continues its dramatic way in the small cliffside a few metres above the shore until you come across another sign, decoratively telling you that you are leaving "Esquimalt Parks Property"—but not making clear whether you are forbidden to carry on.

**Beach** Strolling languidly along the shore is not the reason for coming here, though it is possible to climb down the solid rock to explore sea life. Doing so, in fact, at least at low tide, is something that you should seriously consider, especially if you are not used to the intertidal life of the west coast of Vancouver Island. Here you will see species you generally find only on the exposed coast farther into the Strait of Juan de Fuca. Most obviously, look for the striking green surf grass and the Martian-looking gooseneck barnacles. You may be tempted to consider this a good spot for casting your rod from the rocks, but do be aware—as the offshore kelp beds will signal to you—that the water is not very deep directly in front of the rocky shore.

**Suitability for children** Bring older children for a bit of a walk and an opportunity to look at unusual shore life. Don't bring them here for free-spirited romping and running while you lose yourself in your thoughts—or you may lose more than just yourself.

**Suitability for groups** You will want to put this spot high on your list as a place to explore with a few like-minded friends, but more than a few friends or family members will be falling all over each other on the cramped little path.

**View** Photographers and artists will purr with pleasure here. Diversity reigns—everything from the thickly forested Saxe Point to your left, through the Olympics fading into the distance, and to the right, the rocky little Brothers Islands just offshore from the jutting rocks leading to the National Defence Dockyard area.

**Winds, sun and shade** If you wish to linger at this spot, you can find shade in the grassy area under the odd tree. Otherwise, from mid morning throughout the rest of the day this area soaks up almost every ray available. Much the same is true of winds. If you want to strike a romantic figure, let your tresses down on a windy day, or perch on the rocks, knowing that you will be windblown within an inch of your life.

**Beachcombing** Although the concrete walkway invites relaxed strolling, the steep, jagged shore does not. The rocks exposed at low tide do invite some casual poking around the unusual sea life.

**Seclusion** This little park is in a heavily populated area and, unsurprisingly, can be a favourite place for early morning strollers. Don't, however, expect to see more than the odd person and do expect, once you've gone along the walkway a short distance, to feel wonderfully hidden.

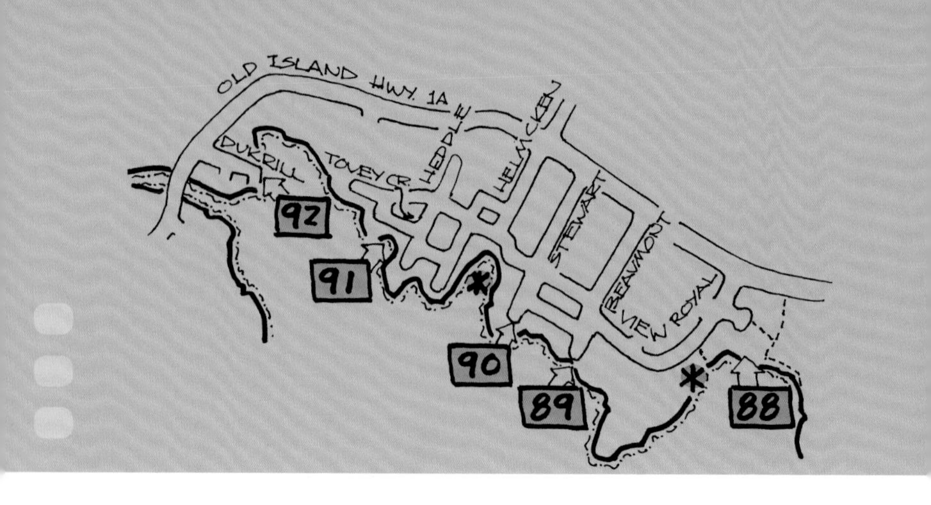

# 88

## PORTAGE REGIONAL PARK

A little-known and secluded park with pebble and sand beach and views of Thetis Cove

**Location, signs and parking** Although Portage Regional Park is large and beautiful, don't be surprised if not even many residents living in close proximity know it exists or how to get into it. Development of the immediate surroundings has meant that the park is virtually invisible to all but informed insiders. But take heart. Once you know where to go, the getting there is comparatively easy. The park actually stretches along part of the Island Highway (1A) just south of Four Mile Pub, but unless you are on foot or on a bicycle, don't try to approach from here. If you do want to use the old, largely unmarked entrance close to the pub, you might treat yourself to a pub lunch and then walk a short distance down the highway until you see a closed fire gate and a crushed-gravel service road leading into the woods. If you put aside the lunch for later, turn off the old highway onto View Royal Avenue and immediately left past the pub into the parking area for the View Royal Municipal Hall. Look carefully for a concrete structure indicating the entrance to the park and more parking. The lot can be crowded when the goings-on of municipal governance are of more interest than the park, so you might want to choose a weekend or evening for your visit. Unsurprisingly, you are not allowed to leave your car overnight, between 10 p.m. and an unusually early 5 a.m. Another sign of particular interest to owners of free-spirited chihuahuas tells you that this is an off-leash area.

**Path** Large, welcoming signs will direct you to the wide and well-maintained trail. After a short distance, the trail descends down a dozen or so wooden steps but generally is level and smooth, so those with only slight walking difficulties should be fine here. When you come to a junction in the path, turn right for the shore. A total of about 100 m will bring you to a grassy area above a curious steep, pebbly bank at the head of Thetis Cove. From here you may choose to walk directly onto the pebbly beach or, if you prefer, you can take a smaller dirt track running above the shore to the left. Because this is the site of an ancient First Nations village, some of the shore is closed for archeological work. The user-made trail leads all the way toward a housing area and to a fairly steep dirt track to the east end of the cove.

**Beach** Because Thetis Cove, tucked deep within Esquimalt Harbour, is so well protected from the sound and fury of the open straits—hence its choice by First Nations people of long ago—the shore itself is a little squelchy. The pebbly part of the upper shore, where the main path leads, is probably the choice for those who want to feast on celery sticks or sunshine. Those who want sand, however, can climb over the rocky outcropping to the left, and find a considerable stretch of fine but fairly soft, wet sand.

**Suitability for children** Although the path can be a bit of a trek for stubby little legs and there are no facilities by the beach, this is a safe, pleasant spot for the young 'uns. If sand pies are on the menu for the afternoon, head to the left down the beach, but be prepared for a slightly messy cleanup.

**Suitability for groups** The park may be large, but it does not offer the washrooms and picnic tables some groups might want. Other groups, however, bent on other pleasures, will find lots of room to wander and chat, sketch or munch.

**View** Be prepared to be charmed and surprised by the view, even if you are familiar with most of the views from the obvious spots around the

Victoria waterfront. Richards Island in the middle of the cove will lead your eyes past private boat docks, across the bumps and protrusions of Esquimalt, and to the surprisingly woody shores of east Colwood and the distant Olympic Mountains.

**Winds, sun and shade** The First Nations people who sometimes sheltered here knew what they were about. No waves and only a little wind from the west make their way into the recesses of the cove. Since there are no trees in the main, pebbly area, come prepared with all the sun protection you need for an extended stay here, though the sun is largely from the back and side until afternoon. Shade aplenty is available under the thick trees of the park.

**Beachcombing** Most of your walking will be through the trails. You can walk 100 m or so along the shore, if you can make it over the rocky outcropping at high tide, but will feel little temptation to explore the low-tide line.

**Seclusion** The spot is used by local dogs who bring their owners here, but otherwise it is amazingly quiet. You will feel that you have discovered an oasis of wooded solitude in an otherwise suburban area.

* **Also nearby** A GREEN AREA is signposted on the bend of **View Royal Avenue** shortly after the turnoff for Portage Regional Park. While you could make your way along the winding dirt track down the wet, wooded bank, you will find yourself merely at the west end of Thetis Cove. If you need a fast and dirty route to the cove to check out the bird count, this is a good alternative to the long path through the adjoining park, but otherwise it has few charms to make it preferable to the park route.

# 89

## BEAUMONT AVENUE

**A park-like approach to a sun-baked solid-rock shore with beautiful views beyond Esquimalt Harbour to Fisgard Lighthouse**

**Location, signs and parking** Since Beaumont Avenue leaves Highway 1A, you need only follow it to its end and find one of many parking spots along the shoulder of the road or immediately in front of the park-like entrance. The mulch pathway, waste bin and short bit of fencing are obvious indications that you've reached the right spot. In any case, you will see two signs, one announcing this to be the BEAUMONT SHORELINE ACCESS and bearing the characteristic logo of many View Royal access points. Another sign will implicitly remind you that you will have to take your midnight carousing or snoozing elsewhere. On the way to the shore, which runs along Tovey Bay, you will see another sign warning you that you are in a TSUNAMI HAZARD ZONE. You will be forgiven for being puzzled by the sign since the shoreline is high here and since you might discover an identical sign is posted at the end of nearby Norquay Road, where the even higher shore has no open shore access at all. To add yet more puzzlement, you will find that there is no such sign at the Tovey Crescent shoreline access, also nearby. Presumably, whoever was in charge of such signs calculated that a tsunami could funnel into the bay in such a way as to produce a huge surge at this particular high spot. Presumably.

**Path** After descending gradually for 30 or so metres, the wood mulch path arrives at a park bench and a set of stairs leading in two stages down about 25 steps onto a small area of rock.

**Beach** The use of the term "shoreline" rather than "beach" in the sign at the beginning of the path could hardly be more appropriate. You will find yourself on a small area of largely rounded, solid rock. Even at low tide, not much shore is exposed since it drops steeply toward the water. You might expect to be able to fish from the rocks here, and perhaps can, but beware: the bottom drops quickly to only about 8 m and then levels out. To your left, under a huge arbutus, you will see a small cove with a pebbly upper beach. Technically, you could make your way there and use the beach but, since it is in front of a private residence that is set well back at the top of a bank, you will probably feel most inclined to stay where you are. In fact, you may well find this a comfortable spot to perch with just an iPod, your thoughts or a honeybunch, and plenty of sunscreen.

**Suitability for children** This is a spot for adults, not children. The area is much too confined—and the shoreline too steep—for children to feel happy and their parents to feel comfortable.

**Suitability for groups** Only a small group, with a specific purpose, will come here, not one that wishes to spend a few hours lounging on the shore or picnicking.

**View** The view is really the main reason for coming here, especially if you are interested not just in drinking it in but also in capturing it on film or sketchpad. Although the view is actually quite confined, the combination of elements is striking: small boat jetties, rocky shores with overhanging arbutus, offshore reefs, the wooded shore of the National Defence land, Fisgard Lighthouse (a national historic site) on the far side of Esquimalt Harbour and, of course, the Olympic Mountains, with Mount Olympus itself in the centre of your frame.

**Winds, sun and shade** Although this can be a real sun-and-heat trap on a hot afternoon, most will find this the most pleasant time to visit. The westerlies that can whip up Juan de Fuca Strait are significantly reduced here and no other winds can make their way over the headlands.

**Beachcombing** Picking your way a short distance over the rocks in either direction is as much as you will want to do here.

**Seclusion** The spot is surprisingly secluded—and quiet—given that it is at the edge of a residential area. The configuration of shoreline and vegetation is such that you can expect neither to be seen by others nor to see them.

## 90

### STEWART AVENUE

**A beautiful bit of sunny shore, combining a rocky bluff and miniature pebble beach**

**Location, signs and parking** Stewart Avenue leaves the Island Highway and leads directly to this access spot. Parking for a few cars is comparatively easy near the access strip, though you will find that you are not welcome to park between 10 p.m. and a surprisingly early 5 a.m. You might guess that local residents have either some worries or bad experiences in their minds, too, since an eye-catching black and yellow sign vehemently asserts that no matter where you park you are not welcome on the beach between dawn and dusk. A more welcoming sign bears the View Royal logo and identifies the spot as STEWART SHORELINE ACCESS. A tsunami warning sign tells you to move to higher ground in case of an earthquake, even though you might feel you are already on something that approximates high ground.

**Path** Only a few steps will take you from asphalt, past a hideous, functional-looking metal construction and a park bench to 33 steps down the bank. This is where the path becomes—beautifully—distinctive. Instead of dropping you directly onto the shore, it takes you down to a small, solid-rock peninsula and, perched on top, another bench. To one side of this area, too, there is a slip-retardant metal ramp leading onto the adjoining pebble beach. This particular feature makes this spot the only one in View Royal where launching a kayak is feasible, though, of course, the 30-plus steps would hardly make the undertaking easy.

**Beach** In the smallest possible area, this beach has a little bit of everything—except sand. The small, rocky promontory is rounded enough that it invites you to ensconce yourself comfortably on this viewpoint. Picnickers or sunbathers might prefer the welcoming, tiny beach, with its significant area of loose pebbles above the high-tide line, though usually without the logs some require of a Proper Beach. Another beach, to the left of the promontory, lies within the realm of the neighbours on that side and, in any case, is not as suitable for lounging.

**Suitability for children** Along with Portage Park, this is the best place in View Royal to bring a child. The small beach is for a toddler to toddle and splash a little. An older child will also enjoy mooching around the rocky promontory, particularly at low tide when various slimy creatures are available for prodding.

**Suitability for groups** The area is too confined and the parking too limited for more than one or two families' worth of visitors. It would, however, be criminal not to bring your watercolouring friends here.

**View** Choose mid to high tide and early afternoon if you want to see a pretty spot at its prettiest. Though fairly confined, the view is full of charming elements. You might not be charmed by the Esquimalt dockyards in the distance on your left, but if you can ignore these, you will be more than charmed by the combination of foreground reefs, wooded peninsulas, Fisgard Lighthouse and Olympic Mountains.

**Winds, sun and shade** It can get more than a little warm here on a hot afternoon, since westerly breezes are muted by the angle of the shore and

Stewart Avenue

the headland to the west. Since shade isn't available during the afternoon, make sure your arsenal of sun-protection gear is well stocked.

**Beachcombing** Don't come here expecting to walk more than a few steps in any direction. This is a spot for drinking in sunshine and the view, not for exploring the coast.

**Seclusion** Only by turning toward the shorefront house on your left will you find your seclusion broken. Otherwise, come to this spot expecting to find large portions of peace and quiet, to be either enjoyed alone or shared with another.

* **Also nearby** **Helmcken Road** ends at a prettily maintained, tiny park with a flower planter, a park bench and a gravel path. A LIMEKILN SHORELINE ACCESS sign suggests access to a shore, though the 28 wooden steps lead only to a viewing platform overlooking a deep, little bay. Although few will tempted to do so, you can venture down a rough, bushy track to the shore. Of primary interest here, other than the view itself, is a venerable historic cairn, itself dating from 1959, and, in weathered bronze, telling you that the "gallant ships" from the "old world" came to this spot for water when British Columbia was an "infant colony." It is not clear where the water was to be found since there is now no stream visible.

## 91

### TOVEY CRESCENT

**A hidden, sheltered cover with pebbly upper shore**

**Location, signs and parking** Turn off Highway 1A onto Helmcken. After a right turn onto View Royal, look for Tovey Crescent on your left and follow it to its intersection with Governor's Point Road. You won't see any of the usual signs indicating that you've found a public beach access—signs about parking overnight or leashing dogs, for example—but you will see a meticulously kempt area with a winding crushed gravel path leading through an area of lawn toward a park bench and glimpses of the bay beyond. Parking on the shoulders of the adjoining roads is easy since you won't be running the common gauntlet of NO PARKING signs.

**Path** The level gravel path leads to the edge of a bank and morphs into a recently constructed set of approximately 20 beautifully engineered, broad gravel-and-wood steps set into the wooded bank. Unlike most such steps in the area, these have a handrail—and a very solid one—but on only one side.

**Beach** The path emerges onto a smooth beach of fine gravel at the head of a small, heavily wooded cove. You will find yourself in one of those intriguingly hidden spots that conjure up fantasies of ancient smuggling stories. Who would have thought this spot existed? Nearly enclosed by a forested rocky point on either side, the circular little cove stretches along the beach about 70 or 80 m to your right. Throughout its length the shore is overhung with firs and arbutus. Because it is so protected, it has none of the logs and dry upper shore you would expect on a more exposed shore. While you will find this a fascinating place to visit and commit to photographs or sketches, you will find little inducement to linger. Even then, you will find the spot prettiest at mid or high tide since low tide reveals a somewhat muddy shore.

**Suitability for children** You wouldn't choose this spot if you were looking for somewhere to entertain your child for an afternoon. This is not to say, however, that a child accompanying a curious parent won't immediately start making use of the water and rocks for the purposes nature intended.

**Suitability for groups** This is the kind of spot you visit when you decide to explore a unique shoreline, not the kind of spot where you bring a group.

**View** The charm of the view is that there is no view—at least not in the conventional watery sense. You will feel yourself very much in a hidden world. The cove itself is surrounded by trees. The National Defence land on the opposite side of Esquimalt Harbour not far away adds to the complete visual circle of forest.

**Winds, sun and shade** Choose afternoon for visiting the spot, when the sun floods into the dark little cove and brings it to life. And don't worry about your hat being blown off: the chances of more than a gentle breeze reaching this hidden shore are tiny.

**Beachcombing** You will probably want to walk the short distance around the curving bay to savour the view and appreciate the sense of isolation, but this will be the extent of your shorefront wandering.

**Seclusion** Although houses surround the cove, you and yours will likely be alone and unseen in this emerald world.

## 92 DUKRILL ROAD—MILLSTREAM ESTUARY

**A sheltered view of the south shore of View Royal, and a kilometre-long path along the Millstream Creek estuary**

**Location, signs and parking** Dukrill Road leaves Highway 1A on the Victoria (east) side of the bridge and beside the Capital Regional District Water Services office. Because of parking restrictions, it is easiest to park in the CRD parking lot and walk the 50 m down Dukrill to its end. You will have to find a "visitor" spot with its 30-minute time limit, but on a weekend the time limit doesn't seem to apply. At the junction of Dukrill and Buddy roads you will see a stylish sign identifying this as DUKRILL SHORELINE ACCESS.

**Path** The path begins as a well-maintained, level, crushed-gravel trail bordered by wooden railings and kempt grass. After a few dozen paces you will find yourself at the top of a well-built sequence of concrete steps with wooden railings. Thirty-eight steps take you down, over two stages, to a small, railed concrete platform and access to a level concrete and gravel walkway running parallel to the shore for perhaps 20 m. Once there, another path to the right heads into Parson's Bridge Park, up above the estuary and extending for about a kilometre over several hills and staircases.

**Beach** The beach you encounter at the foot of the stairs is the kind to visit for an intriguing perspective on familiar geography and for a good close-up, at high tide, on the bird population. It is not the kind of place to linger very long, though, in part because there is so little space to do so. Marine charts identify the extensive low-tide flats as "mud" and for good reason. Come at high tide, though, when the flats are covered—and the spot is charming. Immediately below the bottom of the stairs is a tiny, offshore, rocky area that you can reach even when the tide is in by stepping along an awkward but passable walkway of chunks of concrete.

**Suitability for children** A child might accompany a curious adult for a short visit, but will be more intrigued by the path beckoning off to the right.

**Suitability for groups** While groups may also enjoy the path along the estuary to the right and watching for birds, the shore itself provides no space for groups to spread out.

**View** The view is this spot's greatest appeal. While you can just glimpse the open straits beyond the distant bits of the Esquimalt dockyard, the more immediate view will capture your imagination. Your eye will rove along the forests and bluffs of View Royal, where houses peer out of the trees and little private docks extend into this enclosed end of Esquimalt Harbour. Enjoy the picturesque details of the wooded point immediately to your right and Cole Island out in the middle of the bay, an island once used by the Royal Navy for storage and now a national historic site—you can just glimpse the old buildings.

Walk along the Parsons Bridge Park path until you can see down below the outlet of Millstream Creek. Depending on the tide, you can witness the mixing of the creek's fresh water and the ocean's salt water. The creek's bed is clearly visible at low tide, when the low-tide flats glisten with squelchy mud. Birds often flock there, and the view of this area is well worth the trek up the hills and into the valleys.

**Winds, sun and shade** Expect dappled sun and shade for much of the day and increasing shade in the afternoon. The view is probably most attractive in late afternoon when the sun comes from your right and illuminates the shoreline. Wind is almost an alien concept here. Winds can be blustering away out in the straits and barely felt here—a fact not overlooked by the canny seabirds that find shelter in this area.

**Beachcombing** There is no beach to comb, only squelchy low-tide flats. If you don't insist on beach walking, head out on the Parsons Bridge Park path and expect to make a complete circle back to your car. The path snakes around the high shore above the estuary all the way to Parsons Bridge. Intrepid children might, at low tide, venture down rocky cliffs at a few accessible spots to explore the exposed rocks, but the mud is quite possessive of anything that sinks into it, so be forewarned! When the path reaches the bridge, you or the intrepid child could cross under the bridge along a maintenance walkway to the other side, with traffic rumbling overhead, where there is a well-used skateboarders' paradise. You could also take the more staid path and head on up the long flight of steps beside the bridge. You will emerge at the busy highway, across from Six Mile Pub, and can then walk along the highway back to Dukrill Road.

**Seclusion** The spot at the base of Dukrill Road is little visited and seems to have seclusion built into it, overhung by surrounding trees and inset into this cove at the head of the bay, all defining that "hidden feeling." The path along the estuary, however, runs along the front yard of a condominium development, and condo dwellers use the path for walking their dogs. The happy skateboarders seem content with their side of the bridge.

## BEST BETS

All beachgoers will find favourite spots, and for the most personal of reasons. Perhaps one beach will become a favourite because of the configuration of tidal pools. Another one might have a particularly cozy little nest among beach logs. Yet another might have much-needed public toilets. As a starting point, however, many will find the following recommendations handy. (An asterisk indicates that the best bet is described in the entry's "Also nearby" text.)

**1. Launching kayaks or canoes**

2 Mark Lane
7 Ardmore Drive—South
11 Briarwood Place
16 Moses Point Road
18 Seabreeze Road
29 Goddard Road (high tide only)
31 Rothesay Road (high tide only)
32 Tulista Boat Ramp
54 Telegraph Bay
57 Baynes Road (a little awkward)
58 McAnally Road—Smuggler's Cove Road
67 Rutland Road (a little cramped)
70 Lane Street (high tide)
71 Beach Drive—Orchard Avenue
72 Radcliffe Lane—East (high tide)
80 Russell Street
82 Fleming Bay—Macaulay Point Park

**2. Bringing small children**

6 Coles Bay Regional Park
9 Braemar Avenue
11 Briarwood Place
14 Cromar Road
20 Beach Road
22*A Resthaven Park
28 Beaufort Road
30 Amherst Avenue
38 Island View Beach Regional Park
39 Parker Park
43 Cordova Bay Road
44 Gloria Place
45 Cordova Bay Beach Park
50 Arbutus Cove Park
54 Telegraph Bay
58 McAnally Road—Smuggler's Cove Road
62 Telegraph Bay Road—South
63 Killarney Road
69 Bowker Avenue
77 Foul Bay Road—Gonzales Bay
82 Fleming Bay—Macaulay Point Park (high tide)
88 Portage Regional Park

**3. Bringing adventurous children**

1 Gowlland Tod Provincial Park—Mark Lane
6 Coles Bay Regional Park
7 Ardmore Drive—South
8 Aboyne Avenue
13 Towner Park Road
16 Moses Point Road
21 Nymph Point Park
22 Lillian Hoffar Park
23 Bigrock Road
28 Beaufort Road
29 Goddard Road
35 Arthur Drive
36 James Island Road—Saanichton Bay Public Dock
41 Walema Avenue
46 D'Arcy Lane
48 Glencoe Cove Kwatsech Park—North
51 Hollydene Park
66 Lansdowne Road
67 Rutland Road
68 Surrey Road
70 Lane Street
72 Radcliffe Lane—East
76 Crescent Road—Chinese Cemetery
90 Stewart Avenue

**4. Long beach walks or jogs**

- 10 Ardmore Drive—Glenelg Avenue
- 11 Briarwood Place
- 12 Patricia Bay Park
- 13 Towner Park Road
- 23 Bigrock Road
- 24 Bowden Road
- 26 Fifth Street
- 28 Beaufort Road
- 31* Sidney Harbour
- 38 Island View Beach Regional Park
- 39 Parker Park
- 41 Walema Avenue
- 43 Cordova Bay Road
- 44 Gloria Place
- 45 Cordova Bay Beach Park
- 48, 49 Glencoe Cove Kwatsech Park
- 62 Telegraph Bay Road—South
- 63 Killarney Road
- 64 Hibbens Close
- 69 Bowker Avenue
- 70 Lane Street
- 76 Crescent Road—Chinese Cemetery
- 77 Foul Bay Road—Gonzales Bay
- 79*A, B Dallas Road and the Inner Harbour
- 80* Westsong Walkway
- 82 Fleming Bay—Macaulay Point Park

**5. Birdwatching**

- 12 Patricia Bay Park
- 15 Setchell Road
- 20 Beach Road
- 21 Nymph Point Park
- 22 Lillian Hoffar Park
- 23 Bigrock Road
- 24 Bowden Road
- 25 Ardwell Avenue
- 26 Fifth Street
- 27 Third Street
- 28 Beaufort Road
- 29 Goddard Road
- 37 Saanichton Bay Park
- 38 Island View Beach Regional Park (walk to Cordova Spit)
- 46 D'Arcy Lane
- 52 Haro Place
- 57 Baynes Road
- 60 Seaview Road
- 69 Bowker Avenue
- 70 Lane Street
- 72 Radcliffe Lane—East
- 73 Radcliffe Lane—McMicking Point
- 76 Crescent Road—Chinese Cemetery
- 82 Fleming Bay—Macaulay Point Park
- 85 Sturdee Street
- 87 Grafton Street—Denniston Park
- 88 Portage Regional Park
- 89 Beaumont Avenue
- 92 Dukrill Road—Millstream Estuary

**6. Kite flying or Frisbee throwing**

- 12 Patricia Bay Park
- 22 Lillian Hoffar Park (grassy area for Frisbees)
- 28 Beaufort Road
- 29 Goddard Road
- 30 Amherst Avenue
- 38 Island View Beach Regional Park
- 39 Parker Park
- 41 Walema Avenue
- 43 Cordova Bay Road
- 44 Gloria Place
- 45 Cordova Bay Beach Park
- 50 Arbutus Cove Park
- 51 Hollydene Park
- 54 Telegraph Bay (a little limited)
- 62 Telegraph Bay Road—South
- 63 Killarney Road
- 69 Bowker Avenue
- 77 Foul Bay Road—Gonzales Bay
- 82 Fleming Bay—Macaulay Point Park

**7. Bringing groups**

- 6 Coles Bay Regional Park
- 12 Patricia Bay Park
- 21 Nymph Point Park
- 22 Lillian Hoffar Park
- 25 Ardwell Avenue
- 33*A Cy Hampson Park
- 38 Island View Beach Regional Park
- 39 Parker Park
- 43 Cordova Bay Road
- 45 Cordova Bay Beach Park
- 48, 49 Glencoe Cove Kwatsech Park
- 50 Arbutus Cove Park
- 54 Telegraph Bay
- 62 Telegraph Bay Road—South
- 63 Killarney Road

76 Crescent Road—
Chinese Cemetery
77 Foul Bay Road—Gonzales Bay
82 Fleming Park—
Macaulay Point Park
88 Portage Regional Park

**8. Afternoon sunbathing**

3 Keene Way
4 Brentwood Drive
7 Ardmore Drive—South
11 Briarwood Place
12 Patricia Bay Park
14 Cromar Road
23 Bigrock Road
26 Fifth Street
28 Beaufort Road
29 Goddard Road
30 Amherst Avenue
38 Island View Beach Regional Park
43 Cordova Bay Road
45 Cordova Bay Beach Park
54 Telegraph Bay
58 McAnally Road—
Smuggler's Cove Road
59 Tudor Avenue
62 Telegraph Bay Road—South
63 Killarney Road
67 Rutland Road
69 Bowker Avenue
70 Lane Street
72 Radcliffe Lane—East
77 Foul Bay Road—Gonzales Bay
85 Sturdee Street
86 Foster Street
88 Portage Regional Park
89 Beaumont Avenue
90 Stewart Avenue

**9. Seclusion**

1 Gowlland Tod Provincial Park—
Mark Lane
7 Ardmore Drive—South
8 Aboyne Avenue
15 Setchell Road
17 Woodcreek Drive
19 Gullhaven Road
40 Fenn Avenue
41 Walema Avenue
46 D'Arcy Lane
48, 49 Glencoe Cove Kwatsech Park
52 Haro Place
53 Guinevere Road
59 Tudor Avenue
65 Humber Road
67 Rutland Road
72 Radcliffe Lane—East
75 Lorne Terrace
82 Fleming Bay—Macaulay Point Park
85 Sturdee Street
86 Foster Street
87 Grafton Street—Denniston Park
88 Portage Regional Park
89 Beaumont Avenue
90 Stewart Avenue
91 Tovey Crescent
92 Dukrill Road—Millstream Estuary

**10. Protection from northwest winds**

6 Coles Bay Regional Park
17 Woodcreek Drive
21 Nymph Point Park
23 Bigrock Road
24 Bowden Road
28 Beaufort Road
30 Amherst Avenue
58 McAnally Road—
Smuggler's Cove Road
59 Tudor Avenue
62 Telegraph Bay Road—South
68 Surrey Road
71 Beach Drive—Orchard Avenue
72 Radcliffe Lane—East
75 Lorne Terrace
80 Russell Street
88 Portage Regional Park
90 Stewart Avenue
91 Tovey Crescent
92 Dukrill Road—Millstream Estuary

**11. Protection from southeast winds**

4 Brentwood Drive
8 Aboyne Avenue
9 Braemar Avenue
14 Cromar Road
15 Setchell Road
16 Moses Point Road
17 Woodcreek Drive
22 Lillian Hoffar Park
29 Goddard Road

35 Arthur Drive
47 Balmacarra Road
48 Glencoe Cove Kwatsech Park—North (beach)
50 Arbutus Cove Park
51 Hollydene Park
53 Guinevere Place
54 Telegraph Bay
65 Humber Road
68 Surrey Road
92 Dukrill Road—Millstream Estuary

### 12. Off-leash dog walking

33*A Cy Hampson Park
39 Parker Park
43 Cordova Bay Road (winter months)
44 Gloria Place (winter months)
69 Bowker Avenue (winter months)
77 Foul Bay Road—Gonzales Bay (winter months)
82 Fleming Bay—Macaulay Point Park
83* Saxe Point Park (one area only)
88 Portage Regional Park

### 13. Foul-weather car picnicking

12 Patricia Bay Park
17* West Saanich Road
24 Bowden Road
25 Ardwell Avenue
53 Guinevere Place
56 White Rock Street
57 Baynes Road
69 Bowker Avenue
71 Beach Drive—Orchard Avenue
76 Crescent Road—Chinese Cemetery
80 Russell Street
83 Kinver Street (high tide only)

### 14. Combining with forest walking

1 Gowlland Tod Provincial Park—Mark Lane
6 Coles Bay Regional Park
17 Woodcreek Drive
21 Nymph Point Park
47 Balmacarra Road
50 Arbutus Cove Park
88 Portage Regional Park

### 15. Fishing from the rocks

1 Gowlland Tod Provincial Park—Mark Lane
15 Setchell Road
19 Gullhaven Road
21 Nymph Point Park
36 James Island Road—Saanichton Bay Public Dock (crabbing from docks)
48 Glencoe Cove Kwatsech Park—North (bluffs)
52 Haro Place
55 Mount Baker View Road
56 White Rock Street
82 Fleming Bay—Macaulay Point Park
89 Beaumont Avenue

### 16. For a variety of shore types

7 Ardmore Drive—South
8 Aboyne Avenue
11 Briarwood Place
16 Moses Point Road
17 Woodcreek Drive
21 Nymph Point Park
22 Lillian Hoffar Park
28 Beaufort Road
29 Goddard Road
46 D'Arcy Lane
48, 49 Glencoe Cove Kwatsech Park
51 Hollydene Park
66 Lansdowne Road
69 Bowker Avenue
70 Lane Street
71 Beach Drive—Orchard Avenue
77 Foul Bay Road—Gonzales Bay
82 Fleming Bay—Macaulay Point Park
83* Saxe Point Park
88 Portage Regional Park

### 17. A wedding or family photo shoot

15 Setchell Road
21 Nymph Point Park
24 Bowden Road
25 Ardwell Avenue
33*A Cy Hampson Park
38 Island View Beach Regional Park
43 Cordova Bay Road
49 Glencoe Cove Kwatsech Park—South
54 Telegraph Bay
56 White Rock Street

58 McAnally Road—Smuggler's Cove Road
62 Telegraph Bay Road—South
63 Killarney Road
69 Bowker Avenue
71 Beach Drive—Orchard Avenue
76 Crescent Road—Chinese Cemetery
80 Russell Street
83* Saxe Point Park

**18. A high-point view**

4 Brentwood Drive
9 Braemar Avenue
15 Setchell Road
22*B Harbour Road
23 Bigrock Road
24 Bowden Road
40 Fenn Avenue
46 D'Arcy Lane
46*A Timber Lane
46*B Mount Douglas Park
47 Balmacarra Road
52 Haro Place
55 Mount Baker View Road
56 White Rock Street
64 Hibbens Close
75* Trafalgar Park
76 Crescent Road—Chinese Cemetery (Harling Point)
85 Sturdee Street

**19. Those who have walking difficulties**

7 Ardmore Drive—South
9 Braemar Avenue
12 Patricia Bay Park
24 Bowden Road
25 Ardwell Avenue
26 Fifth Street
33*A Cy Hampson Park
34 Newman Farm Park
36 James Island Road—Saanichton Bay Public Dock
38 Island View Beach Regional Park
44 Gloria Place
54 Telegraph Bay
58 McAnally Road—Smuggler's Cove Road
62 Telegraph Bay Road—South
67 Rutland Road
69 Bowker Avenue
70 Lane Street
71 Beach Drive—Orchard Avenue
72 Radcliffe Lane—East
80 Russell Street
81 Robert Street—Rainbow Park
82 Fleming Bay—Macaulay Point Park
83 Kinver Street (high tide)
83*A Saxe Point Park
87 Grafton Street—Denniston Park

**20. Viewing sunsets**

4 Brentwood Drive
5 Senanus Road
8 Aboyne Avenue
10 Ardmore Drive—Glenelg Avenue
12 Patricia Bay Park
13 Towner Park Road
15 Setchell Road
60 Seaview Road
73 Radcliffe Lane—McMicking Point
76 Crescent Road—Chinese Cemetery
82 Fleming Bay—Macaulay Point Park
83*A Saxe Point Park
84 Nelson Street
85 Sturdee Street
86 Foster Street
87 Grafton Street—Denniston Park
88 Beaumont Avenue

# INDEX TO ENTRIES

## PART 1 SAANICH INLET TO NORTH SIDNEY



## PART 2 SIDNEY TO CADBORO BAY



## PART 3 OAK BAY TO VIEW ROYAL

**THEO DOMBROWSKI** is a retired teacher who was involved for many years in international education, primarily at Lester B. Pearson College of the Pacific outside Victoria, BC. A writer, photographer and artist, he has a PhD in English and spent many years teaching literature and writing. He studied drawing and painting at the Banff School of Fine Arts and the University of Victoria Fine Arts Department and has worked as a professional artist. Theo is donating his proceeds from sales of this book to the local environmental group Georgia Strait Alliance and to the international humanitarian support group Médecins Sans Frontières/Doctors Without Borders (MSF). He lives in Nanoose Bay, BC. Theo is also the author of *Secret Beaches of Southern Vancouver Island: Qualicum to the Malahat*.

**ACKNOWLEDGEMENTS** Thanks to Eileen Dombrowski, Bruce Whittington, Anne Dombrowski, Bill Cavers, Louise Kadar, Vickie Jackson and Charlotte Gann for their help in many ways, including providing materials or information.